Healthy

MEAT AND POTATOES

Healthy
MEAT AND POTATOES

Charles Knight
David Knight

First edition: April 2001
Second edition: March 2006

Library of Congress Cataloging-in-Publication Data

Knight, Charles, 1947-
  Healthy meat and potatoes / Charles Knight
    1. low-fat-diet–Recipes. I.Title.

RM237.7.K635 2001
641.5'638–dc21

                            00-046105

Printed in the United States of America

10 9 8 7 6 5

This book is dedicated to my mother, Lucille Knight, and my wife, LeAnn Knight.

Some men are fortunate to have one woman in their life that is encouraging, supportive and motivating. I have been more than blessed by having two.

Contents

Preface   xi

Acknowledgments   xiii

Introduction   xv

Waterless, Greaseless Cooking   1

Healthy Hors d'Oeuvres and Appetizers   7

Healthy Soups and Stews   27

Healthy Meats and Other Entrees   63

Healthy Potatoes and Vegetables   127

Healthy Sauces   183

Healthy Stocks   213

Healthy Desserts   223

Metric Conversion Charts   231

Index   233

Preface

MORE THAN TWENTY years ago, while making a personal appearance at the Buffalo Food Show for *PM Magazine*, I met a young man selling cookware and pitching the benefits of waterless, greaseless cooking to a rather large, and interested audience. I was impressed not only by his delivery and promotional abilities but by what he had to say about this unique method of cooking foods without water or grease. He gave me a couple of pans to use in my performance, or I should say to "promote for him," and I have to admit I was impressed with both the product and the method. Our paths crossed again in Hartford, Charlotte and again in Tampa, and from that point in time we have become good personal friends, business associates and, for a few years, even neighbors. I encouraged him to design his own cookware and start his own company. For once, somebody listened to good advice and today Charles Knight has become one of the foremost experts on cookware designed specifically for the home cook, as well as on the methods of waterless, greaseless cooking.

It only takes good common sense to cook good healthy food. If you start with mediocre ingredients you end up with a mediocre dish, and life is too short to eat lousy food. If you use lousy cookware . . . well you know what happens. Waterless, greaseless cookware is designed specifically for the home cook, but professionals can employ the methods used in *Healthy Meat and Potatoes* as well. I use this cookware in my restaurant and have employed the cooking methods and you should too. Don't kill your food, destroying minerals and vitamins, with grease and fat and all the other unhealthy stuff. I still use a few drops of olive oil for flavor, but with good-quality ingredients, good sound methods and good cookware, you can make cooking easier and more enjoyable, and you'll not only feel healthy you'll be healthier!

So go for it! Let the world know how simple and easy it is to cook healthy. Don't just talk about good food; cook good food in your own kitchen with waterless, greaseless cookware and the great recipes you will find in *Healthy Meat and Potatoes*. Just do it! Your friends and family will love you for it.

"I See You."
Chef Tell

Acknowledgments

T O MY OLD neighborhood in Rahway, New Jersey, you made my childhood an unforget-
table culinary experience. Thank you for feeding me when I was a kid, especially Queen-
ie Fedyk for your great Southern dishes; Marie Zawislak for your neighborhood-famous
Polish cuisine and baked goods, and most notably Melio Paolantonio and Aunt Florence Sica
for your Italian influence.

To Uncle Vince, thanks for sharing the art of Tampa's Cuban-Italian cuisine.

Special thanks, Dorothy Heywood, for sharing your great recipe ideas.

To my good buddies, Executive Chef Hans Hinkle of the Hyatt Regency and Tony and
Angelo from Cafe Amaretto in Tampa, thank you for providing guidance and inspiration.

To my employees and distributors, who allowed me the luxury of time to accomplish
this undertaking: Jim, Sandy, "little" Sandy, Dave P., Garcia, John, Dave G., Adrianne, Kristen,
Billy, Anthony, Rob, Steve, Jeef, Lenny, Alex, Jeff, Jay, Lee, Max, Tom H. Russ, Charlie, Paul M.,

Paul B., Scott, Lance, Greg, George, Tony, Randy, Bill and, most notably, Tom Walsh, Ashok Tandon and Kristie McBride. Thank you for assisting me in making our dreams come true.

To Bob Swanson, you are the best copywriter in the world.

To the television crew of Harris & Co., NBC affiliate WFLA-TV Channel 8 in Tampa, especially Rob and Joe. You sampled the recipes after every television performance for nearly 10 years. If you didn't like it, it isn't in the book.

To my good friend, business associate, mentor and former neighbor, Chef Tell. When you weren't looking, I was learning; not only how to cook, but how to perform on television. In my book, you're the best chef in the world.

To my best friend and television partner, Jack Harris and his wife, Joy, you provided continuous encouragement, support and undying friendship. No one could have better friends.

To my father-in-law, Dave Pergola, you make the best Italian gravy in the world, and you and Jan provided me with the best wife in the world as well.

To my children: Joshua, you make great macaroni and cheese; Christina, you're the best baker in the world—I love your cookies; David, someday soon you'll have your own television cooking show, and you'll be writing cookbooks. Thanks for being great kids.

Special thanks to the community of dedicated cookware salespeople who have spent a lifetime educating people on how to cook the waterless, greaseless way.

Introduction

GOOD FOOD IS a unique, delightful "language" spoken through tempting tastes, stimulating aromas and attractive presentations. It's the oldest art form of every civilization and culture. A salivating link to our past, continuously rediscovered, refined and reshaped in our present. Good food is the essence of friendships and neighborhoods, the frosting that tops exciting events and the surprising highlight of any party or celebration.

Hearty and delightful meals are created with gentle hands and warm hearts. This I learned as a youngster growing up in the wonderful ethnic mix of New York and New Jersey, with home kitchens brimming with incredible dishes brought with care from the Old World. To those around me, good food was the nourishment of both body and soul. This harvest of flavors was the great influence of my boyhood. From the time I was old enough to know my way around the neighborhood family kitchens, I wanted to be a chef. All my dreams came true as I moved into the fascinating culinary world.

In *Healthy Meat and Potatoes*, I have assembled many of the fondest ethnic tastes and American favorites I enjoyed in my boyhood. Other ideas came from my high school years working in butcher shops and as a short-order cook. More came from the inspiration of Chef Tell and culinary education. Even more came in preparation for my weekly television appearances on WFLA-TV in Tampa and from developing the curriculum for the Health Craft Cooking School. And now, living in Tampa, I have added some Southern delights and the ethnic mix of Ybor City's Italian, Spanish and Cuban cuisine, all to come in the pages that follow.

I have also included what I have learned from three decades in the cookware business: a practical way to create the old classics and family favorites with reduced fat, less sodium, lower cholesterol and calories without compromising taste or culinary training. Better tasting meals that help develop better health, a winning combination! The secret is waterless, greaseless cooking.

Yes, good food is a delightful, unique language, and I sincerely hope the ideas you will find in *Healthy Meat and Potatoes* will help you express yourself in healthful and wonderful ways.

To your good health!

WATERLESS, GREASELESS COOKING

THE ANSWER TO better health is exercise and the food we eat. Nutritious, low-fat low-sodium meals are fundamental to today's health-conscious lifestyles; meals that help reduce dangerous cholesterol cut unwanted calories and retain important minerals and vitamins. All of our fresh foods have a built-in natural goodness. But the wonderful health-giving values you paid for at the food store may soon disappear in your kitchen. With 'old-fashioned conventional cooking methods, fresh vegetables must be peeled, boiled and subjected to high heat, not to mention the use of cooking fats and oils. All of this results in the irreplaceable loss of a large share of the vital minerals and vitamins that we need for good health.

Waterless, greaseless food preparation creates wholesome, great-tasting meals without sacrificing vitamins and minerals. Furthermore, the methods you will learn thoroughly capture the wonderful flavors we expect in our meals. It's possible because of this unique cooking method. Foods are cooked on low heat, below the boiling temperature, in a vapor seal. This vapor seal method is the secret that retains vital nutritional values. By eliminating the need for peeling and boiling, vegetables come to the table with a "garden fresh" taste, and meats are gently browned and cooked in their own natural juices, without the need for high-calorie oils. It's a whole new experience in cooking and taste, and a key benefit for better health.

Because food preparation is easy and efficient, waterless, greaseless cooking has become the preferred method of millions of home cooks who are dedicated to better health through healthier cooking techniques. *Healthy Meat and Potatoes* contains exciting recipes that will bring nature's goodness to your table everyday.

Two sound fundamentals are to always underscore anything we include in this cookbook. First, the recipes must be quick and easy to prepare, with ingredients that are readily available. And second, every recipe must be healthful.

Waterless, Greaseless Cookware

Waterless, greaseless cookware, in many ways, is different from both the less expensive pots and pans on display in most discount stores and the popular commercially designed cookware available in the upscale market. First and foremost, waterless, greaseless cookware is designed specifically for the home cook. Secondly, it's not available in retail stores. Historically, it has only been available through factory representatives who either come to your home by appointment to explain the facts, benefits and features, or through distributors who demonstrate at fairs and home shows. Why this method of marketing? Prior to *Healthy Meat and Potatoes*, there was no other way, besides through demonstration, to explain the values and principles of waterless, greaseless cooking. Today, waterless, greaseless cookware, in addition to the methods of marketing mentioned previously, is now available on the Internet. Beware, not all of the cookware that claims to be waterless and greaseless is truly waterless and greaseless.

The quality of waterless, greaseless cookware varies from company to company and from set to set, as do the features and benefits. I know firsthand that good cookware is expensive to produce, and as the designer and manufacturer of one of America's premier lines of waterless, greaseless cookware, there is no such thing as getting more than what you pay for. Waterless, greaseless cookware is expensive but no more so than the popular commercially designed cookware, and certainly equal to the value of the refrigerator you use to keep your foods fresh and the range you use to cook with. Waterless, greaseless cookware is more than a lifetime investment: It's an investment in a lifestyle.

When buying waterless, greaseless cookware, purchase from a reputable company and a reputable individual. And even more important, compare before you buy. Once you own a good set of waterless, greaseless cookware, it will be very difficult to settle for less. However, the high price and quality in no way signifies that the cookware will take care of itself. Even a Rolls Royce needs periodic maintenance.

CLEANING

In order to get the maximum value for this worthwhile investment, clean the pans after every use with a good-quality stainless steel cleaner. An easy scrub with the cleaner, using a damp paper towel or dishcloth, and a good rinse in hot water is all that's necessary to keep these pans bright and shiny and to keep foods from sticking to the pan.

COOKING METHODS

The following cooking methods are used with waterless, greaseless cookware.

DRY SAUTÉING: Cooking vegetables or meats in a hot dry pan over medium heat, until slightly browned (see Sautéing Without Fat, below).

WET SAUTÉING: Cooking vegetables in a small amount of stock over medium heat.

WATERLESS VEGETABLE COOKING: The pan must be at least three-quarters full. Rinse with water and drain. Cover the pan, close the vent and cook over low heat. When the cover spins freely on a cushion of water, the vapor seal has formed, 3 to 5 minutes. After forming the seal, cook for the time specified. Don't peek. Removing the cover will destroy the vapor seal, lengthen the cooking time and may cause the vegetables to burn.

To reestablish the vapor seal: Cover the pan, close the vent and add 2 tablespoons water to the rim. Cook over low heat for 5 to 10 minutes.

SAUTÉING WITHOUT FAT

Many recipes call for sautéing vegetables, particularly a *mirepoix* (a mixture of carrots, celery and onions used for seasoning), in oil. Although we do need some oil in our diet, and some oils are better than others, the problem with sautéing vegetables in oil or butter is not so much the oil or butter itself, but the process. When vegetables are sautéed in oil, they do not properly caramelize and release the aromatic flavors into the dish being cooked. For example: When professional chefs need extra flavor in a particular dish, at times they will take a peeled whole or quartered onion, stick a fork in it and hold it over an open flame and actually burn the onion. The onion is then placed into the sauce, gravy, soup or stew and allowed to simmer with the ingredients. This is done to brown the onion to bring the natural flavor-filled sugars and salts to the surface.

Then why would the same chef add oil to the pan to brown a *mirepoix*? The answer is simple: Cheap, thin pans, even the coated ones, cannot cook vegetables sans oil without the vegetables sticking and burning. Likewise, professional or commercially designed pans are too large for most home cooking. A small quantity of vegetables cooked in a large pan over high heat will burn; therefore, oil is needed. In addition, costly time spent by a professional cook or chef in such a menial application is time and money wasted. So oil is used, and lots of it, sometimes as much as ¼ cup or more. Unfortunately, the oil coats the vegetables and prevents them from properly caramelizing and releasing their natural flavor. As a result, oil is now incorporated into the dish itself, and extra flavoring in the form of salt must be added to make up for what has been lost.

Comparisons of Fats, Salts and Mirepoix *(carrot, celery and onion):*

Olive Oil, per tablespoon: 119 Calories; 13.5g Fat (100% calories from fat); 1.8g Saturated Fat; 9.9g Monounsaturated Fat; 1.1g Polyunsaturated Fat

Vegetable Oil, per tablespoon: 120 Calories; 14.6g Fat (100% calories from fat); 1.6g Saturated Fat; 8.1g Monounsaturated Fat; 2.9g Polyunsaturated Fat

Clarified Butter, per tablespoon: 119 Calories; 13.6g Fat (99.9% calories from fat); 8.4g Saturated Fat; 3.9g Monounsaturated Fat; 0.5g Polyunsaturated Fat

Table Salt, per teaspoon: 2,132mg Sodium

Kosher Salt and Sea Salt, per teaspoon: 1,880mg Sodium

Simple *Mirepoix* (carrot, celery and onion): 69 Calories; 0.3g Fat (4.1% calories from fat); 2.4g Protein; 15g Carbohydrates; 0mg Cholesterol; 612mg Sodium

Maximize Flavor

As you can see from the comparisons above, the sodium (612mg) in the *mirepoix* is one-third that of 1 teaspoon of salt. When caramelized properly, dry sautéed using no oil, the natural sugars and salts of the *mirepoix* are allowed to combine with the natural flavors of the other ingredients. The end result is more nutritional, flavorful meals without the extra calories from oil and the dangers of added sodium (salt). Even the Culinary Institute of America in Hyde Park, New York, is now teaching and recommending the dry sauté method in their

Nutritional Cuisine Program. The secret, for the home cook as well as the professional chef, is to use a high-quality smaller pan that conducts the heat evenly and gently and to use lower cooking temperatures.

Olive Oil or Butter

If you do decide to add a small amount of olive oil or butter for flavor, as I do in some of the recipes, a good rule of thumb is to add it after the vegetables have been dry sautéed or cooked the waterless way. I believe you'll thoroughly enjoy the results, and your body will benefit, in both the short and the long term.

COMPARISON OF CONVENTIONAL AND WATERLESS, GREASELESS COOKING OF MEATS

Broiling

Oven and charcoal broiling subjects the meat to extremely high heat, whether it is a gas flame, electric element or glowing charcoal, with a space of only a few inches of air. It's an extremely hot process—gas burns at 3,000°F (1,649°C), the electric element glows at about 2,000°F (1,093°C). The high temperatures involved in broiling limits its usefulness; the whole piece of meat must be cooked through before the outside surface is browned (caramelized). For this reason, oven broiling is traditionally limited to relatively thin and tender cuts like chops, steaks, small poultry parts and fish. Meat with a lot of connective tissue is less suited to broiling because collagen does not have the time, or reach the temperature necessary, to soften and liquify.

The one advantage of broiling or grilling is that the very high temperatures at the meat's surface are ideal for a browning reaction; thus broiled meats have a characteristically intense caramelized flavor. A drawback is that these same temperatures are high enough to burn fat, creating potentially carcinogenic hydrocarbons. Deposited on the meat, they may be as dangerous as smoking cigarettes.

Sautéing

Sautéing, or pan-frying, depends largely on the conductive transfer of heat. With waterless, greaseless cookware, fats and oil do not need to be added to the pan to prevent the meat from sticking. Frying is a fairly hot and rapid cooking method, so it is limited to the same thin, tender meats best suited for broiling. Frying temperatures are significantly lower than broiling temperature; however, this is primarily because the smoke point of the fat must not be exceeded if burnt flavors are to be avoided.

Conventional pan frying with fat is not recommended because different fats have different smoke points, and the choice of fat determines the maximum cooking temperature. Because heat is conducted very efficiently through quality waterless, greaseless cookware to the meat, the meat's surface tends to be browned very quickly, in 1 to 2 minutes. To prevent the meat's surface from toughening while the inside cooks, the heat is usually reduced after the initial browning. If the pan is covered, water vapor is trapped and a process more like basting results. Therefore, you must open the vent when pan-frying.

Roasting

With roasting, or more accurately oven baking, we return to the controversy of high-heat drying out the meat that was discussed previously. Roasting depends on heat radiation from the oven walls and on convection (the transfer of heat via currents of air), which have a much lower heat capacity than water, oil or metal. It is a method well suited to large pieces of meat.

Meats with connective tissue require longer cooking processes at higher temperatures to be converted into gelatin, while muscle proteins, once they have coagulated at about 160°F (71°C), will only get drier and tougher with time until the fibers themselves begin to disintegrate. If you brown first, and then roast on top of the stove at medium to medium-high temperatures for a given doneness, your meats will have been cooked in a relatively short period of time.

Healthy
HORS D' OEUVRES
AND APPETIZERS

H ORS D'OEUVRE SOUNDS French, and it is as French as costly Burgundy wines, but don't let that intimidate you. Hors d'oeuvre (literally translated) means "before or outside the main work." So "work," in a culinary sense, is a dinner. And "before" is the period of time before the dinner is served. We will concentrate on the before aspect, as that is where hors d'oeuvres (or "appetizers," as many Americans prefer) play a very important role in the ultimate success of any dinner and an area where many home cooks need an infusion of new ideas.

It is a personal compliment to be invited to a private home for a dinner party. Be it a formal affair, or a backyard cookout, invited guests feel they are "special." Each will be looking forward to an enjoyable gathering and good food. After the guest list has been confirmed, it is important to plan the dinner from a logistical viewpoint. The party's start may be set for 7:00 P.M., with dinner to be served at 8:00 P.M. That leaves a time period of up to an hour that requires careful planning. There are two factors to be considered. First, invitees will undoubtedly arrive at various times, presenting a challenge to serve a small number that is rapidly growing into a larger group. Therefore, a variety of two or three appetizers should be offered, with cold appetizers served first and warm or hot ones offered when all or most of your guests have arrived, or are at the dinner table. Secondly, guests frequently do not know one another, needing a common interest to create a convivial atmosphere that food can help provide.

In the time period between arrival and dinner service, attractive, flavorful hors d'oeuvres are an excellent way to break the social ice and start sparkling conversations. Hors d'oeuvres are a delightful catalyst to start any party off on the right foot, pleasantly filling the minutes before dinner with tempting morsels and interesting conversation. But if the guests are offered an unimaginative collection of store-bought dips and chips, the atmosphere of the affair may unfortunately be subdued and little will be expected of the dinner to follow. The conversation may still be inspired, but may not be the conversation you had in mind.

Eye-appealing appetizers and hors d'oeuvres are not difficult to make. They may be prepared earlier in the day and created with healthful, low-calorie ingredients. The pages that follow contain some time-proven recipes; from zesty Caribbean Crab Cakes, to flavor-packed Bruschetta. The critical "before" dinner time frame is an excellent stage for you to display your culinary accomplishments. Delight your guests with what you have created in your own home kitchen and stand by for the compliments!

Angelic Deviled Eggs

To enjoy a bright yellow-orange egg yolk instead of the normal yellow-green, insert a pin into the pointed end of the egg to allow the sulfur to dissipate during the cooking process. Protein begins to toughen at 170°F (75°C), and water boils at 212°F (100°C). Therefore, it is important not to boil the eggs. This recipe will teach you how to make hard-cooked eggs the angelic way.

EQUIPMENT: **Medium covered sauté skillet, measuring cup and spoons, French chef's knife, cutting board and mixing bowl**

PREPARATION TIME: **40 minutes**   O   **Makes 24 appetizers**

12 eggs

½ cup sour cream or mayonnaise

½ teaspoon Dijon mustard

6 green olives, minced

¼ teaspoon freshly ground black pepper

¼ teaspoon hot pepper sauce

1 tablespoon chopped fresh parsley

½ stalk celery, finely minced

¼ teaspoon sweet paprika

Place a wet paper towel in the bottom of the skillet and place the eggs on the paper towel. Cover the skillet, close the vent and cook over medium-low heat. When the cover spins freely on a cushion of water, the vapor seal has formed, 3 to 5 minutes. After forming the seal, cook for 10 to 12 minutes. Do not peek. Removing the cover will destroy the vapor seal and lengthen the cooking time.

To cool the eggs before peeling, remove the cover and place the pan under cold running water for 3 to 5 minutes. Let the hard-cooked eggs sit in the cold water for 10 to 15 minutes.

Peel the shells from the eggs and cut the eggs in half lengthwise. Place the yokes in a mixing bowl and the egg white halves on a serving platter. To the mixing bowl, add the sour cream, mustard, olives, pepper, hot sauce, parsley and celery and mix well.

Spoon the egg yolk mixture into the egg white halves and sprinkle with paprika. Cover and chill before serving.

PER APPETIZER, WITH SOUR CREAM: 51 Calories • 3.8g Fat (68% calories from fat) 3.3g Protein • 0.6g Carbohydrates • 108mg Cholesterol • 45mg Sodium

PER APPETIZER, WITH MAYONNAISE: 73 Calories • 6.4g Fat (79% calories from fat) 3.2g Protein • 0.5g Carbohydrates • 109mg Cholesterol • 69mg Sodium

Baked Artichoke Dip

EQUIPMENT: French chef's knife, cutting board, measuring cup and spoons, food cutter (grating blades) and 10-inch gourmet skillet with metal handle

PREPARATION TIME: 20 minutes ○ Makes 30 to 36 cracker-size servings

2 cups diced cooked fresh or canned artichoke hearts (6 to 8 artichoke hearts)

½ cup freshly grated Parmesan cheese

1 cup sour cream or mayonnaise

¼ cup canned diced mild green chiles

¼ cup prepared horseradish

¼ cup chopped green onions

Gourmet crackers, to serve

In the skillet, combine the artichoke hearts, ¼ cup of the Parmesan cheese, sour cream, chiles and horseradish and mix well.

Cover the skillet, close the vent and cook over medium-low heat. When the cover spins freely on a cushion of water, the vapor seal has formed, 3 to 5 minutes. After forming the seal, cook for 5 to 7 minutes. Don't peek. Remove from the heat.

Preheat broiler. Uncover and broil until the top of the artichoke dish is slightly browned, 3 to 5 minutes. Using a pot holder, remove the skillet to a trivet and serve directly from the skillet.

To serve, top with the remaining Parmesan cheese and sprinkle with the green onions. Serve with crackers.

PER SERVING, WITH SOUR CREAM: 25 Calories • 1.7g Fat (58% calories from fat) • 1g Protein • 1.7g Carbohydrates • 4mg Cholesterol • 35mg Sodium

PER SERVING, WITH MAYONNAISE: 55 Calories • 5.2g Fat (82% calories from fat) • 1g Protein • 1.7g Carbohydrates • 4mg Cholesterol • 66mg Sodium

Barbecued Turkey Meatballs

EQUIPMENT: **Measuring cup and spoons, medium mixing bowl, French chef's knife, cutting board, slotted serving spoon and a large, covered sauté skillet or electric skillet**

PREPARATION TIME: **50 minutes** ○ **Makes 25 to 30 meatballs**

½ cup rolled oats

½ cup lowfat milk

1 pound ground turkey or lean ground beef

2 medium sweet onions, minced

1 clove garlic, minced

1 cup brewed coffee

3 tablespoons tomato paste

¼ cup apple cider vinegar

2 tablespoons Worcestershire sauce

½ cup brown sugar

¼ teaspoon Dijon mustard

¼ teaspoon ground cinnamon

¼ cup ketchup

1 teaspoon chopped fresh parsley

In a mixing bowl, combine the oats and milk and let stand for 15 minutes. Add the turkey and one of the onions. Mix well and form into 1-inch meatballs.

In a hot, dry skillet, covered with vent open, dry sauté the meatballs over medium heat, until brown on all sides, about 15 minutes. Turn occasionally as they release from the skillet. Re-cover the skillet each time the meatballs are turned. Remove the meatballs with a slotted spoon and set aside.

To the skillet, add the remaining onion and the garlic; sauté in the meatball drippings until slightly browned, 3 to 5 minutes, stirring occasionally.

Slowly stir in the coffee and reduce the heat to medium-low. Add the remaining ingredients except parsley, and mix well.

Return the meatballs to the skillet. Cover and close the vent. When the lid spins freely on a cushion of water, the vapor seal has formed, 3 to 5 minutes. After forming the seal, cook for 10 to 12 minutes.

To serve, sprinkle the meatballs with the parsley and serve with cocktail forks or toothpicks.

PER MEATBALL, WITH TURKEY: 47 Calories • 1.4g Fat (27% calories from fat) • 3.3g Protein • 5.4g Carbohydrates • 12mg Cholesterol • 55mg Sodium

PER MEATBALL, WITH LEAN BEEF: 64 Calories • 3.3g Fat (46% calories from fat) 3.3g Protein • 5.4g Carbohydrates • 12mg Cholesterol • 52mg Sodium

Broccoli Hors d'Oeuvre, Italian Style

EQUIPMENT: **Measuring spoons, French chef's knife, cutting board, 1¼ quart covered saucepan, mixing bowl, colander and whisk**

PREPARATION TIME: **40 minutes** ○ **Makes 10 to 12 appetizers or 6 to 8 salads**

1 large head broccoli, broken in florets

1 teaspoon chopped fresh parsley

½ teaspoon freshly ground black pepper

DRESSING

1 egg yolk (see Note, below)

3 tablespoons water

3 tablespoons balsamic vinegar

1 teaspoon fresh lemon juice

¼ teaspoon freshly ground black pepper

1 teaspoon Dijon mustard

3 cloves garlic, finely minced

2 teaspoons extra-virgin olive oil

4 or 5 leaves Boston lettuce

2 ripe plum tomatoes, cut in ¼-inch-thick slices

20 to 25 black olives

Place the broccoli stem-side down in the pan. Rinse with cold water and pour the water off. The water that clings to the broccoli is sufficient for cooking the waterless way. Cover the pan, close the vent and cook over medium-low heat. When the cover spins freely on a cushion of water, the vapor seal has formed, 3 to 5 minutes. After forming the seal, cook for 5 to 7 minutes.

Remove the pan from the heat, and using a slotted spoon, transfer broccoli to an ice water bath and chill for 3 to 5 minutes. Drain the broccoli in a colander.

Meanwhile, make the dressing: In a mixing bowl, combine the egg yolk, water, balsamic vinegar, lemon juice, pepper, mustard, garlic and olive oil and whisk vigorously until the dressing becomes light in color and increases in volume, about 3 to 5 minutes.

To serve, place the lettuce leaves on a large serving plate. Arrange the tomato slices and olives in the center and the broccoli around the outer edge of the plate. Top with dressing and sprinkle with parsley and freshly ground black pepper. Serve with cocktail forks.

PER APPETIZER SERVING: 28 Calories • 1.8g Fat (52% calories from fat) •
1g Protein • 2.7g Carbohydrates • 18mg Cholesterol • 51mg Sodium

VARIATION

Serve as a cold salad, garnishing each serving with Boston lettuce and arrange the broccoli, tomatoes and olives on salad plates. Sprinkle with freshly grated Parmesan cheese.

PER SALAD SERVING: 42 Calories • 2.7g Fat (52% calories from fat) •
1.5g Protein • 4.1g Carbohydrates • 27mg Cholesterol • 76mg Sodium

NOTE: Anyone who is ill or has a compromised immune system, including the very young and the elderly, should avoid raw eggs because they may contain salmonella. Pasteurized raw eggs are available in some markets and are safe to use.

Buffalo Chicken Wings

If you love buffalo chicken wings, but want to cut the fat and avoid the process of deep-frying, this is an excellent alternative. Deep-fried wings have almost three times the calories and six times the fat.

EQUIPMENT: French chef's knife, cutting board, large covered sauté skillet or electric skillet, measuring cup and spoons and small serving bowl

PREPARATION TIME: 30 minutes O Makes 48 appetizers

24 large chicken wings

4 stalks celery

1 cup Low-Sodium Chicken Stock (page 217 or canned) or 1 stick (8 tablespoons) unsalted butter

1 to 3 tablespoons hot sauce

¼ cup dry bread crumbs

DIPPING SAUCE

½ cup sour cream

¼ cup crumbled blue cheese

¼ teaspoon Worcestershire sauce

¼ teaspoon hot sauce

¼ teaspoon Dijon mustard

With a knife or poultry shears, trim off the tip of the chicken wings and discard. Cut the wings in half at the joint and trim the skin from the meat.

In a hot, dry skillet over medium heat, cook the wings to a crisp golden brown, 6 to 7 minutes per side. Cook covered with the vent open.

Meanwhile, prepare the Dipping Sauce: In a mixing bowl, combine the sour cream, cheese, Worcestershire sauce, hot sauce and Dijon mustard and set aside.

With a knife, cut each celery stalk into 3 or 4 equal-size portions and then slice each portion into 3 or 4 bite-size celery sticks. Place the Dipping Sauce in the middle of a serving platter and arrange the celery sticks around the sauce.

Slowly stir the stock in with the chicken wings. Reduce the heat to low. Add the hot sauce and bread crumbs and mix well.

To serve, remove the wings and bread crumb gravy to a warm platter. Serve with the celery sticks and Dipping Sauce.

PER PIECE, WITH STOCK: 47 Calories • 1.3g Fat (26% calories from fat) • 8g Protein • 0.5g Carbohydrates • 20mg Cholesterol • 44mg Sodium

PER PIECE, WITH BUTTER: 64 Calories • 3.2g Fat (47% calories from fat) • 8g Protein • 0.5g Carbohydrates • 25mg Cholesterol • 3mg Sodium

DIPPING SAUCE, PER SERVING: 8 Calories • 0.7g Fat (82% calories from fat) • 0.2g Protein • 0.1g Carbohydrates • 2mg Cholesterol • 12mg Sodium

Caribbean Crab Cakes

EQUIPMENT: French chef's knife, cutting board, mixing bowls, large covered sauté skillet or electric skillet and flexible (pancake turner) spatula

PREPARATION TIME: 20 minutes   ○   Makes 8 to 10 bite-size crab cakes

COCKTAIL DIPPING SAUCE

¼ cup ketchup

1 tablespoon prepared horseradish

CARIBBEAN CRAB CAKE DIPPING SAUCE

3 tablespoons mayonnaise

3 tablespoons sour cream

1 tablespoon minced sweet pickles

1 tablespoon minced shallots or red onion

2 teaspoons minced capers

1 dash sweet paprika

CARIBBEAN CRAB CAKES

1 cup chopped cooked fresh lump crabmeat

1 medium shallot, minced

¼ stalk celery, minced

¼ cup dry bread crumbs

1 teaspoon mayonnaise

¼ teaspoon Worcestershire sauce

¼ teaspoon Dijon mustard

1 egg white or 1 whole egg

½ teaspoon chopped fresh dill

1 dash ground red pepper

1 dash freshly ground black pepper

1 dash ground cloves

1 dash ground allspice

1 dash ground ginger

1 dash sweet paprika

romaine lettuce leaves
1 medium lime, cut into 8 to 10 wedges
1 teaspoon chopped fresh parsley

Prepare the sauces. To make the Cocktail Dipping Sauce: In a small mixing bowl, combine the ketchup and horseradish. Mix well, cover and chill.

To make the Caribbean Crab Cake Dipping Sauce: In a small mixing bowl, combine the mayonnaise, sour cream, pickles, shallot, capers and paprika. Mix well, cover and chill.

Make the Caribbean Crab Cakes: In a mixing bowl, combine the crabmeat, shallot, celery, bread crumbs, mayonnaise, Worcestershire sauce, mustard, egg white or egg, dill and spices and mix well.

With a tablespoon, form the crab mixture into 8 or 10 small round balls.

Place the crab balls in a hot, dry skillet over medium heat. With a flexible spatula, press down on each ball to form a small, round, flat crab cake. Cover the pan, close the vent and cook for 3 to 4 minutes. With a flexible spatula, turn the crab cakes and slightly brown the other side, 2 to 3 minutes. Remove to a platter and serve warm.

To serve, line a serving platter with the lettuce leaves. Place the sauce in the center and surround with the crab cakes and fresh lime wedges. Sprinkle with the parsley and serve with cocktail forks or toothpicks.

PER CRAB CAKE, WITHOUT SAUCE: 27 Calories • 0.4g Fat (12% calories from fat) • 3.2g Protein • 2.7g Carbohydrates • 11mg Cholesterol • 68mg Sodium

Cocktail Dipping Sauce:

PER SERVING: 8 Calories • 0g Fat (3% calories from fat) • 0.2g Protein • 2.2g Carbohydrates • 0mg Cholesterol • 76mg Sodium

Caribbean Crab Cake Dipping Sauce:

PER SERVING: 28 Calories • 2.8g Fat (88% calories from fat) • 0.1g Protein • 0.7g Carbohydrates • 3mg Cholesterol • 35mg Sodium

VARIATION

Crab cakes can be served chilled.

Bruschetta

EQUIPMENT: French chef's knife, cutting board, measuring spoons, mixing bowl, sieve, tongs and large sauté skillet or electric skillet

PREPARATION TIME: 40 minutes ○ Makes 10 to 12 servings

4 medium tomatoes, seeded and chopped

1 medium shallot, minced, or ½ medium onion, minced

4 tablespoons chopped fresh parsley or cilantro

10 fresh basil leaves, chopped

4 cloves garlic, finely minced

¼ teaspoon freshly ground black pepper

1 tablespoon olive oil

1 teaspoon fresh lime juice

1 tablespoon balsamic vinegar

¼ teaspoon sugar (optional)

1 loaf French bread, cut into 1-inch-thick slices

2 tablespoons freshly grated Parmesan cheese

In a mixing bowl, combine the tomatoes, shallot, parsley, basil, garlic and pepper with the olive oil, lime juice, vinegar and sugar, if using. Cover and chill for at least 30 minutes or up to 3 to 4 hours. The longer chilling further intensifies the flavors.

Using a sieve, strain the vegetables and herbs from the juice and set both aside.

Lightly brush each bread slice with the reserved juice.

In a hot, dry skillet, place the bread on the hot surface and toast each side for 2 to 3 minutes.

To serve, top the toasted bread with the vegetable mixture and sprinkle with the Parmesan cheese.

PER SERVING: 78 Calories • 2.1g Fat (24% calories from fat) • 2.6g Protein
2.9g Carbohydrates • 1mg Cholesterol • 135mg Sodium

VARIATION

Serve the vegetable topping as a relish or garnish without the French bread.

Hot and Spicy Cornbread

EQUIPMENT: **Mixing bowl, measuring cup and spoons and 1-quart covered saucepan**

PREPARATION TIME: **30 minutes** ○ **Makes 6 or 8 servings**

1⅓ cups cornbread mix or 1 (9-ounce) package

2 eggs

1 (4-oz.) can cream-style corn

2 tablespoons maple syrup

1 small jalapeño chile, minced

3 tablespoons honey

Combine the cornbread mix, eggs, corn, maple syrup and chile in a mixing bowl. Mix well.

Coat the saucepan with vegetable spray and pour the cornbread mixture into the pan. Cover the pan, close the vent and cook over medium-low heat for 20 to 25 minutes. Test for doneness with a fork. If not done, cover the pan, close the vent and return to medium-low heat and cook for 5 to 10 minutes more.

To release the cake from the pan, place the hot pan on a cold, damp dish towel. Uncover the pan and place an inverted serving plate over the top of the pan. Invert the pan so the cake releases on top of the serving plate.

To serve, cut into 6 to 8 pieces and drizzle with honey.

PER SERVING: **183 Calories • 4g Fat (18% calories from fat) • 4g Protein • 35g Carbohydrates • 53mg Cholesterol • 409mg Sodium**

VARIATIONS

Serve as an appetizer with Salsa (page 211).

Substitute 1 (4-ounce) can chopped mild green chiles for the cream-style corn. Omit the jalapeño chile, if desired.

Stuffed Zucchini Johnsonville

This is an exceptional appetizer that I created while doing television recipes for Johnsonville Sausage. I strongly recommend their products for the consistency of flavor and the quality of ingredients . . . especially in the absence of a local Italian butcher.

EQUIPMENT: **French chef's knife, cutting board, measuring spoons, medium sauté skillet, 13-inch chef's skillet with metal handle, food cutter (grating blades) and tongs**

PREPARATION TIME: **30 minutes** ◦ **Makes 16 servings**

1 medium onion, minced

2 cloves garlic, minced or pureed

2 Italian sausage links, removed from casing

1 medium tomato, chopped

1 tablespoon Italian bread crumbs

3 tablespoons freshly grated Parmesan cheese

½ teaspoon Italian seasoning

1 egg, beaten

8 small zucchini

1 tablespoon fresh basil, chopped

In a hot, dry skillet over medium heat, dry sauté the onion and garlic until slightly browned. Add the sausage and sauté until cooked through, about 5 minutes, stirring occasionally.

Add the tomato, bread crumbs, 1 tablespoon of the Parmesan cheese, Italian seasoning and egg to the sausage mixture and mix well. Remove from the heat and set aside.

Cut each zucchini in half lengthwise and remove the seeds with a teaspoon. In a hot, dry chef's skillet over medium heat, place the zucchini cut-side down and grill until slightly browned, about 3 minutes. Remove with tongs, set aside and cool enough to handle.

Preheat broiler. Fill each zucchini half with a liberal amount of the stuffing and return to the chef's skillet. Broil until the stuffing is slightly browned and crisp, about 3 minutes.

To serve, place the stuffed zucchini on a serving platter and top with remaining Parmesan cheese and freshly chopped basil.

PER SERVING: 73 Calories • 5g Fat (62% calories from fat) • 4g Protein • 3g Carbohydrates • 25mg Cholesterol • 174mg Sodium

Sweet and Sour Meatballs

This recipe is an absolutely wonderful hors d' oeuvre or appetizer for any kind of party or celebration.

EQUIPMENT: 2 large mixing bowls, measuring cup and spoons, French chef's knife, cutting board and large covered sauté skillet or electric skillet

PREPARATION TIME: 45 minutes ○ Makes 25 to 30 meatballs

1 pound ground turkey or beef

½ pound Italian sausage, removed from casing

1 medium onion, minced

2 cloves garlic, minced

2 eggs, beaten

½ cup dry bread crumbs

SWEET AND SOUR SAUCE

⅔ cup apple cider vinegar

¼ cup cornstarch

1 (8-oz.) can pineapple chunks in juice, undrained

1 (8-oz.) can bamboo shoots, undrained

⅔ cup packed light brown sugar

1 (8-oz.) jar maraschino cherries, undrained

¼ cup soy sauce

Combine the ground turkey or beef, Italian sausage, onion, garlic, eggs and bread crumbs in a mixing bowl. Mix well and shape mixture into 25 to 30 1-inch meatballs.

In a hot, dry skillet over medium heat, dry sauté the meatballs with the cover on and the vent open until browned on all sides, 15 minutes, turning occasionally.

Meanwhile, prepare the sauce: In a mixing bowl, combine the vinegar and cornstarch. Stir in remaining ingredients and mix well.

Slowly stir the sauce mixture into the meatballs. Cook, stirring, until thickened. Remove the skillet from the heat and let stand for 5 minutes before serving.

To serve, place toothpicks into the meatballs and serve straight from the skillet or transfer them to a warm serving dish.

PER 2 MEATBALLS WITH SAUCE: 418 Calories • 9g Fat (18% calories from fat) •
12g Protein • 77g Carbohydrates • 64mg Cholesterol • 502mg Sodium

Spinach Dip

EQUIPMENT: French chef's knife, cutting board, measuring cups, 2-quart covered saucepan or electric skillet and food cutter (shredding blades)

PREPARATION TIME: 25 minutes O Makes about 24 cracker-size servings

1 medium onion, minced

½ medium carrot, minced

½ stalk celery, minced

1 clove garlic, minced

1 medium jalapeño chile, minced

1 (4-oz.) can mild green chiles

2 medium tomatoes, finely chopped

1 (8-oz.) package frozen spinach, thawed and drained

2½ cups shredded Monterey Jack cheese

½ cup half-and-half

Gourmet crackers or tortilla chips, to serve

In a hot, dry saucepan over medium heat, dry sauté the onion, carrot, celery and garlic until tender, about 5 minutes, stirring occasionally. Do not brown.

Add the remaining ingredients to the saucepan, mix well and reduce the heat to medium-low. Cover the pan, close the vent and cook until the cheese melts, about 10 minutes, stirring occasionally.

Serve from the pan accompanied by gourmet crackers or tortilla chips.

PER SERVING WITHOUT CRACKERS: 84 Calories • 4g Fat (45% calories from fat)
6g Protein • 6g Carbohydrates • 12mg Cholesterol • 160mg Sodium

Healthy
SOUPS AND STEWS

O NE OF THE most admired skills in any cook's repertoire is the ability to create wholesome, tasty soups and stews. Cooks with these admirable attributes frequently utilize
soups and stews as highly versatile comfort foods, and with good reason. Picture a bitterly
cold day and exhilarating hot soups and stews come to mind. During a boring bout in bed,
throat-soothing soups are the best restorative medicine. On sizzling summer days, rejuve-
nating cold soups quickly lower our thermostats. Hot or cold, soups are time-proven delights,
ready to add zest and variety to our lifestyles.

Soups and stews are truly the most broad-based of any food group. Their range of
enchanting flavors stems from almost endless choice of vegetables, meats and fish. With this
variety, there's a compatible soup for any menu you may plan. Soups are most popularly
served as a separate course in luncheons or dinners. Some soups and stews are excellent as a
main course. In any event, soups are always welcome. Among your acquaintances, can you

recall anyone who does not like soup? Well-rounded home cooks and professional chefs soon develop a knack for preparing a number of these table delights; ready to enhance the pleasures of a widespread array of luncheons and dinners.

Most soups are uncomplicated to create, and for convenience, most can be prepared several hours before serving. The secret to making great soups is simple. Always use good basic ingredients. The best *mirepoix* (carrots, celery and onions), herbs (thyme, parsley stems and bay leaf) and chicken, beef or veal stock is essential. In the following section, you will find recipes and step-by-step techniques for dozens of delightful soups and stews. With these taste wonders in your repertoire, you will develop an understanding of the chemistry of the world's finest dishes.

About Sodium and Salt

ONIONS, CARROTS AND CELERY

A natural source of sodium can be found in the most basic of vegetables, and sodium (salt), as we all know, does provide flavor. However, sodium can be a problem for some people, especially those with congestive heart disease or hypertension. In general, high amounts of sodium should be avoided. To achieve maximum natural flavor without the need to add sodium in the form of table salt, kosher salt or sea salt, we will use three basic vegetables—onions, carrots and celery—in most soups and stews. They provide natural vegetable flavor and natural sodium content. When onions, carrots and celery are dry sautéed using no oil, the natural flavors are released into the dish. When sautéed in oil, the natural flavors cannot escape the coating of oil and additional sodium (salt) is necessary to flavor the food. These basic vegetables provide the following:

- 1 medium onion: 54mg sodium

- 1 medium carrot: 28mg sodium

- 1 stalk celery: 35mg sodium

TOMATOES AND BEANS

Many of the most popular soup recipes use either tomatoes or dried beans as another source of flavor. When tomatoes are called for, always try to use fresh, ripe tomatoes; plum tomatoes are the best. When the recipe calls for dried beans, home-cooked beans are always the first choice, and we have provided a simple recipe (page 30) that is easy to follow and prepare and that has better flavor than the canned varieties. When using canned goods, always consult the Nutrition Facts on the label. (It is now possible to find some dried beans that are canned without added salt.)

Tomatoes and beans provide the following:

○ 1 cup Homemade Beans (page 30): 356mg sodium

○ 1 cup canned beans: 750mg sodium

○ 1 cup chopped fresh tomatoes: 16mg sodium

○ 1 cup canned tomatoes: 391mg sodium

Homemade Beans

EQUIPMENT: Measuring cup and spoons, 2-quart covered saucepan, serving spoon

PREPARATION TIME: 2½ hours ○ Makes 1½ to 2 cups, depending on the bean

1 cup dried beans

1 small onion, diced

1 clove garlic, minced

½ teaspoon dried thyme

1 small bay leaf

1 ham hock or 2 slices bacon (optional)

About 3 cups Low-Sodium Chicken Stock (page 217) or canned

Rinse and sort the beans; set aside.

In a hot, dry saucepan over medium heat, dry sauté the onion and garlic until slightly browned. Place the beans, thyme, bay leaf and ham hock or bacon, if using, in the pan and cover with about 3 inches of stock and stir to combine. Bring to a rapid boil. Remove from the heat, cover the pan and close the vent, and let stand about 1 hour. Don't peek.

To resume cooking, check the liquid level in the pan. The beans should be covered by at least 1 to 2 inches of liquid. If they have absorbed the liquid, add water as needed. Cover the pan, close the vent and cook over low or medium-low heat until the beans are tender, 1 to 1½ hours. Remove the ham hock, if used.

Serve the beans as a side dish or use in recipes as needed. The cooked beans can be covered tightly and refrigerated for up to 3 days or even frozen for longer storage.

PER ½ CUP: 132 Calories • .5g Fat (3% calories from fat) • 13.5g Protein
23g Carbohydrates • 0mg Cholesterol • 356mg Sodium

Baked Potato Soup

EQUIPMENT: Measuring cup and spoons, French chef's knife, cutting board, 4-quart covered soup pot or electric saucepan, blender or food processor, food cutter (shredding blade), large serving spoon and ladle

PREPARATION TIME: 20 minutes ○ Makes 7 or 8 servings

2 cups Low-Sodium Chicken Stock (page 217) or canned

1 medium onion, diced

1 medium parsnip, diced

2 stalks celery, diced

¼ teaspoon Italian seasoning

¼ teaspoon freshly ground black pepper

1 medium baked russet potato, cubed

2 medium baked russet potatoes, quartered

2 cups whole milk

1 tablespoon chopped fresh parsley

¼ cup shredded cheddar cheese (optional)

2 slices bacon, crisp-cooked, crumbled (optional)

In a hot soup pot over medium heat, wet sauté the onion, parsnip and celery in ½ cup of the stock until tender, about 5 minutes, stirring occasionally. Add the remaining stock, Italian seasoning, pepper and cubed potato. Mix well and bring to a simmer. Do not boil.

In a blender or food processor, combine the quartered potatoes and milk. Puree on medium speed. Add the mixture to the soup pot and mix well. Cover the pan and open the vent. Reduce the heat to low and simmer until vegetables are tender and soup is thickened, about 10 minutes. Do not allow soup to boil.

To serve, top with bacon and the cheddar cheese, if using. Serve with warm French bread.

PER SERVING: 93 Calories • 2.2g Fat (19% calories from fat) • 6g Protein • 15g Carbohydrates • 8mg Cholesterol • 241mg Sodium

VARIATION

Substitute 3 cups mashed potatoes when baked potatoes are not available.

Black Bean Chili

EQUIPMENT: Boning knife, French chef's knife, cutting board, measuring cup and spoons, 4-quart covered soup pot or electric saucepan, food cutter (shredding blade), large serving spoon and ladle

PREPARATION TIME: 40 minutes O Makes 9 or 10 servings

1 pound pork loin chops, trimmed and meat cubed

2 medium onions, diced

½ green bell pepper, diced

1 clove garlic, minced

1 cooked chorizo or hot Italian sausage link, cubed

½ cup Chardonnay or other dry white wine

1 cup Low-Sodium Chicken Stock (page 217) or canned

4 cups cooked black beans with liquid (page 30) or 4 cups canned black beans
   with liquid

1 pinch ground cloves

1 pinch red pepper flakes

¼ teaspoon ground cumin

½ teaspoon dried oregano

½ teaspoon white distilled vinegar

½ cup shredded mozzarella cheese (optional)

1 tablespoon minced jalapeño chile

In a hot, dry soup pot over medium heat, brown the bones and meat on all sides, about 10 minutes, turning occasionally. Discard the bones. Add the onions, bell pepper and garlic and sauté until slightly browned, about 5 minutes, stirring occasionally. Add the sausage and cook, stirring until the mixture thickens.

Slowly stir in the wine and simmer until it has nearly evaporated. Stir in the stock, black beans, cloves, red pepper, cumin, oregano and vinegar. Cover the pan and open the vent. Reduce the heat to low and simmer for about 20 minutes. Do not allow the chili to boil.

To serve, top with the cheese, if using, and sprinkle with the jalapeño. Serve with warm Cuban bread.

PER SERVING: **227 Calories** • **8.4g Fat (34% calories from fat)** • **18g Protein** • **19g Carbohydrates** • **34mg Cholesterol** • **260mg Sodium (canned beans add about 469mg Sodium per serving)**

Beef Stew

EQUIPMENT: French chef's knife, cutting board, measuring cup and spoons, 4-quart covered soup pot or electric saucepan, large serving spoon and ladle

PREPARATION TIME: 45 minutes O Makes 9 or 10 servings

1 pound lean beef, trimmed and cubed

1 medium onion, diced

1 clove garlic, minced

1 teaspoon dried thyme

½ teaspoon chopped fresh parsley

3 cups Low-Sodium Brown Beef or Veal Stock (page 219) or canned

½ teaspoon Worcestershire sauce

¼ teaspoon freshly ground black pepper

2 medium russet potatoes, unpeeled, cubed

2 medium carrots, cut into ¼-inch-thick rounds

2 stalks celery, cut into ½-inch-thick slices

1 bay leaf

1 tablespoon Low-Cholesterol Roux (page 190)

In a hot, dry soup pot over medium heat, brown the beef on all sides, about 10 minutes, turning occasionally.

Add the onion and garlic and sauté in the beef drippings until slightly browned, about 5 minutes, stirring occasionally. Stir in the thyme and parsley.

Slowly stir in the stock. Stir in the Worcestershire sauce, pepper, potatoes, carrots, celery and bay leaf.

Stir in the roux. Cover the pan, open the vent and reduce the heat to low. Simmer until the vegetables are tender, 25 to 30 minutes. Do not allow the stew to boil. Discard the bay leaf.

To serve, ladle into soup bowls or a tureen and serve with rye bread and butter.

PER SERVING: 105 Calories • 2.9g Fat (23% calories from fat) • 14g Protein
8g Carbohydrates   28mg Cholesterol   253mg Sodium

Brunswick Stew

EQUIPMENT: **French chef's knife, cutting board, measuring cup and spoons, 4-quart covered soup pot or electric saucepan, large serving spoon and ladle**

PREPARATION TIME: **40 minutes**   ○   **Makes 9 or 10 servings**

1 medium onion, diced

1 medium carrot, diced

1 stalk celery, diced

1 clove garlic, minced

2 cups Low-Sodium Brown Veal or Beef Stock (page 219) or canned

1 tablespoon Low-Cholesterol Roux (page 190)

2 cups seeded and diced plum tomatoes or 2 cups canned whole tomatoes

1 (8-ounce) can low-sodium or no-salt-added cream-style corn

1 cup frozen lima beans

1 medium russet potato, unpeeled, cubed

1 pinch cayenne pepper

1 teaspoon dried thyme

1 bay leaf

1 teaspoon chopped fresh parsley

2 boneless, skinless chicken breasts halves, cubed

In a hot, dry stockpot over medium heat, dry sauté the onion, carrots, celery and garlic until slightly browned, about 5 minutes, stirring occasionally.

Slowly stir in the stock and roux. Add in the tomatoes, corn, lima beans, potato, cayenne, thyme, bay leaf, parsley and chicken. Mix well, cover the pan, open the vent and reduce the heat to low and simmer, about 30 minutes. Do not allow the stew to boil. Discard the bay leaf.

To serve, ladle into soup bowls and serve with warm Italian bread.

PER SERVING: **95 Calories** • **1g Fat (11% calories from fat)** • **9g Protein** • **15g Carbohydrate** • **12mg Cholesterol** • **183mg Sodium (canned tomatoes add 75mg Sodium per serving)**

Butternut Squash Soup

EQUIPMENT: French chef's knife, cutting board, food cutter (grater blade), measuring cup and spoons, 4-quart covered soup pot or electric saucepan, large serving spoon, blender or food processor and ladle

PREPARATION TIME: 45 minutes   O   Makes 7 or 8 servings

1 tablespoon unsalted butter

1 medium onion, diced

1 stalk celery, diced

1 (about 2-pound) butternut squash, peeled and grated

¼ teaspoon grated nutmeg

¼ teaspoon ground cinnamon

3 cups Low-Sodium Chicken Stock (page 217) or canned

1 cup whole milk or half-and-half

½ teaspoon sugar

¼ teaspoon freshly ground black pepper

½ teaspoon sweet paprika

1 teaspoon chopped parsley

½ teaspoon grated lemon zest

In a hot soup pot over medium-low heat, sauté the onion and celery in the butter until tender, about 5 minutes, stirring occasionally. Add the squash (do not add water). Cover the pan, close the vent and cook over medium-low heat. When the cover spins freely on a cushion of water, the vapor seal has formed, 3 to 5 minutes. After forming the seal, cook for 20 minutes. Don't peek. Removing the cover will destroy the vapor seal, lengthen the cooking time and may cause the vegetables to burn.

Drain off the excess water and puree the squash mixture in a food processor or blender.

Return the pureed squash mixture to the soup pot and stir in the nutmeg, cinnamon, stock, milk or half-and-half, sugar and pepper. Bring to a simmer over medium-low heat and cook for about 10 minutes, stirring occasionally. Do not allow the soup to boil.

To serve, ladle into soup bowls or a tureen and sprinkle with the paprika, parsley and lemon zest. Serve with warm bread.

PER SERVING, WITH MILK: 96 Calories   3g Fat (21% calories from fat)
6g Protein • 17g Carbohydrate • 8mg Cholesterol • 283mg Sodium

PER SERVING, WITH HALF-AND-HALF: 116 Calories •
5g Fat (34% calories from fat) • 6g Protein • 17g Carbohydrate •
15mg Cholesterol • 281mg Sodium

VARIATION

For a cool summer dish, cover and chill the soup in the refrigerator for about 1 hour before serving.

Chicken Noodle Soup

EQUIPMENT: Measuring cup and spoons, French chef's knife, cutting board, 6½-quart covered stockpot with steamer basket, large serving spoon and ladle

PREPARATION TIME: 1 hour ○ Makes 9 or 10 servings

3 pounds whole chicken, cut up and skin removed

About 4 quarts water

1 large onion, coarsely chopped

2 medium carrots, coarsely chopped

2 stalks celery with leaves, coarsely chopped

1 bay leaf

2 sprigs of fresh thyme or 1 teaspoon dried thyme

3 sprigs fresh parsley with stems

4 whole peppercorns

½ cup frozen green peas

½ pound egg noodles

1 teaspoon chopped fresh parsley

Place the steamer basket inside the stockpot, place the chicken in the basket and cover with water. Bring to a boil over medium-high heat. With a large serving spoon, skim off the froth (fat and scum) that rises to the surface. Reduce the heat to low. Add the onion, carrots, celery, bay leaf, thyme, parsley and peppercorns. Cover the pan, open the vent and simmer until the chicken is tender, about 40 minutes.

To strain the broth, lift the steamer basket up and allow the liquid to drain back into the stockpot. Remove the chicken to a cutting board and discard the vegetables and herbs. Continue to simmer the broth for about 10 minutes.

When the chicken has cooled sufficiently to handle, remove the meat from the bones with a knife and cut the meat into cubes. Return the chicken meat to the broth and stir in the peas and egg noodles. Cover the pan, open the vent and simmer until the egg noodles are cooked, about 15 minutes. Do not allow the soup to boil.

To serve, ladle into soup bowls or a tureen and sprinkle with the parsley. Serve with sour-dough bread.

PER SERVING: 283 Calories • 3.6g Fat (12% calories from fat) • 24g Protein •
38g Carbohydrates • 91mg Cholesterol • 151mg Sodium

Collard Greens Soup

EQUIPMENT: French chef's knife, cutting board, measuring cup and spoons, 6½-quart covered stockpot, large serving spoon and ladle

PREPARATION TIME: 1 hour   O   Makes 9 or 10 servings

1 large Spanish onion, diced

2 cloves garlic, minced

½ cup chopped ham or 1 small ham hock

1 cooked chorizo or hot Italian sausage link, cut into ¼-inch-thick slices

½ cup Chardonnay or other dry white wine

1 bunch fresh collard greens, washed, stems remove and chopped

3 cups Low-Sodium Chicken Stock (page 217) or canned

2 cups cooked white (cannellini) beans with liquid (page 30) or 2 cups canned beans
   with liquid

1 large russet potato, cubed

1 teaspoon dried thyme

1 teaspoon chopped fresh parsley

1 bay leaf

¼ teaspoon white pepper

1 teaspoon distilled white vinegar

In a hot, dry stockpot over medium heat, dry sauté the onion and garlic until slightly browned, about 5 minutes, stirring occasionally. Add the ham or ham hock and sausage and cook, stirring, until the mixture thickens.

Slowly stir in the wine and simmer until reduced by half. Reduce the heat to low. Add the collard greens. Cover the pan, close the vent and cook until the collard greens are tender, about 25 minutes.

Stir in the remaining ingredients. Cover the pan, open the vent and simmer until the potatoes are tender, about 30 minutes. Do not allow the soup to boil. Discard the bay leaf and ham hock, if using.

To serve, ladle into soup bowls or a tureen. Serve with warm Cuban bread.

PER SERVING: **146 Calories** • **5g Fat (29% calories from fat)** •
11g Protein • **16g Carbohydrates** • **18mg Cholesterol** •
243mg Sodium (canned beans add about 75mg Sodium per serving)

Cream of Asparagus Soup

EQUIPMENT: French chef's knife, cutting board, 2-quart covered saucepan, measuring cups and spoons, large serving spoon and ladle

PREPARATION TIME: 1 hour   ○   Makes 5 or 6 servings

1 bunch asparagus (about 1½ pounds), trimmed and cut into 1-inch pieces

1 medium onion, diced

1 medium carrot, diced

1 stalk celery, diced

½ tablespoon Low-Cholesterol Roux (page 190)

1 cup Low-Sodium Chicken Stock (page 217) or canned

2 cups whole milk or half-and-half

¼ teaspoon Italian seasoning

¼ teaspoon white pepper

1 pinch fennel seeds

¼ teaspoon sweet paprika

Place the asparagus, onion, carrot and celery in the saucepan. Rinse with cold water and pour the water off. The water that clings to the vegetables is sufficient for cooking the waterless way (see Note, page 3). Cover the pan, close the vent and cook over medium-low heat. When the cover spins freely on a cushion of water, the vapor seal has formed, 3 to 5 minutes. After forming the seal, cook for 20 minutes. Don't peek. Removing the cover will destroy the vapor seal, lengthen the cooking time and may cause the vegetables to burn.

In a measuring cup, combine the roux with the chicken stock.

Add the stock mixture, milk or half-and-half, Italian seasoning, white pepper and fennel seeds to the saucepan. Mix well and bring the soup to a simmer over medium-low heat, stirring as it begins to thicken. Do not allow the soup to boil.

To serve, ladle the soup into soup bowls or a tureen and sprinkle with paprika. Serve with warm French bread.

PER SERVING WITH WHOLE MILK: 78 Calories • 3.3g Fat (35% calories from fat)
5g Protein   9g Carbohydrates • 12mg Cholesterol   229mg Sodium

10g Fat (63% calories from fat) • 5g Protein • 9g Carbohydrates •
31mg Cholesterol • 222mg Sodium

VARIATION

When the vegetables are finished cooking, puree all the ingredients in a blender or food processor and finish the cooking process as directed above.

Cuban Clam Chowder

EQUIPMENT: French chef's knife, cutting board, measuring cup and spoons, vegetable brush, 4-quart covered soup pot or electric saucepan, large serving spoon and ladle

PREPARATION TIME: 45 minutes ○ Makes 9 to 10 servings

20 fresh chowder clams in shells or 1 cup canned clams

1 large Spanish onion, diced

1 large green bell pepper, diced

2 cloves garlic, minced

1 teaspoon dried thyme

1 teaspoon dried oregano

1 cooked chorizo or hot Italian sausage link, cut into ¼-inch-thick slices

2½ cups Low-Sodium Fish Stock (page 218) or Low-Sodium Chicken Stock
    (page 217) or canned

2 cups seeded and chopped plum tomatoes or 2 cups canned whole tomatoes

1 bay leaf

1 medium russet potato, cubed

½ teaspoon chopped fresh parsley

¼ teaspoon red pepper flakes

½ teaspoon distilled vinegar

1 tablespoon Low-Cholesterol Roux (page 190)

Under cold running water, with a vegetable brush, clean the clams well and set aside. Clams that appear heavy or do not close tightly when tapped are either filled with sand or near death and must be discarded.

In a hot, dry stockpot over medium heat, dry sauté the onion, bell pepper and garlic until slightly browned, about 5 minutes, stirring occasionally. Add the thyme, oregano and sausage and cook, stirring, until the mixture thickens.

Add the remaining ingredients. Reduce the heat to low, cover the pan and open the vent. Simmer for about 25 minutes. Do not allow the chowder to boil. Discard the bay leaf.

To serve, ladle the chowder into soup bowls. Serve with warm Cuban bread.

> **PER SERVING:** 91 Calories • 3g Fat (33% calories from fat) •
> 8g Protein • 8g Carbohydrates • 13mg Cholesterol •
> 197mg Sodium (canned clams and tomatoes add 79mg Sodium per serving)

Hungarian Goulash

EQUIPMENT: French chef's knife, cutting board, measuring cup and spoons, 4-quart covered soup pot or electric saucepan, large serving spoon, and ladle

PREPARATION TIME: 40 minutes O Makes 11 or 12 servings

1 kielbasa (Polish sausage) link, cut into ¼-inch-thick slices

1 pound turkey tenderloin, cut into small cubes

1 medium onion, diced

1 stalk celery, diced

1 medium green bell pepper, cut into small pieces

2 cloves garlic, minced

3 cups Low-Sodium Brown Veal or Beef Stock (page 219) or canned

3 medium red potatoes, unpeeled, cubed

2 cups seeded and chopped plum tomatoes or 2 cups canned
    whole tomatoes

1 tablespoon sweet Hungarian paprika

1 dash cayenne pepper

1 bay leaf

1 teaspoon dried thyme

½ teaspoon caraway seed

1 teaspoon chopped fresh parsley

In a hot, dry soup pot over medium heat, brown the kielbasa and turkey on all sides, about 10 minutes, turning occasionally.

Add the onion, celery, bell pepper and garlic and sauté until slightly browned, about 5 minutes, stirring occasionally.

Slowly stir in the stock. Stir in the remaining ingredients. Reduce the heat to low, cover the pan and open the vent. Simmer until the vegetables are tender, about 30 minutes. Do not allow the goulash to boil.

To serve, ladle the goulash into individual soup bowls. Sprinkle with the parsley. Serve with pumpernickel bread and butter.

PER SERVING: 118 Calories   5g Fat (37% calories from fat)
10g Protein   •   8g Carbohydrates   •   29mg Cholesterol   •
152mg Sodium (canned tomatoes add 63mg Sodium per serving)

Hearty Chicken Stew

EQUIPMENT: French chef's knife, cutting board, measuring cup and spoons, 4-quart covered soup pot or electric saucepan, large serving spoon and ladle

PREPARATION TIME: 45 minutes ○ Makes 7 or 8 servings

4 cups Low-Sodium Chicken Stock (page 217) or canned

1 tablespoon Low-Cholesterol Roux (page 190)

2 medium boneless, skinless chicken breast halves, cubed

1 medium onion, quartered and cut into ½-inch-thick slices

3 medium carrots, sliced ½-inch thick

2 stalks celery, sliced ½-inch thick

2 medium red potatoes, unpeeled, quartered

3 cloves garlic, peeled

¼ teaspoon freshly ground black pepper

½ teaspoon poultry seasoning

½ teaspoon chopped fresh parsley

1 bay leaf

In the soup pot, combine the stock and roux and mix well. Add the remaining ingredients. Cover the pan, open the vent and simmer until vegetables are tender, about 40 minutes, stirring occasionally. Do not allow the stew to boil. Discard the bay leaf.

To serve, ladle the stew into individual soup bowls or a tureen and sprinkle with the parsley. Serve with warm sourdough bread and butter.

PER SERVING: 96 Calories • 1g Fat (10% calories from fat) • 12g Protein
14g Carbohydrates • 15mg Cholesterol • 364mg Sodium

Italian Turkey Soup

EQUIPMENT: French chef's knife, cutting board, 4-quart covered soup pot or electric saucepan, measuring cup and spoons, large serving spoon and ladle

PREPARATION TIME: 40 minutes   ○   Makes 11 or 12 servings

1 medium onion, diced

1 medium carrot, diced

2 stalks celery, diced

1 medium red bell pepper, diced

1 clove garlic, minced

6 cups Low-Sodium Chicken Stock (page 217) or canned

1 teaspoon poultry seasoning

1 pound turkey dark meat, skinless

1 cup frozen green peas

8 ounces spinach-filled tortellini

1 tablespoon chopped fresh parsley

In a hot, dry stockpot over medium heat, dry sauté the onion, carrot, celery, bell pepper and garlic until slightly browned, about 5 minutes, stirring occasionally.

Slowly stir in the stock. Stir in the remaining ingredients, except parsley. Reduce the heat to low, cover the pan and open the vent. Simmer until the turkey is tender, about 30 minutes. Do not allow the soup to boil.

To serve, ladle the soup into soup bowls or a tureen and sprinkle with the parsley. Serve with warm Italian garlic bread.

PER SERVING: 110 Calories   •   3g Fat (23% calories from fat)   •   16g Protein   •   8g Carbohydrates   •   51mg Cholesterol   •   392mg Sodium

Light Lobster Bisque

This is a huge favorite around our house, but it does take some time and effort to prepare. So when you have a free afternoon, take the time and you will thoroughly enjoy the results. This is an excellent way to make two lobsters serve a crowd.

PLEASE READ THE ENTIRE RECIPE BEFORE BEGINNING.

EQUIPMENT: Butcher knife, measuring cup and spoons, French chef's knife, cutting board, extra-large sauté pan or large wok, large serving spoon, lighter stick or long match, blender or food processor, fine strainer, 4-quart covered soup pot or electric saucepan, 10-inch gourmet skillet and ladle

PREPARATION TIME: 1 hour 30 minutes　○　Makes 11 or 12 servings

2 (1- to 1½-pound) live Maine lobsters

1 medium onion, diced

1 medium carrot, diced

2 stalks celery, diced

¼ cup tomato puree

½ cup Chardonnay or other dry white wine

½ cup brandy

2 teaspoons dried thyme

2 bay leaves

4 cups Low-Sodium Fish Stock (page 218) or Chicken Stock (page 217) or canned

2 tablespoons unsalted butter

2 tablespoons all-purpose flour

2 cups whole milk or half-and-half

½ cup dry sherry

½ teaspoon sweet paprika

1 tablespoon chopped fresh parsley

2 tablespoons sour cream

To kill the lobsters, dip their heads into boiling water for 3 to 4 minutes.

With a butcher knife, split the lobster in half from head to tail and remove the sack at the top of the head. Under cold running water, clean the carcass and separate the claws, legs and tail from the body. Set aside.

In a hot, large dry sauté skillet or wok, dry sauté the onion, carrot and celery until slightly browned, about 5 minutes, stirring occasionally. Stir in the tomato puree and cook, stirring, until reddish-brown in color.

Slowly stir in the wine. Place the claws, tail, legs and body, meat-side down, on top of the vegetable mixture. Reduce the heat to medium-low, cover the pan and close the vent. Simmer until the shells turn red and the meat is cooked through, 8 to 10 minutes.

Remove the lid and increase the heat to medium-high. When the mixture begins to boil, pour in the brandy and ignite with a long match or lighter stick. CAUTION: *Be careful to keep your face away from the flames because they will temporarily flare up.* Using a long serving spoon, stir until the flames are extinguished. Stir in the thyme and bay leaves and simmer until reduced by one-half. Reduce the heat to low, remove the lobster parts to a cutting board. Stir in the stock and simmer for about 10 minutes.

When the lobster parts have cooled sufficiently to handle, remove the meat from the shells and set aside. Retain the soft-shell pieces, legs and underbelly, and discard the hard-shell pieces. (Hard shell is any part that does not easily give when squeezed between your forefinger and thumb.) Place the soft-shell parts and the lobster stock in a blender or food processor and puree on medium speed. (You may need to do this in stages depending on the capacity and power of your blender or food processor.) Strain though a fine strainer into the soup pot.

Melt the butter in the soup pot over medium-low heat. Stir in the flour and cook, stirring, until a light golden color. Add the strained lobster stock and 5 cups of the reduced lobster cooking liquid. Stir in the milk or half-and-half and simmer to desired thickness. Do not boil the bisque.

Chop the lobster meat into bite-size pieces. In a hot skillet over medium heat, wet sauté the lobster with the sherry and paprika for 1 to 2 minutes and add it to the bisque.

To serve, ladle the bisque into individual soup bowls or a tureen. Sprinkle with chopped fresh parsley and top with a dollop of sour cream.

PER SERVING, WITH MILK: 119 Calories • 3g Fat (29% calories from fat) •
13g Protein • 4.4g Carbohydrates • 56mg Cholesterol • 317mg Sodium

PER SERVING, WITH HALF-AND-HALF: 137 Calories • 5g Fat (41% calories from fat)
13g Protein • 4.3g Carbohydrates   62mg Cholesterol   314mg Sodium

Manhattan Clam Chowder

EQUIPMENT: **French chef's knife, cutting board, measuring cup and spoons, 4-quart covered soup pot or electric saucepan, large serving spoon and ladle**

PREPARATION TIME: **40 minutes** ○ **Makes 9 or 10 servings**

16 chowder or cherrystone clams in shells or 1 cup canned clams

1 hot Italian sausage link, removed from casing (optional)

1 medium onion, diced

2 medium carrots, diced

2 stalks celery, diced

1 medium green bell pepper, diced

1 clove garlic, minced

1 teaspoon dried thyme

1 teaspoon dried oregano

½ teaspoon freshly ground black pepper

1 teaspoon chopped fresh parsley

2 cups Low-Sodium Fish Stock (page 218) or Chicken Stock (page 217) or canned

2 cups seeded and chopped plum tomatoes or canned whole tomatoes

1 bay leaf

1 teaspoon fresh lemon juice

2 medium red potatoes, unpeeled, cubed

1 cup no-salt-added V-8 juice

Under cold running water, with a vegetable brush, clean the clams well and set aside. Clams that appear heavy or do not close tightly when tapped are either filled with sand or near death and must be discarded.

In a hot, dry soup pot over medium heat, dry sauté the Italian sausage until cooked through. Add the onion, carrots, celery, bell pepper and garlic and sauté until slightly browned, 8 to 10 minutes, stirring occasionally. Stir in the thyme, oregano, pepper and parsley.

Slowly stir in the stock. Add the remaining ingredients. Reduce the heat to low, cover the pan, open the vent and simmer for about 25 minutes. Do not allow the chowder to boil.

To serve, ladle the chowder into soup bowls. Serve with rye bread and butter.

PER SERVING, WITHOUT SAUSAGE: 63 Calories • 0.4g Fat (6% calories from fat) 6g Protein • 10g Carbohydrates • 8mg Cholesterol • 192mg Sodium (canned tomatoes add 75mg sodium per serving)

PER SERVING, WITH SAUSAGE: 92 Calories • 3g Fat (29% calories from fat) • 7g Protein • 10g Carbohydrates • 14mg Cholesterol • 254mg Sodium (canned tomatoes add 75mg Sodium per serving)

Minestrone

EQUIPMENT: French chef's knife, cutting board, measuring cup and spoons, 4-quart covered soup pot or electric saucepan, large serving spoon, food cutter (grating blade) and ladle

PREPARATION TIME: 40 minutes   o   Makes 9 or 10 servings

1 medium onion, diced

1 medium carrot, diced

1 stalk celery, diced

1 clove garlic, minced

½ teaspoon dried thyme

½ teaspoon Italian seasoning

2 sprigs fresh parsley

1 bay leaf, stem removed and finely crumbled

½ cup Chianti or Cabernet Sauvignon wine

2 cups Low-Sodium Brown Veal or Beef Stock (page 219)

2 cups seeded and chopped plum tomatoes or 2 cups canned whole tomatoes

2 medium red potatoes, unpeeled, diced

1 small zucchini, cut into ½-inch cubes

¼ head of green cabbage, finely chopped

2 cups cooked white (cannellini) beans in liquid (page 30) or 2 cups canned beans
   with liquid

¼ cup tagliatelle or ditalini pasta

½ teaspoon freshly ground black pepper

2 tablespoons freshly grated Parmesan cheese

4 fresh basil leaves, cut into ¼-inch strips

In a hot, dry soup pot over medium heat, dry sauté the onion, carrot, celery and garlic until slightly browned, about 3 to 5 minutes, stirring occasionally. Stir in the thyme, Italian seasoning, parsley and bay leaf.

Slowly stir in the wine. Stir in the stock, tomatoes, potatoes, zucchini, cabbage, beans, pasta and pepper. Reduce the heat to low, cover the pan, open the vent and simmer for 20 to 25 minutes. Do not allow the soup to boil.

To serve, ladle the soup into soup bowls or a tureen. Sprinkle with the Parmesan cheese and basil. Serve with warm Italian bread.

PER SERVING: 147 Calories • 1g Fat (6% calories from fat) •
8g Protein • 22g Carbohydrates • 1mg Cholesterol •
195mg Sodium (canned beans and tomatoes add 309mg Sodium per serving)

New Orleans–Style Seafood Filé Gumbo

EQUIPMENT: French chef's knife, cutting board, 4-quart covered soup pot or electric saucepan, measuring cup and spoons, large serving spoon and ladle

PREPARATION TIME: 40 minutes   O   Makes 9 or 10 servings

1 andouille sausage link

1 medium onion, diced

1 medium bell pepper, diced

2 cloves garlic, minced

1 tablespoon Low-Cholesterol Roux (page 190)

½ teaspoon dried thyme

½ teaspoon dried oregano

½ teaspoon filé powder

2 cups Low-Sodium Fish Stock (page 218) or Low-Sodium Chicken Stock (page 217) or canned

2 cups seeded and chopped plum tomatoes or canned whole tomatoes

1 pound okra, sliced crosswise into ¼-inch-thick rounds

½ cup lump crabmeat

½ pound bay scallops

4 drops hot pepper sauce

2 cups cooked long-grain rice

4 fresh basil leaves, cut into ¼-inch strips

In a hot, dry soup pot over medium heat, brown the sausage on all sides, about 15 minutes, turning occasionally. Remove the sausage to a cutting board and slice into ¼-inch-thick rounds.

Add the onion, bell pepper and garlic to the pot and sauté until slightly browned, 3 to 5 minutes, stirring occasionally. Add the remaining ingredients and the sausage. Stir to combine and reduce the heat to low. Cover the pan, open the vent and simmer, 15 to 20 minutes, stirring occasionally. Do not allow the gumbo to boil.

To serve, ladle the gumbo over the rice and sprinkle with the basil. Serve with Hot and Spicy Cornbread (page 21).

PER SERVING: 144 Calories • 3g Fat (18% calories from fat) • 11g Protein • 20g Carbohydrates • 19mg Cholesterol • 317mg Sodium (canned tomatoes add 75mg Sodium per serving)

Pasta é Fagioli

EQUIPMENT: French chef's knife, cutting board, measuring cup and spoons, 4-quart covered soup pot or electric saucepan, large serving spoon, food cutter (grating blade) and ladle

PREPARATION TIME: 40 minutes ○ Makes 9 or 10 servings

1 medium onion, minced

1 medium carrot, diced

1 stalk celery, diced

1 medium green bell pepper, diced

2 cloves garlic, minced

½ teaspoon dried thyme

½ teaspoon Italian seasoning

3 cups Low-Sodium Chicken Stock (page 217) or Pan-Roasted Vegetable Stock (page 221) or canned

4 cups cooked white (cannellini) beans in liquid (page 30) or 4 cups canned beans with liquid

¼ cup tagliatelle or ditalini pasta

1 teaspoon distilled white vinegar

2 tablespoons freshly grated Parmesan cheese

4 fresh basil leaves, cut in ¼-inch strips

In a hot, dry stockpot over medium heat, dry sauté the onion, carrot, celery, bell pepper and garlic until slightly browned, about 10 minutes, stirring occasionally. Stir in the thyme and Italian seasoning.

Slowly stir in the stock. Stir in the beans, pasta and vinegar. Reduce the heat to low. Cover the pan, open the vent and simmer until the vegetables and pasta are tender, about 30 minutes. Do not allow the soup to boil.

To serve, ladle the soup into soup bowls or a tureen and top with the Parmesan cheese and basil. Serve with warm Italian garlic bread.

PER SERVING: 106 Calories • 1g Fat (5% calories from fat) •
9g Protein   19g Carbohydrates • 1mg Cholesterol
236mg Sodium (canned beans add 352mg Sodium per serving)

Spanish Bean Soup

EQUIPMENT: French chef's knife, cutting board, measuring cup and spoons, 4-quart covered soup pot or electric saucepan, large serving spoon and ladle

PREPARATION TIME: 45 minutes ○ Makes 9 or 10 servings

1 medium Spanish onion, minced

1 stalk celery, diced

2 cloves garlic, minced

1 teaspoon dried oregano

½ cup chopped ham or 1 small ham hock

1 cooked chorizo or hot Italian sausage link, cut into ¼-inch-thick slices

½ cup Chardonnay or other dry white wine

2 cups Low-Sodium Chicken Stock (page 217) or Pan-Roasted Vegetable Stock
   (page 221) or canned

4 cups cooked garbanzo beans with liquid (page 30) or 4 cups canned beans
   with liquid

1 teaspoon chopped fresh parsley

1 bay leaf

¼ teaspoon white pepper

1 large russet potato, unpeeled, cubed

1 teaspoon white distilled vinegar

In a hot, dry soup pot over medium heat, dry sauté the onion, celery and garlic until slightly browned, 3 to 5 minutes, stirring occasionally. Add the oregano, ham or ham hock and sausage and cook, stirring, until the mixture thickens slightly, 3 to 5 minutes.

Slowly stir in the wine and simmer until reduced by half. Stir in the remaining ingredients. Cover the pan, open the vent and simmer until the potatoes are cooked through, 25 to 30 minutes. Do not allow the soup to boil. Discard the bay leaf and ham hock, if using.

To serve, ladle the soup into soup bowls or a tureen. Serve with Cuban bread.

PER SERVING: 193 Calories • 5g Fat (23% calories from fat) •
13g Protein   24g Carbohydrates • 18mg Cholesterol
188mg Sodium (canned beans add 469mg Sodium per serving)

White Chili

EQUIPMENT: French chef's knife, cutting board, measuring cup and spoons, 4-quart covered soup pot or electric saucepan, large serving spoon, food cutter (julienne blade) and ladle

PREPARATION TIME: 30 minutes ✺ Makes 9 or 10 servings

1 medium onion, diced

1 medium parsnip, diced

1 stalk celery, diced

3 cloves garlic, minced

2½ cups Low-Sodium Chicken Stock (page 217) or canned

½ teaspoon ground cumin

½ teaspoon dried oregano

¼ teaspoon ground cloves

1 dash red pepper flakes

2 large boneless, skinless chicken breast halves, cubed

4 cups cooked white (cannellini) beans with liquid (page 30) or 4 cups canned beans
    with liquid

¼ cup grated Monterey Jack cheese

1 small jalapeño chile, minced

2 tablespoons sour cream

In a hot soup pot over medium heat, wet sauté the onion, parsnip, celery and garlic in ½ cup of the stock until tender, 3 to 5 minutes, stirring occasionally.

Stir in the cumin, oregano, cloves and red pepper. Add the remaining stock, chicken and beans. Cover the pan and open the vent and simmer until chicken and vegetables are tender, 20 to 25 minutes.

To serve, ladle the chili into soup bowls. Sprinkle with the cheese and jalapeño chile and top with the sour cream. Serve with warm sourdough bread.

PER SERVING: 148 Calories • 2g Fat (13% calories from fat) •
14g Protein   21g Carbohydrates   14mg Cholesterol
216mg Sodium (canned beans add 354mg sodium per serving)

Swiss Broccoli Soup

EQUIPMENT: **Measuring cup and spoons, French chef's knife, cutting board, 4-quart covered soup pot or electric saucepan**

PREPARATION TIME: **20 minutes ○ Makes 5 or 6 servings**

1 medium onion, diced

½ cup diced broccoli stems

1 medium carrot, diced

1½ cups Low-Sodium Chicken Stock (page 217) or canned

1½ cups lowfat milk

1 cup grated low-sodium Swiss cheese

1 tablespoon Low-Cholesterol Roux (page 190)

¼ teaspoon white pepper

¼ teaspoon grated nutmeg

Florets from 1 head broccoli

Sweet paprika

In the 4-quart soup pot over medium heat, wet sauté the onion, broccoli stems and carrot in ½ cup of the stock until tender, 3 to 5 minutes, stirring occasionally.

Add the remaining stock, milk, Swiss cheese and roux. Cook, stirring occasionally, until the soup thickens slightly and begins to simmer, 5 to 7 minutes.

Reduce the heat to low, stir in the white pepper, nutmeg and chopped broccoli. Cover the pan, open the vent and simmer 5 to 7 minutes.

To serve, sprinkle with paprika and serve with warm French bread.

PER SERVING: **135 Calories • 7g Fat (43% calories from fat) • 11g Protein • 9g Carbohydrates • 20mg Cholesterol • 266mg Sodium**

Healthy
MEAT AND OTHER ENTREES

T HERE ARE THREE different techniques for cooking meats the waterless, greaseless way on top of the stove: pan broiling, roasting and sautéing.

Throughout this section, you will learn the methods of cooking a roast on top of the stove, how to cook the perfect steak, how to bake, the methods associated with braising, and the quick and easy methods of sautéing. All the recipes are cooked on top of the stove.

PAN BROILING AND SAUTÉING

Because heat is conducted very efficiently through quality waterless, greaseless cookware to the meat, the meat's surface tends to brown very quickly, in 1 to 2 minutes. No fat is needed for cooking. Once the meat is browned sufficiently, it will release easily from the pan for turning. To prevent the meat's surface from toughening while the inside cooks, the heat is usually reduced after the initial browning. If the pan is covered, water vapor is trapped and a process more like basting results. Therefore, you must open the vent when pan-frying.

ROASTING

If you brown first and then roast on top of the stove at medium to medium-high temperatures for a given doneness, your meats will have been cooked in a relatively short period of time.

Instructions for roasting on top of the stove are relatively simple to follow. Preheat the pan's bottom over medium or medium-high heat. Sprinkle a few water droplets into the pan. If the water droplets "dance," then the pan is hot enough to quickly brown the meat. If they just evaporate, then the pan is not hot enough. Place the meat in the pan and brown on all sides.

Cover the pan and reduce the heat to medium-low. When bubbles begin to form around the cover, you have reached the proper cooking temperature for roasting on top of the stove. If there are no bubbles, the heat is too low. If the moisture around the top of the pan is spitting, the heat is too high. It's that simple to start roasting your meats the waterless, greaseless healthy way on top of the stove.

Marinated Orange Rosemary Chicken

EQUIPMENT: Mixing bowl, large covered sauté skillet or electric skillet, measuring cup and spoons, French chef's knife and cutting board

PREPARATION TIME: 30 minutes ❍ Makes: 4 servings

1½ cups fresh orange juice

4 sprigs rosemary

½ teaspoon freshly ground black pepper

4 skinless chicken breast halves

1 teaspoon brown sugar (optional)

¼ cup Light Béchamel Sauce (page 188)

1 tablespoon chopped fresh rosemary leaves

4 orange slices

To prepare the marinade, in a mixing bowl or large freezer bag, combine the orange juice, rosemary sprigs and pepper. Place the chicken breasts into the marinade, cover or seal the bag and refrigerate for 1 hour.

Place the chicken in a hot, dry skillet over medium-high heat. Cover the pan, open the vent and cook until golden brown and until the chicken releases easily from the pan, 12 to 15 minutes. Turn the chicken, cover the pan and roast for 5 to 10 minutes on the other side. Remove the chicken to a warm platter and keep warm.

Slowly stir the marinade into the chicken drippings and simmer until reduced by about half, 3 to 4 minutes. Stir in the brown sugar, if using, and béchamel and simmer until sauce thickens, 1 to 2 minutes. Remove the rosemary sprigs and serve.

To serve, top the chicken with the sauce, sprinkle with chopped rosemary and garnish with a slice of orange. Serve with Parsnips and Cream (page 148) and Pan-Roasted Potatoes (page 155).

PER SERVING: 272 Calories • 2.6g Fat (9% calories from fat) • 35g Protein • 27g Carbohydrates • 82mg Cholesterol • 100mg Sodium

Barbecue Rosemary Chicken

EQUIPMENT: Butcher knife, French chef's knife, cutting board, measuring cup and spoons and large covered sauté skillet or electric skillet

PREPARATION TIME: 45 minutes ○ Makes 6 to 8 servings

2 skinless chicken breast halves

2 skinless chicken thighs

2 skinless chicken legs

2 chicken wings, skinned

2 medium sweet onions, diced

2 cloves garlic, minced

2 tablespoons tomato paste

2 cups brewed coffee

½ cup apple cider vinegar

2 tablespoons Worcestershire sauce

1 cup packed light brown sugar

¼ teaspoon red pepper flakes

¼ teaspoon Dijon mustard

¼ teaspoon ground cinnamon (optional)

1 tablespoon minced dried rosemary

1 tablespoon chopped fresh parsley

Place the chicken in a hot, dry skillet over medium heat. Cover the pan, open the vent and cook until golden brown and the chicken releases easily from the pan, 12 to 15 minutes. Turn the chicken, cover the pan and brown the other side, 5 to 7 minutes. Remove the chicken to a warm platter and keep warm.

Add the onions and garlic to the chicken drippings and sauté until slightly browned, 3 to 5 minutes, stirring occasionally. Add the tomato paste and stir until the paste turns reddish-brown in color, about 5 minutes. Do not allow the residue that forms on the bottom of the pan to burn.

Slowly stir in the coffee. Add the remaining ingredients, except the parsley, and stir to combine. Return the chicken to the skillet and reduce the heat to medium-low. Cover the pan, open the vent and simmer for 10 to 15 minutes. Do not allow to boil.

To serve, top the chicken with barbecue sauce, sprinkle with the parsley and serve with Fresh Corn on the Cob (page 143) and Stovetop Baked Barbecue Beans (page 138).

PER SERVING: **238** Calories   •   **4g** Fat (15% calories from fat)   •   **27g** Protein   •
23g Carbohydrates   •   **89mg** Cholesterol   •   **160mg** Sodium

Chicken Cacciatore

EQUIPMENT: Large covered sauté skillet, French chef's knife, cutting board, measuring cup and spoons, 6½-quart stockpot, 6-quart pasta/steamer inset, and food cutter (grating blade)

PREPARATION TIME: 45 minutes ○ Makes 8 servings

8 skinless chicken thighs

1 medium onion, diced

1 medium carrot, diced

1 stalk celery, diced

1 clove garlic, minced

1 tablespoon Italian seasoning

½ teaspoon freshly ground black pepper

½ cup port wine

1 cup sliced mushrooms (about 2 ounces)

1 cup Low-Sodium Chicken Stock (page 217 or canned)

2 cups seeded and chopped plum tomatoes or canned whole tomatoes

½ pound linguini

2 tablespoons freshly grated Parmesan cheese

2 tablespoons chopped fresh basil

In a hot, dry skillet over medium heat, place the chicken thighs. Cover the pan, open the vent and cook until golden brown and release easily from the skillet, 7 to 8 minutes per side. Remove the chicken to a warm platter and keep warm. Discard excess chicken fat from the skillet.

Add the onion, carrot, celery and garlic and sauté in the chicken drippings until slightly browned, 3 to 5 minutes, stirring occasionally. Stir in the Italian seasoning and black pepper.

Slowly stir in the wine. Simmer until reduced by half, 2 to 3 minutes, stirring occasionally.

Add the mushrooms, chicken stock and tomatoes. Mix well and reduce the heat to medium-low. Return the chicken thighs to the skillet and baste with the sauce. Cover the pan, open the vent and simmer for 15 to 20 minutes.

Meanwhile, with the 6-quart steamer/pasta insert in the steamer/spaghetti cooker, cook the linguini according to the package directions.

To serve, divide the linguini among 8 plates and divide the sauce over the linguini. Place one chicken thigh on each serving. Sprinkle with the Parmesan cheese and basil.

PER SERVING WITH FRESH TOMATOES: 270 Calories •
4.8g Fat (17% calories from fat) • 25g Protein • 29g Carbohydrates •
79mg Cholesterol • 252mg Sodium (canned tomatoes add 94mg sodium per serving)

VARIATION

For a Spanish flair, add 1 minced chorizo sausage link, ½ cup sliced black olives and 2 tablespoons capers. Serve over yellow rice.

PER SERVING: 298 Calories • 8.7g Fat (28% calories from fat) • 25g Protein •
26g Carbohydrates • 85mg Cholesterol • 455mg Sodium

Chicken Chow Mein

EQUIPMENT: 1¼–quart covered saucepan, French chef's knife, cutting board, food cutter (slicing blade) measuring cup and spoons, small mixing bowl, medium covered sauté skillet or 2-quart covered saucepan

PREPARATION TIME: 30 minutes ○ Makes 5 or 6 servings

1 cup basmati or other long-grain rice

1 teaspoon unsalted margarine or butter (optional)

2 medium onions, halved and sliced

1 medium red bell pepper, cut into ¼-inch-thick slices

2 stalks celery, cut into ¼-inch-thick slices

½ cup canned sliced water chestnuts

1 teaspoon grated fresh ginger

2 boneless, skinless chicken breast halves, cut into ¼-inch-thick slices

1¼ cups Low-Sodium Chicken Stock (page 217) or canned

1 tablespoon Low-Cholesterol Roux (page 190)

1 pinch white pepper (optional)

1 (5-ounce) package chow mein noodles, cooked

½ cup chopped green onions

In the 1¼–quart saucepan, bring the water to a boil and stir in the rice and margarine or butter, if using. Boil the rice for about 1 minute and stir. Cover the pan, close the vent and remove from heat. Let stand 25 to 30 minutes.

To the medium skillet, add the onions, bell pepper, celery, water chestnuts, ginger and chicken. Rinse with cold water and pour the water off. The water that clings to the ingredients is sufficient for cooking the waterless way (see Note, page 3). Cover the pan, close the vent and cook over medium-low heat. When the cover spins freely on a cushion of water, the vapor seal has formed, 3 to 5 minutes. After forming the seal, cook for 10 to 15 minutes. Don't peek. Removing the cover will destroy the vapor seal, lengthen the cooking time and may cause the vegetables to burn.

While the vegetables and chicken are cooking, combine the stock, roux and white pepper, if using, in a measuring cup. Mix well and set aside.

Add the stock mixture to the skillet and increase the heat slightly. Simmer, uncovered, until the mixture thickens, 3 to 5 minutes, stirring occasionally. Do not boil.

To serve, spoon the rice onto a serving platter. Top with the chow mein noodles and the chicken and vegetable mixture. Sprinkle with the green onions.

PER SERVING: 242 Calories • 4.7g Fat (17% calories from fat) • 13g Protein • 38g Carbohydrates • 17mg Cholesterol • 348mg Sodium

Chicken Cordon Bleu

EQUIPMENT: Butcher knife, large covered conventional skillet or electric skillet, measuring cup and spoons and 10-inch stainless steel wok

PREPARATION TIME: 35 minutes ○ Makes 6 servings

6 medium boneless, skinless chicken breast halves

3 slices low-sodium Swiss cheese

3 extra-lean ham slices,

1¼ cups Low-Sodium Chicken Stock (page 217) or canned

1 tablespoon Low-Cholesterol Roux (page 190)

1 pinch cayenne pepper

½ cup Chardonnay or other dry white wine

¼ cup half-and-half (optional)

1 tablespoon chopped fresh parsley

With a butcher knife, butterfly each chicken breast half by slicing about three-quarters of the way through and laying the breast open. Place a half slice of Swiss cheese and a half slice of ham on the open breast. Fold over and secure with a toothpick. Trim off any excess cheese and ham.

Place the chicken in a medium-hot dry skillet over medium-high heat. Cover the pan, open the vent and cook until chicken is golden brown and releases easily from the pan, 7 to 8 minutes per side.

While the chicken is cooking, combine the chicken stock, roux and cayenne pepper in a hot wok over medium heat. Cook, stirring, until the roux is incorporated into the stock and the mixture thickens slightly, 3 to 5 minutes. Remove from the heat and set aside.

Transfer the chicken to a warm platter and keep warm.

Slowly stir in the wine. Bring to a simmer and cook until reduced by half, 2 to 3 minutes, stirring occasionally. Add the reduced stock mixture. Cook, stirring, until the sauce thickens, 1 to 2 minutes. Stir in the half-and-half, if using.

To serve, remove the toothpicks from the chicken. Top the chicken with the sauce and sprinkle with the parsley. Serve with Candied Carrots (page 142) and Spinach, Italian Style (page 169).

PER SERVING: 363 Calories • 19g Fat (48% calories from fat) • 42g Protein • 3.7g Carbohydrates • 110mg Cholesterol • 480mg Sodium

PER SERVING, WITH HALF-AND-HALF: 376 Calories • 20g Fat (49% calories from fat) • 42g Protein • 4g Carbohydrates • 114mg Cholesterol • 384mg Sodium

Creamed Chicken and Basmati Rice

EQUIPMENT: 1-quart saucepan, French chef's knife, cutting board, measuring cup and spoons, large covered sauté skillet or electric skillet and food cutter (slicing blade)

PREPARATION TIME: 55 minutes ○ Makes 7 or 8 servings

1¼ cups Low-Sodium Chicken Stock (page 217) or canned

1 tablespoon Low-Cholesterol Roux (page 190)

1 medium onion, diced

1 medium parsnip or carrot, diced

1 stalk celery, diced

2 cloves garlic, minced

1 teaspoon dried thyme or poultry seasoning

1 bay leaf, stem removed and finely crushed

1 teaspoon chopped fresh parsley

¼ teaspoon freshly ground black pepper

¼ cup Chardonnay or other dry white wine

2 cups sliced mushrooms (about 4 ounces)

1½ cups lowfat or whole milk

1 cup basmati or other long-grain rice

4 boneless, skinless chicken breast halves, cut into ¼-inch-thick slices

½ teaspoon sweet paprika

1 tablespoon chopped fresh parsley

To prepare a light velouté sauce, in a saucepan, combine the chicken stock and roux over medium-low heat. Simmer, stirring as the sauce thickens slightly, 7 to 8 minutes. Remove from heat, cover and set aside.

In a hot, dry skillet over medium heat, dry sauté the onion, parsnip, celery and garlic until tender (do not brown), 3 to 4 minutes, stirring occasionally. Stir in the thyme, bay leaf, parsley and pepper.

Add the wine and mushrooms and simmer until the mushrooms are reduced by half, 5 to 6 minutes, stirring occasionally. Stir in the milk and rice and simmer (do not boil) 3 to 4 minutes, stirring occasionally.

Add the reserved sauce and stir in the sliced chicken breasts. (If you prefer to cook the chicken breasts whole, place them on top of the mixture.)

Reduce the heat to medium-low, cover the pan, open the vent and simmer (do not boil) for about 30 minutes.

To serve, sprinkle with the paprika and parsley and serve from the skillet.

PER SERVING: **201 Calories** • **2.2g Fat (10% calories from fat)** • **16g Protein** • **28g Carbohydrates** • **27mg Cholesterol** • **210mg Sodium**

Creamed Saffron Chicken with Tortellini and Peas

EQUIPMENT: 3-quart covered saucepan, 2-quart steamer/strainer inset, measuring cup and spoons, large covered sauté skillet or electric skillet, 1-quart covered saucepan, food cutter (grating blade), butcher knife, French chef's knife and cutting board

PREPARATION TIME: 40 minutes o Makes 7 or 8 servings

10 ounces precooked spinach-filled tortellini

4 boneless skinless chicken breast halves

SAFFRON SAUCE

1 cup Low-Sodium Chicken Stock (page 217) or canned

¼ cup whole milk or half-and-half

5 to 6 threads of saffron

1 tablespoon Low-Cholesterol Roux (page 190)

½ cup frozen green peas, thawed and drained

½ teaspoon freshly ground black pepper

¼ cup freshly grated Parmesan cheese

2 tablespoons chopped fresh basil

In the 3-quart saucepan, bring the water to a simmer; do not boil. Place the tortellini into the steamer/strainer inset and place the inset into the 3-quart saucepan. Cover the pan, open the vent and steam the tortellini until al dente (cooked through, yet firm).

In a hot, dry skillet over medium heat, place the chicken. Cover the skillet, open the vent and cook until golden brown and the chicken releases easily from the skillet, 7 to 8 minutes per side.

While the chicken is cooking, prepare the sauce: In a 1-quart saucepan, combine the chicken stock, milk or half-and-half, saffron and roux and bring to a simmer over medium-low heat. Simmer, stirring until the mixture thickens, 4 to 5 minutes. Add the peas and cook for 3 to 5 minutes, stirring occasionally. Remove from the heat and cover.

Transfer the chicken to a cutting board and cut into ¼-inch-thick slices.

To serve, arrange equal portions of chicken, and tortellini on each plate and top with Saffron Sauce. Sprinkle with pepper, Parmesan cheese and basil.

PER SERVING, WITH WHOLE MILK: 174 Calories • 6g Fat (32% calories from fat) • 18g Protein • 12g Carbohydrates • 77mg Cholesterol • 282mg Sodium

PER SERVING, WITH HALF-AND-HALF: 184 Calories • 7.4g Fat (36% calories from fat) • 18g Protein • 10g Carbohydrates • 81mg Cholesterol • 280mg Sodium

VARIATIONS

The chicken breasts may be served whole to make 4 servings.

Replace the peas with broccoli florets.

Use dried tortellini pasta; cook according to package directions.

Garlic Roasted Stuffed Chicken with Port Marinara

EQUIPMENT: **French chef's knife, cutting board, food cutter (grating blade), mixing bowl, measuring cup and spoons, paring knife and large covered sauté skillet or electric skillet**

PREPARATION TIME: **45 minutes** ○ **Makes: 6 servings**

3 slices whole-wheat bread, chopped

1 medium shallot, minced

1 stalk celery, minced or grated

2 cloves garlic, minced

½ teaspoon poultry seasoning

6 medium chicken breast halves, skin removed

1 medium onion, diced

2 cloves garlic, sliced paper thin

1 tablespoon dried oregano

1 tablespoon tomato paste

½ cup good-quality port wine

2 cups seeded and chopped plum tomatoes or canned whole tomatoes

2 tablespoons freshly grated Parmesan cheese

1 tablespoon chopped fresh basil

In a mixing bowl, combine the bread, shallot, celery, minced garlic and poultry seasoning. Using your hands, mix the ingredients until combined and are moist and firm. Form into 6 equal portions. Set aside.

With a paring knife, make a pocket by inserting the knife into the side of the chicken breast between the rib cage and the meat. Place a portion of stuffing into the pocket of each chicken breast half.

In a hot, dry skillet over medium heat, add the chicken breasts. Cover the pan, open the vent and cook until golden brown and the chicken breast releases easily from the skillet, 12 to 15 minutes. Turn the chicken, cover the pan and roast for 5 to 10 minutes on the other side. Transfer the chicken to a warm platter and keep warm.

To the skillet, add the onion and sliced garlic, sauté in the chicken drippings until lightly browned, 2 to 3 minutes, stirring occasionally. Stir in the oregano and tomato paste and cook, stirring, until the paste turns reddish-brown in color, 3 to 4 minutes.

Slowly stir in the wine. Stir in the tomatoes and return the chicken to the sauce. Reduce the heat to medium-low. Cover the pan, open the vent and simmer for 10 to 12 minutes.

To serve, top the chicken with the sauce and sprinkle with Parmesan cheese and basil. Serve with Mustard Greens, Italian Style (page 146).

PER SERVING: 254 Calories • 3g Fat (12% calories from fat) • 35g Protein • 15g Carbohydrates • 83mg Cholesterol • 295mg Sodium

Stovetop Roast Stuffed Turkey

EQUIPMENT: French chef's knife, cutting board, measuring cup and spoons, 10-inch gourmet skillet, large sauté skillet with hi-dome cover or electric skillet with hi-dome cover

PREPARATION TIME: 1 hour 15 minutes   ○   Makes 4 or 5 servings

1 small onion, diced

½ stalk celery, diced

½ apple, cored, seeded and chopped

1 teaspoon poultry seasoning

1 teaspoon chopped fresh parsley

¼ teaspoon freshly ground black pepper

2 to 3 slices raisin bread, chopped

1 (3½- to 4-pound) turkey breast without skin

½ cup Chardonnay or other dry white wine

2 cups Low-Sodium Chicken Stock (page 217) or canned

1½ tablespoons Low-Cholesterol Roux (page 190)

¼ teaspoon poultry seasoning

1 tablespoon chopped fresh parsley

In a hot, dry gourmet skillet over medium heat, dry sauté the onion and celery until slightly browned, 3 to 5 minutes, stirring occasionally. Reduce the heat to medium-low and add the chopped apple and sauté for 1 to 2 minutes. Stir in the poultry seasoning and parsley. Add the bread and remove from heat. If the dressing is slightly dry, add 1 or 2 teaspoons chicken stock. Mix well and allow dressing to cool sufficiently before handling.

To stuff the turkey breast, with a knife, make an incision between the meat of the breast and the rib cage. Work the knife in and form a large pocket and fill the pocket with the stuffing. Secure the opening with toothpicks.

In a hot, dry skillet over medium heat, brown the turkey by pressing the breast meat side to the hot surface of the pan. Cover the pan, close the vent and allow the vapor seal to form, 5 to 6 minutes. Once the seal has formed, roast for about 15 minutes per pound. The proper roasting temperature is developed when tiny bubbles appear between the rim of the pan and the cover. If the cover spits moisture, the heat is too high. If there are no bubbles, the heat is too low. Adjust the heat and roast. Don't peek. Removing the cover will destroy the vapor seal, lengthen the cooking time and may cause the turkey to burn.

When finished roasting the turkey, turn the breast, cover the pan, close the vent and roast the other side, about 5 to 7 minutes. Remove the turkey to a warm platter and keep warm.

Slowly stir in the wine and reduce by about half. Stir in the stock, roux and poultry seasoning. Cook, stirring, until the gravy reaches the desired thickness, 2 to 4 minutes.

To serve, carve the turkey breast, top with gravy and sprinkle with the parsley. Serve with Amaretto Sweet Potatoes (page 178) and Cranberry Sauce (page 212).

PER SERVING: 289 Calories • 5g Fat (15% calories from fat) • 47g Protein • 11g Carbohydrates • 109mg Cholesterol • 400mg Sodium

Sloppy Gobblers

EQUIPMENT: French chef's knife, cutting board, measuring cup and spoons and medium covered sauté skillet

PREPARATION TIME: 30 minutes O Makes 7 or 8 servings

1 medium onion, diced

1 medium green bell pepper, diced

1 stalk celery, diced

2 cloves garlic, minced

1 tablespoon Italian seasoning

1 Italian sausage link, removed from casing (optional)

¾ pound ground turkey or extra-lean ground beef

1½ teaspoons steak sauce

1½ teaspoons reduced-sodium soy sauce

1 teaspoon chopped pickled jalapeño pepper

1 cup Spaghetti Sauce (Salsa de Pomodoro) (page 204)

4 hamburger buns

In a hot, dry skillet over medium heat, dry sauté the onion, bell pepper, celery and garlic until slightly browned, 3 to 5 minutes. Stir in the Italian seasoning.

To the skillet, add the sausage if using, and cook, stirring to break up, until cooked through, 3 to 4 minutes. Add the turkey or beef and cook until slightly browned, stirring to break up, 7 or 8 minutes.

Reduce the heat to medium-low, stir in the steak sauce, soy sauce, chile pepper and spaghetti sauce. Cover the pan, open the vent and simmer for 8 to 10 minutes. Do not allow the mixture to boil.

To serve, top the hamburger buns with Sloppy Gobbler and serve with Home Fries (page 154) or Pan-Roasted Potatoes (page 155).

PER SERVING WITH TURKEY AND SAUSAGE: 180 Calories •
8g Fat (41% calories from fat) • 12g Protein • 15g Carbohydrates •
42mg Cholesterol   351mg Sodium

PER SERVING WITH TURKEY AND NO SAUSAGE: 144 Calories
5g Fat (30% calories from fat)   •   10g Protein   •   15g Carbohydrates   •
34mg Cholesterol   •   273mg Sodium

PER SERVING WITH BEEF AND SAUSAGE: 216 Calories   •
12g Fat (50% calories from fat)   •   12g Protein   •   15g Carbohydrates   •
37mg Cholesterol   •   339mg Sodium

PER SERVING WITH BEEF AND NO SAUSAGE: 180 Calories   •
9g Fat (43% calories from fat)   •   11g Protein   •   15g Carbohydrates   •
29mg Cholesterol   •   285mg Sodium

Mama's Sneaky Meatloaf

Can you get any sneakier than to hide the vegetables inside of a great tasting meatloaf?

EQUIPMENT: **Large covered sauté skillet or electric skillet, French chef's knife, cutting board and measuring cup and spoons**

PREPARATION TIME: **50 minutes**   ✿   **Makes 8 to 10 servings**

1½ **pounds ground turkey or extra-lean ground beef**

1 **medium onion, diced**

1 **medium carrot, minced or grated**

1 **stalk celery, minced or grated**

2 **cloves garlic, minced**

1 **medium red potato, grated**

2 **egg whites or 1 egg**

1 **cup dry bread crumbs**

1 **tablespoon Italian seasoning**

1 **cup Spaghetti Sauce (Salsa de Pomodoro) (page 204)**

½ **medium green bell pepper, cut into ¼-inch-thick slices**

½ **cup grated cheddar cheese**

1 **tablespoon chopped fresh parsley**

In the cold skillet, combine the turkey, onion, carrot, celery, garlic, potato, egg whites, bread crumbs and Italian seasoning. Mix well and form into a loaf. Top with the sauce, cheese and 3 or 4 green bell pepper slices.

Place the skillet over medium heat. Cover the skillet and close the vent. When the cover spins freely on a cushion of water, the vapor seal is formed, 3 to 5 minutes. After forming the seal, adjust the heat to produce tiny moisture bubbles between the rim of the skillet and the cover. If the cover spits moisture, the heat is too high. If no bubbles appear, the heat is too low. Bake for about 30 minutes after forming the proper vapor seal.

To serve, sprinkle with the parsley and cut into 8 to 10 slices. Serve with Yellow Squash Parmesan (page 171) and Candied Carrots (page 142).

PER SERVING, WITH TURKEY: 197 Calories • 8g Fat (39% calories from fat) • 16g Protein • 14g Carbohydrates • 60mg Cholesterol • 254mg Sodium (whole egg adds 20mg Cholesterol per serving)

PER SERVING, WITH BEEF: 253 Calories • 15g Fat (52% calories from fat) • 17g Protein • 14g Carbohydrates • 53mg Cholesterol (whole egg adds 20mg Cholesterol per serving) • 231mg Sodium

Momma LeAnnie's Stovetop Lasagna

EQUIPMENT: 10-inch gourmet skillet, electric skillet with cover, food cutter (julienne and grating blades) and measuring cup and spoons

PREPARATION TIME: 1 hour 15 minutes   O   Makes 10 to 12 servings

1 medium onion, diced

3 cloves garlic, minced

1 tablespoon Italian seasoning

1 pound ground turkey or extra-lean ground beef

8 ounces part-skim ricotta cheese

2 cups Spaghetti Sauce (Salsa de Pomodoro) (page 204)

8 ounces lasagna noodles

4 ounces part-skim mozzarella cheese, shredded

4 ounces low-sodium cheddar cheese, shredded

½ cup freshly grated Parmesan cheese

In a hot, dry skillet over medium-high heat, dry sauté the onion and garlic until slightly browned, 3 to 5 minutes, stirring occasionally. Stir in the Italian seasoning.

Add the ground turkey and sauté until the turkey is cooked through, 4 to 5 minutes, stirring to break up turkey. Remove from the heat and allow to cool slightly. Stir in the ricotta cheese and set aside.

To prepare the lasagna, cover the inside bottom of the electric skillet with about ½ cup of the spaghetti sauce. Place 4 uncooked lasagna noodles in the bottom of the skillet on top of the sauce (trim the corner of the noodles to fit the skillet). Sprinkle about one-fourth of the mozzarella and cheddar cheeses over the noodles and top with about half of the turkey mixture. Spread about ½ cup of the spaghetti sauce over the turkey layer.

Place a layer of lasagna noodles on the sauce and repeat the previous steps until the skillet is full, making 2 thick layers and topping the final layer with lasagna noodles. Top the lasagna noodles with the remaining sauce and sprinkle with the remaining mozzarella and cheddar cheeses.

Cover the skillet, close the vent and bake at 210°F (100°C) for about 50 minutes. Don't peek. Removing the cover will destroy the vapor seal, lengthen the cooking time and may cause the lasagna to burn.

Turn the heat off and allow the lasagna to rest for about 15 minutes.

To serve, slice into 10 to 12 equal portions, sprinkle with the Parmesan cheese and serve with warm Italian garlic bread.

PER SERVING WITH TURKEY: 285 Calories • 13g Fat (42% calories from fat) • 22g Protein • 19g Carbohydrates • 60mg Cholesterol • 389mg Sodium

PER SERVING WITH BEEF: 318 Calories • 17g Fat (47% calories from fat) • 22g Protein • 19g Carbohydrates • 56mg Cholesterol • 378mg Sodium

VARIATIONS

Meatless Lasagna

Omit the turkey and use the ricotta cheese as its own layer.

PER SERVING: 229 Calories • 10g Fat (40% calories from fat) • 15g Protein • 19g Carbohydrates • 30mg Cholesterol • 353mg Sodium

White Lasagna with Chicken and Spinach

Replace the Spaghetti Sauce with Alfredo Sauce (page 202) and replace the turkey with ground chicken and 16 ounces fresh spinach. Cook the spinach with the chicken.

PER SERVING: 315 Calories • 13.5g Fat (39% calories from fat) • 27g Protein • 21g Carbohydrates • 65mg Cholesterol • 364mg Sodium

Turkey Piccata

When cooking the greaseless way, there are times when you must use some oil, especially when browning meats dredged in flour. The advantage of cooking with waterless, greaseless cookware is that when oil is called for, you can use a minimal amount to accomplish the task.

EQUIPMENT: **Meat mallet, mixing bowl, measuring cup and spoons, French chef's knife, cutting board and large covered sauté skillet or electric skillet**

PREPARATION TIME: **20 minutes ○ Makes 4 servings**

2 tablespoons all-purpose flour

1 teaspoon freshly ground black pepper

1 teaspoon sweet paprika

1 teaspoon garlic powder

4 slices turkey cutlets (about ¾ pound), pounded flat

1 tablespoon olive oil

½ cup Chardonnay or other dry white wine

½ cup Low-Sodium Chicken Stock (page 217) or canned

2 tablespoons fresh lemon juice

2 tablespoon capers

1 tablespoon chopped fresh parsley

In a mixing bowl, combine the flour, pepper, paprika and garlic powder and coat the cutlets in the flour mixture.

Place the olive oil in a hot skillet over medium heat. Add the cutlets and cook until browned, 2 to 4 minutes per side. Remove the cutlets to a warm platter and keep warm.

Add the wine to the hot skillet and simmer until reduced by half, 1 to 2 minutes. Stir in the stock, lemon juice and capers. Cook, stirring, until the sauce thickens, 1 to 2 minutes.

To serve, spoon the sauce over the turkey and sprinkle with the parsley.

PER SERVING: **205 Calories** • **9g Fat (46% calories from fat)** • **21g Protein**
5g Carbohydrates   55mg Cholesterol   156mg Sodium

Braised Breast of Duck with Persimmons and Prunes

EQUIPMENT: Large covered sauté skillet or electric skillet, measuring cup and spoons, French chef's knife, cutting board and food cutter (grating blade)

PREPARATION TIME: 20 minutes ○ Makes 4 servings

2 (about 4-ounce) skinless duck breasts, preferably Maple Leaf Farms brand

1½ cups fresh orange juice

¼ cup packed light brown sugar

½ teaspoon ground cinnamon

1 medium persimmon, cut crosswise into ¼-inch-thick slices

4 prunes, cut into ¼-inch-thick pieces

1 tablespoon grated orange zest

In a hot, dry skillet over medium heat, place the duck. Cover the pan, open the vent and sear until slightly browned and when duck releases easily from the skillet, 3 to 4 minutes per side. Do not overcook the duck; it should be rare when served. Transfer the duck to a warm platter and keep warm.

Slowly stir in the orange juice. Stir in the brown sugar and cinnamon and add the persimmon and prunes. Reduce the heat to low and simmer for 4 to 5 minutes.

Return the duck to the skillet. Cover the skillet, open the vent and simmer for 3 to 4 minutes. Transfer the duck to a cutting board and cut into ¼-inch-thick slices.

To serve, top the sliced duck with the sauce, persimmons and prunes. Sprinkle with the orange zest. Serve with crisp Hash Brown Potatoes (page 153) and Candied Carrots (page 142).

PER SERVING: 173 Calories • 3.6g Fat (19% calories from fat) • 11g Protein • 25g Carbohydrates • 44mg Cholesterol • 46mg Sodium

Duck Orecchiette

EQUIPMENT: 6½–quart stockpot, pasta/steamer basket, large covered sauté skillet, French chef's knife, cutting board, measuring cup and spoons and food cutter (grating blades)

PREPARATION TIME: 25 minutes ○ Makes 7 or 8 servings

1 pound orecchiette pasta

4 (about 4-ounce) skinless duck breasts, preferably Maple Leaf Farm brand

½ medium onion, diced

½ medium carrot, diced

½ stalk celery, diced

4 cloves garlic, minced

1 teaspoon chopped fresh parsley

1 teaspoon Italian seasoning

½ teaspoon freshly ground black pepper

1 small bay leaf, stem removed and finely crushed

1¼ cups Low-Sodium Brown Veal or Beef Stock (page 219) or canned

1 tablespoon Low-Cholesterol Roux (page 190)

1 cup seeded and chopped fresh plum or canned whole tomatoes

¾ cup fresh or frozen asparagus tips

2 tablespoons freshly grated Parmesan cheese

2 tablespoons chopped fresh basil

In the 6½–quart stockpot, using the pasta/steamer basket, cook the pasta until al dente (cooked through, yet firm) in water according to package directions, 12 to 15 minutes.

In a hot, dry skillet over medium heat, sear the duck breasts until browned and they release easily from the pan, 3 to 4 minutes per side. Remove the duck to a warm platter and keep warm. Do not overcook the duck; it should be rare when served.

To the skillet, add the onion, carrot, celery and garlic and sauté in the duck drippings until slightly browned, 3 to 5 minutes, stirring occasionally. Stir in the parsley, Italian seasoning, pepper and bay leaf.

Slowly stir in the stock. Add the roux and cook; continue stirring until the sauce begins to thicken, 3 to 5 minutes. Add the tomatoes and asparagus tips and bring to a simmer. Reduce the heat to medium-low.

Return the duck breasts to the skillet, cover and open the vent and cook for 3 to 4 minutes. Remove the duck breasts to a cutting board and cut into ¼-inch-thick slices.

To serve, divide the pasta among the plates, top with the gravy and sprinkle with the Parmesan cheese. Place 2 or 3 slices of duck breasts on each serving and sprinkle with the basil.

PER SERVING: 302 Calories • 4.8g Fat (14% calories from fat) • 18g Protein • 47g Carbohydrates • 34mg Cholesterol • 269mg Sodium (316mg Sodium with canned tomatoes)

Peking Duck in Bourbon Sauce

EQUIPMENT: French chef's knife, cutting board, medium covered sauté skillet, large covered sauté skillet or electric skillet

PREPARATION TIME: 30 minutes   ○   Makes 5 or 6 servings

2 (about 4-ounce) skinless duck breasts, preferably Maple Leaf Farms
  brand

1 medium sweet onion, diced

½ cup bourbon

1 teaspoon dried thyme

½ teaspoon freshly ground black pepper

1 teaspoon sugar (optional)

2 cups sliced mushrooms, about 4 ounces

1 cup Low-Sodium White Veal Stock (page 217) or Low-Sodium Chicken Stock
  (page 217) or canned

1 tablespoon Low-Cholesterol Roux (page 190)

1 tablespoon chopped fresh parsley

In a hot, dry skillet over medium heat, sear the duck breasts until browned and they release easily from the pan, 3 to 4 minutes per side. Remove the duck to a warm platter and keep warm. For the best flavor, duck breasts should be served medium-rare.

Add the onion and sauté in the meat drippings until slightly browned, 3 to 5 minutes. Stir in the thyme, pepper and sugar, if using.

Slowly stir in the bourbon and bring to a simmer. Add the mushrooms. Reduce the heat to medium-low, cover the pan, open the vent and sweat the bourbon and mushrooms until reduced by one-third, 7 to 8 minutes.

Stir in the stock and roux. Cook, stirring, until the gravy begins to thicken, 2 to 3 minutes.

Return the duck breasts to the skillet, cover, open the vent and simmer for 3 to 4 minutes.

Remove the duck breasts to the cutting board and cut into ¼-inch-thick slices.

To serve, place the sliced duck on a bed of Butternut Cinnamon Squash (page 172), top with the gravy and sprinkle with the parsley.

PER SERVING: 125 Calories • 3.4g Fat (36% calories from fat) • 10g Protein • 4g Carbohydrates • 29mg Cholesterol • 207mg Sodium

Beef Stroganoff

EQUIPMENT: Butcher knife, cutting board, French chef's knife, measuring cup and spoons, large covered sauté skillet or electric skillet, slotted serving spoon and 3-quart covered saucepan

PREPARATION TIME: 40 minutes   O   Makes 7 or 8 servings

1½ pounds beef top-round steak, thinly sliced and cut into strips

1 medium onion, diced

1 small carrot, diced

½ stalk celery, diced

2 cloves garlic, minced

½ teaspoon dried thyme

1 small bay leaf, stem removed and finely crushed

1 teaspoon chopped fresh parsley

½ teaspoon freshly ground black pepper

2 cups sliced mushrooms (about 4 ounces)

1 cup Low-Sodium Brown Veal or Beef Stock (page 219) or canned

½ cup sour cream

1 teaspoon Dijon mustard

1 teaspoon fresh lemon juice

½ pound egg noodles

1 tablespoon chopped fresh parsley

Place the beef in a hot, dry skillet over medium heat. Cover the pan, open the vent and sear until slightly browned and the beef releases easily from the pan, 5 to 6 minutes. Turn the beef, cover the pan and slightly brown on the other side, 4 to 5 minutes. With a slotted spoon, remove the beef to a warm platter and keep warm.

Add the onion, carrot, celery and garlic to the beef drippings and sauté until slightly browned, 3 to 5 minutes, stirring occasionally.

Stir in the thyme, bay leaf, parsley and pepper. Add the mushrooms, cover the pan, close the vent and turn the heat to medium-low. Cook until the mushrooms are reduced by one-third, 8 to 10 minutes.

Stir in the stock, sour cream, mustard and lemon juice. Return the beef to the pan. Cover, open the vent and simmer for 10 to 12 minutes. Do not allow to boil!

While the stroganoff is cooking, prepare the egg noodles according to package directions in the 3-quart saucepan.

To serve, top the egg noodles with the stroganoff and sprinkle with the parsley.

PER SERVING WITH NOODLES: 307 Calories • 12g Fat (36% calories from fat) • 25g Protein • 24g Carbohydrates • 85mg Cholesterol • 204mg Sodium

Bourbon-Stuffed Filet Mignon

EQUIPMENT: French chef's knife, cutting board, measuring cup and spoons, mixing bowl, large covered sauté skillet, medium covered sauté skillet, paring knife and 1-quart saucepan

PREPARATION TIME: 40 minutes **O** Makes 4 servings

1 medium onion, diced

1 small carrot, diced

½ stalk celery, diced

4 cloves garlic, minced

½ teaspoon dried thyme

1 small bay leaf, stem removed and finely crushed

1 teaspoon chopped fresh parsley

½ teaspoon freshly ground black pepper

1 cup bourbon

1 teaspoon sugar

1 cup diced mushrooms (about 4 ounces)

½ cup dry bread crumbs

2 egg whites or 1 egg

4 (about 3-ounce) filet mignons

2 cups Low-Sodium Brown Veal or Beef Stock (page 219) or canned

1 tablespoon Low-Cholesterol Roux (page 190)

1 teaspoon finely chopped fresh parsley

In a medium-hot dry skillet over medium heat, dry sauté the onion, carrot, celery and garlic until slightly browned, 3 to 5 minutes, stirring occasionally. Stir in the thyme, bay leaf, chopped parsley and pepper.

Slowly stir in the bourbon and sugar. Add the mushrooms and simmer until mushrooms are reduced by one-third, 8 to 10 minutes, stirring occasionally. Remove from the heat and allow mixture to cool slightly.

In a mixing bowl, combine about one-third of the reduced mushroom mixture with the bread crumbs and egg whites and mix well.

Using a paring knife, insert the knife blade into the side of each filet and make an opening about the size of a teaspoon, then cut a large pocket inside the filet. Using a teaspoon, fill the filets with the stuffing mixture and secure with a toothpick.

Place the filets in a medium-hot dry skillet over medium heat. Cover the skillet, open the vent and sear until slightly browned and the filets release easily from the skillet, 5 to 6 minutes per side for medium-rare, 6 to 7 minutes per side for medium or 7 to 8 minutes per side for medium-well.

While the filets are cooking, in the 1-quart pan combine the stock and roux over medium-low heat and cook, stirring, until the gravy thickens slightly, about 3 minutes.

Remove the filets to a warm platter and keep warm.

Slowly stir in the stock mixture. Stir in the remaining mushroom mixture and cook, stirring, until the gravy thickens, 3 to 4 minutes.

To serve, top the stuffed filets with the mushroom gravy and sprinkle with the finely chopped parsley. Serve on a bed of Sour Cream and Garlic Mashed Potatoes (page 166) with a side of Candied Carrots (page 142).

PER SERVING: 449 Calories • 21g Fat (59% calories from fat) • 24g Protein • 10g Carbohydrates • 60mg Cholesterol • 478mg Sodium

Chateaubriand

EQUIPMENT: **Large sauté skillet, hi-dome Dutch oven cover, French chef's knife, cutting board and food cutter (slicing blade)**

PREPARATION TIME: **about 50 minutes**   ❍   **Makes 9 or 10 servings**

1 (2-to 2½-pound) beef tenderloin

1 medium onion, diced

1 small carrot, diced

½ stalk celery, diced

1 clove garlic, minced

1 small bay leaf, stem removed and finely crushed

1 teaspoon dried thyme

1 teaspoon chopped fresh parsley, plus additional for serving

4 cups sliced mushrooms (about 8 ounces)

¼ cup Chardonnay or other dry white wine

1 tablespoon chopped fresh tarragon leaves

½ teaspoon freshly ground black pepper

1¼ cups Low-Sodium Brown Veal or Beef Stock (page 219) or canned

1 tablespoon Low-Cholesterol Roux (page 190)

1 tablespoon chopped fresh tarragon leaves

In a hot, dry skillet over medium heat, cook the beef tenderloin until browned and the meat releases easily from the pan, turning each time the meat releases easily from the pan, 15 to 20 minutes.

Add the onion, carrot, celery and garlic around the tenderloin and sauté until slightly browned, 2 to 3 minutes, stirring occasionally. Stir in the bay leaf, thyme and parsley. Add the mushrooms and reduce the heat to between medium and medium-low.

Place the hi-dome cover on the skillet. When the cover spins freely on a cushion of water, the vapor seal is formed, 3 to 5 minutes. After forming the seal, adjust the heat to produce tiny moisture bubbles between the rim of the skillet and the hi-dome cover. If the cover spits moisture, the heat is too high. If no bubbles appear, the heat is too low. Once you have reached the proper roasting temperature, cook for about 9 minutes per pound for rare; 10

minutes per pound for medium-rare; 11 minutes per pound for medium. Do not remove the cover. Removing the cover will destroy the vapor seal, lengthen the cooking time and may cause the meat to burn.

Transfer the beef tenderloin to a warm platter and keep warm.

To prepare the sauce, increase the heat to medium or medium-high, stir in the wine, tarragon and pepper. Cook, stirring occasionally until the liquid is reduced by half, 2 to 3 minutes. Stir in the stock and roux. Cook, stirring, until the roux is incorporated into the sauce and the mixture thickens slightly. Remove from heat.

To serve, cut the tenderloin into ½-inch-thick slices, top with the sauce and sprinkle with the parsley. Serve with Asparagus with Lemon Pepper (page 134) and Pan-Roasted Potatoes (page 155).

PER SERVING: 288 Calories • 22g Fat (68% calories from fat) • 19g Protein • 4.4g Carbohydrates • 64mg Cholesterol • 176mg Sodium

VARIATION

Chateaubriand usually refers to beef tenderloin steaks. However, this particular recipe produces equal, if not better results and maximizes the flavors of both the tenderloin and the sauce. Tenderloin steaks can be exchanged for the tenderloin roast. Cook according to weight as given above.

Filet Mignon Bordelaise

Caramelizing or browning the outer surface of the meat in a heavy high-quality stainless steel skillet locks in the natural juices, and tenderizes the meat during the finishing cooking process without toughening the steak.

EQUIPMENT: **Measuring spoons and large covered sauté skillet or electric skillet**

PREPARATION TIME: **30 minutes** o **Makes 4 servings**

4 (about 3-ounce) filet mignons

Bordelaise Sauce (page 206)

1 teaspoon chopped fresh parsley leaves

Preheat the skillet over medium-high heat for 3 to 4 minutes. Sprinkle a few drops of water in the pan. If the water droplets dance, the pan is ready. If the water evaporates, the pan is not hot enough. Place the filets in the hot, dry pan, which will be about 400°F (200°C). Cover the pan, open the vent and dry sauté until the filets release easily from the skillet, 4 to 5 minutes. Turn the filets, cover the pan and brown the other side until the filets release easily from the skillet, 4 to 5 minutes. Cook to desired doneness (see doneness tests following this recipe).

To serve, place the filets on dinner plates and top with the Bordelaise Sauce and sprinkle with the parsley. Serve with Asparagus with Lemon Pepper (page 134) and Home Fries (page 154).

PER SERVING: **308 Calories** • **21g Fat (64% calories from fat)** • **20g Protein**
7g Carbohydrates • **60mg Cholesterol** • **351mg Sodium**

HOW TO COOK THE PERFECT STEAK

During the searing and cooking of steaks and chops, when you cook with the cover on and vent open, the meat will cook quicker and be juicier. However, crowding the pan, or cooking at too low a temperature and covering, may cause the steaks to steam. Practice makes perfect, and a good home chef learns to cook a steak to the desired doneness with good equipment, proper technique and by feel. Because of the different texture, cuts and thickness of the meat, learning the feel of the desired doneness by pushing down on the center of a steak with a fork is by far the best method over attempting to time for desired doneness. These basic rules apply to cooking all meats when attempting to accomplish different stages of doneness. To demonstrate, turn the palm of your left hand up and spread your fingers apart.

DONENESS TESTS

Rare: Rest your left thumb against your left forefinger and press down on the soft fleshy part at the base of your left thumb with your right forefinger. That's what rare feels like.

Medium-Rare: Place the your left thumb directly over the center of your left forefinger and press down on the soft fleshy part at the base of your left thumb with your right forefinger. That's what medium-rare feels like.

Medium: Place your left thumb in between your left forefinger and your left middle finger and press down on the soft fleshy part at the base of your left thumb with your right forefinger. That's what medium feels like.

Medium-Well: Place your left thumb directly over the center of your left middle finger and press down on the soft fleshy part of your left thumb with your right forefinger, that's what medium-well feels like.

Well-Done: Place your left thumb in between your left middle finger and your left ring finger and press down on the soft fleshy part of your left thumb with your right forefinger. That's what well-done feels like. Cook for 8 to 9 minutes more after searing.

Stuffed Peppers

EQUIPMENT: French chef's knife, cutting board, measuring cup and spoons, large sauté skillet with hi-dome cover or electric skillet with hi-dome cover, large serving spoon and food cutter (julienne blade)

PREPARATION TIME: 40 minutes   ○   Makes 6 servings

1 cup cooked rice

6 medium green bell peppers

1 medium onion, diced

2 stalks celery, diced

3 cloves garlic, minced

½ teaspoon dried thyme

1 tablespoon chopped fresh parsley

½ pound extra-lean ground beef or ground turkey

2 cups seeded and chopped plum tomatoes or canned whole tomatoes

½ cup bread crumbs

2 cups Salsa (page 211)

2 tablespoons shredded low-sodium cheddar cheese (optional)

1 tablespoon chopped fresh parsley

When selecting bell peppers for stuffing, select those that will stand upright on their own without tipping. With a knife, slice off the top of the peppers and remove the seeds and ribs. Remove the stems from the tops and discard. Dice the tops for cooking and set the whole peppers aside.

In a medium-hot skillet using no oil, dry sauté the chopped pepper, onion, celery and garlic until slightly browned, 3 to 5 minutes, stirring occasionally. Stir in the thyme and parsley.

Add the beef and sauté, stirring to break up, until cooked through, 5 to 7 minutes.

Reduce the heat to medium-low and stir in the tomatoes, bread crumbs and rice and mix well. Remove the mixture to a mixing bowl and allow it to cool slightly.

Slowly stir in the salsa.

With a large serving spoon, fill the cavity of each pepper with the beef mixture. Place the stuffed peppers in the skillet in the salsa. Cover the pan, close the vent and cook for 15 to 20 minutes. Don't peek. Removing the cover will destroy the vapor seal, lengthen the cooking time and may cause the peppers to burn.

Just before serving, top each pepper with the cheese, if using, and cover the pan to melt the cheese.

To serve, spoon some of the cooking liquid over the peppers and sprinkle with chopped fresh parsley. Serve as an entrée or side dish.

PER SERVING, WITH BEEF: 245 Calories • 8.6g Fat (31% calories from fat) • 12g Protein • 31g Carbohydrates • 28mg Cholesterol • 234mg Sodium (canned tomatoes and bottled salsa add 178mg Sodium per serving)

PER SERVING, WITH TURKEY: 213 Calories • 5g Fat (22% calories from fat) • 12g Protein • 31g Carbohydrates • 32mg Cholesterol • 245mg Sodium (canned tomatoes and bottled salsa add 167mg Sodium per serving)

Osso Bucco with Gremolata

EQUIPMENT: 6-quart Dutch oven with hi-dome cover, French chef's knife, cutting board, mixing bowl and food cutter (grating blade)

PREPARATION TIME: 1 hour 30 minutes ○ Makes 4 to 6 servings

4 center-cut veal shanks, about 2 inches thick

1 medium onion, diced

1 medium carrot, diced

1 stalk celery, diced

1 teaspoon dried thyme

1 teaspoon chopped fresh parsley

1 bay leaf, stem removed and finely crushed

1 teaspoon freshly ground black pepper

3 tablespoons tomato paste

½ cup Chardonnay or other dry white wine

1½ cups Low-Sodium Brown Veal or Beef Stock (page 219) or canned

GREMOLATA

8 cloves garlic, finely minced

¼ cup chopped fresh Italian parsley leaves

¼ cup grated lemon zest

4 anchovy fillets, finely minced (optional)

In a hot, dry Dutch oven over medium-high heat, sear the veal shanks until browned and they release easily from the pan, 7 to 8 minutes per side. Remove the veal to a warm platter and keep warm.

Add the onion, carrot, celery and garlic and sauté in the meat drippings until slightly browned, 3 to 5 minutes. Stir in the thyme, parsley, bay leaf and pepper. Add the tomato paste and cook, stirring, until the paste turns reddish-brown in color. Do not allow the residue that forms on the bottom of the pan to burn.

Slowly stir in the wine and stock. Return the veal shanks to the pan. Reduce the heat to medium-low. Place the hi-dome cover on the Dutch oven. When the cover spins freely on a cushion of water, the vapor seal is formed, 5 to 7 minutes. After forming the seal, adjust the heat to produce tiny moisture bubbles between the rim of the Dutch oven and the hi-dome cover. If the cover spits moisture, the heat is too high. If no bubbles appear, the heat is too low. Once you have reached the proper roasting temperature, roast the veal shanks for about 1 hour and 15 minutes. Do not remove the cover. Removing the cover will destroy the vapor seal, lengthen the cooking time and may cause the meat to burn.

Make the Gremolata: In a mixing bowl, combine the garlic, parsley, lemon zest and anchovies, if using. Mix well, cover and refrigerate until served.

To serve, top the veal shanks with the sauce and sprinkle with the gremolata. Serve on a bed of Parmesan Mashed Potatoes with Spinach (page 158).

PER SERVING: 342 Calories • 8g Fat (21% calories from fat) • 55g Protein •
12g Carbohydrates • 179mg Cholesterol • 509mg Sodium

Roast Stuffed Veal

EQUIPMENT: French chef's knife, cutting board, mixing bowl, butcher knife, 6-quart Dutch oven and hi-dome cover, fine strainer and carving knife

PREPARATION TIME: 1 hour 15 minutes   ○   Makes 8 to 10 servings

1 cup ricotta cheese

1 egg white or 1 whole egg

1 (8-ounce) package frozen spinach, thawed and drained well

2 cloves garlic, finely minced

½ teaspoon ground cinnamon

1 small onion, minced

1 (2- to 2½-pound) top-round veal roast

1 medium onion, diced

1 medium parsnip, diced

1 stalk celery, diced

4 cloves garlic, minced

1 teaspoon dried thyme

1 bay leaf, stem removed and finely crumbled

1 tablespoon chopped fresh parsley

8 to 10 small red potatoes

4 to 5 parsnips, cut in 4 pieces each

1¼ cups Low-Sodium White Veal Stock (page 217) or Low-Sodium Chicken Stock (page 217) or canned

2 tablespoons Low-Cholesterol Roux (page 190)

1 tablespoon chopped fresh parsley

In a mixing bowl, combine the ricotta cheese, egg white, spinach, garlic, cinnamon and onion. Mix well and set the stuffing mixture aside.

Using a knife, make a 2- to 3-inch-wide opening in the side of the veal roast. Insert the knife into the meat and make a large pocket inside the roast. Fill the pocket with the stuffing mixture and secure the opening with toothpicks.

In a hot, dry Dutch oven over medium heat, brown the veal roast on all sides. Turn the meat as it releases easily from the pan, 15 to 20 minutes.

Add the onion, diced parsnip, celery and garlic around the roast and sauté in the meat drippings until slightly tender, 2 to 3 minutes, stirring occasionally. Add the thyme, bay leaf and parsley. Reduce the heat to medium-low and place the potatoes and parsnip pieces around the roast.

Place the hi-dome cover on the Dutch oven. When the cover spins freely on a cushion of water, the vapor seal has formed, 4 to 5 minutes. When roasting meat on top of the stove, tiny bubbles should appear around the rim. If the pan spits moisture, the heat is too high. If tiny bubbles do not appear around the rim, the heat is too low. Adjust the heat and roast for 30 to 40 minutes, 12 to 15 minutes per pound.

Remove the parsnips and potatoes to a warm platter and keep warm. Remove the veal roast to a cutting board and allow to rest.

Add the stock and roux to the drippings in the Dutch oven. Increase the heat to medium-high and stir until the gravy thickens. Remove from the heat and serve or strain the gravy through a sieve.

With a knife, cut the roast into ½-inch-thick slices. To serve, top the roast with gravy and serve with the potatoes and parsnips. Sprinkle with the parsley.

PER SERVING: 325 Calories • 7g Fat (19% calories from fat) • 28g Protein •
40g Carbohydrates • 89mg Cholesterol • 312mg Sodium

Sweet Italian Meatballs

The meatballs can be served as an appetizer or as part of the main course with pasta.

EQUIPMENT: **Mixing bowls, French chef's knife, cutting board, large covered sauté skillet or electric skillet**

PREPARATION TIME: **35 minutes** ❍ **Makes 12 to 16 servings**

1 pound extra-lean ground beef

½ pound ground veal

2 egg whites or 1 egg

1 large onion, finely minced

4 cloves garlic, finely minced

½ cup bread crumbs

⅓ cup freshly grated Parmesan cheese

1 tablespoon Italian seasoning

½ teaspoon freshly ground black pepper

½ cup Chianti or other dry red wine

2 cups Spaghetti Sauce (Salsa de Pomodoro) (page 204)

In a mixing bowl, combine the beef, veal, egg whites, onion, garlic, bread crumbs, cheese, Italian seasoning and pepper. Mix well and form into 1-inch-round meatballs.

In a hot, dry skillet over medium heat, dry sauté the meatballs, covered with vent open, until browned on all sides, 15 to 20 minutes. Turn the meatballs as they release easily from the pan. Re-cover the pan after each turning.

Slowly stir in the wine. Add the spaghetti sauce. Reduce the heat to low, cover the pan, close the vent and cook for about 10 to 15 minutes.

PER SERVING: **145 Calories** • **7g Fat (49% calories from fat)** • **10g Protein**
6g Carbohydrates • **33mg Cholesterol** • **221mg Sodium**

Veal Chops in Red Wine Sauce

EQUIPMENT: French chef's knife, cutting board and large covered sauté skillet

PREPARATION TIME: 30 minutes ○ **Makes 4 servings**

4 (1½-inch-thick) veal chops

1 small shallot, finely minced

2 cloves garlic, finely minced

1 teaspoon finely minced rosemary leaves

¼ cup red wine

¾ cup Low-Sodium Brown Veal or Beef Stock (page 219) or canned

2 teaspoons Low-Cholesterol Roux (page 190)

1 teaspoon chopped fresh parsley

In a hot, dry sauté skillet over medium heat, brown the veal chops for 5 to 7 minutes per side for medium-rare or 6 to 8 minutes for medium.

Transfer the veal chops to a warm platter and keep warm. To the skillet, add the shallots and garlic and sauté in the meat drippings until slightly browned, 2 to 3 minutes, stirring occasionally. Stir in the rosemary.

Slowing stir in the wine. Stir in the veal stock and roux and cook, stirring as the sauce thickens.

To serve, top the veal chops with the sauce and sprinkle with chopped fresh parsley. Serve on a bed of Parmesan Mashed Potatoes with Spinach (page 158).

PER SERVING: 265 Calories • 14g Fat (49% calories from fat) • 29g Protein • 3g Carbohydrates • 112mg Cholesterol • 220mg Sodium

Orange Barbecue Pork Chops

EQUIPMENT: French chef's knife, cutting board, measuring cup and spoons, large covered sauté skillet or electric skillet and food cutter (grating blade)

PREPARATION TIME: 30 minutes ○ Makes 4 servings

4 center-cut pork chops, trimmed

1 medium onion, diced

4 cloves garlic, minced

3 tablespoons tomato paste

1 cup brewed coffee

1 tablespoon light brown sugar

1/8 teaspoon red pepper flakes

1/2 cup orange marmalade

1 teaspoon grated orange zest

1 teaspoon chopped fresh parsley

In a hot, dry skillet over medium-high heat, brown the pork chops until they release easily from the skillet, 4 to 5 minutes per side. Remove the pork to a warm platter and keep warm.

Add the onion and garlic and sauté in the pork drippings until slightly browned, 3 to 5 minutes. Add the tomato paste and cook, stirring, until the paste turns reddish-brown in color. Do not allow the residue that forms on the bottom of the pan to burn.

Slowly stir in the coffee. Add the brown sugar, red pepper and orange marmalade and mix well.

Return the pork chops to the skillet and simmer for 8 to 10 minutes.

To serve, top the pork with the sauce and sprinkle with the orange zest and parsley. Serve over Hash Brown Potatoes (page 153) with Spinach with Cognac Cream (page 170) on the side.

PER SERVING: 446 Calories • 21g Fat (42% calories from fat) • 32g Protein
34g Carbohydrates • 91mg Cholesterol • 234mg Sodium

Roast Pork Chardonnay

EQUIPMENT: Measuring cup, 6-quart Dutch oven and hi-dome cover

PREPARATION TIME: 1 hour 45 minutes o Makes 10 to 12 servings

3 pounds pork tenderloin, trimmed of fat

1 cup Chardonnay or other dry white wine

¼ cup steak sauce

¼ cup white distilled vinegar

½ cup fresh orange juice

1¼ cups Low-Sodium Brown Pork or Beef Stock (page 219) or canned

1 tablespoon Low-Cholesterol Roux (page 190)

In a hot, dry Dutch oven over medium heat, brown the pork tenderloin on all sides, 15 to 20 minutes, turning the roast as it releases easily from the pan.

Slowly stir in the wine, bring to a simmer and reduce by about half. Add the steak sauce, vinegar and orange juice. Reduce the heat to medium-low and cover the pan with the hi-dome cover. When the cover spins freely on a cushion of water and tiny bubbles appear around the rim, the vapor seal has formed, 5 to 7 minutes. If the vapor seal spits moisture, the temperature is too high. If no bubbles appear, the heat is too low. Adjust the temperature and braise the roast for 25 to 30 minutes per pound.

When the pork roast is done, the meat should pull easily from the bone. Remove the pork roast to a warm platter and keep it warm.

To prepare the gravy, turn the heat to medium and add the pork stock and roux to the pan. Cook, stirring, until the gravy thickens.

To serve, slice the roast and transfer to a platter. Spoon the gravy over the pork. Serve with cooked yellow rice and Homemade Beans (page 30), using black beans.

PER SERVING: 151 Calories • 5g Fat (27% calories from fat) • 25g Protein • 2g Carbohydrates • 74mg Cholesterol • 152mg Sodium

VARIATION

Roast 4 or 5 whole onions and cut into quarters with the pork tenderloin.

Braised Roast Pork Tenderloin with Cabbage and Apples

This recipe is usually made with sauerkraut, but it contains as much as 700mg of sodium per serving. When using canned and packaged goods consult the label's Nutrition Facts for nutritional data.

EQUIPMENT: **French chef's knife, cutting board, food cutter (shredding blade), measuring cup and spoons and 6-quart Dutch oven and hi-dome cover**

PREPARATION TIME: **1 hour ○ Makes 8 to 10 servings**

1 (2- to 2½-pound) pork tenderloin roast

2 slices lean bacon, diced

1 medium onion, diced

1 medium parsnip, diced

1 stalk celery, diced

2 cloves garlic, minced

1 bay leaf, stem removed and finely crushed

½ cup apple cider vinegar

¼ cup gin

1 medium head green cabbage (about 2 pounds), shredded

2 medium green apples, unpeeled, cored, seeded and chopped

1 tablespoon granulated sugar

1 teaspoon caraway seeds

1 tablespoon light brown sugar

In a medium-hot dry Dutch oven over medium-high heat, brown the pork tenderloin on all sides, turning each time the meat releases easily from the pan, 15 to 20 minutes.

Add the bacon, onion, parsnip, celery and garlic around the tenderloin, and sauté until slightly browned, 2 to 3 minutes, stirring occasionally. Stir in the bay leaf, vinegar and gin. Cook until the liquid is reduced to about half. Reduce the heat to between medium and medium-low.

Add the cabbage, apples, granulated sugar and caraway seeds. Cover the pan with the hi-dome cover. When the cover spins freely on a cushion of water, the vapor seal is formed, 3 to 5 minutes. After forming the seal, adjust the heat to produce tiny moisture bubbles between the rim of the Dutch oven and the hi-dome cover. If the cover spits moisture, the heat is too high. If no bubbles appear, the heat is too low. Once you have reached the proper braising temperature, cook for 20 to 25 minutes for medium or 25 to 30 minutes for medium well. Do not remove the hi-dome cover. Removing the cover will destroy the vapor seal, lengthen the cooking time and may cause the meat to burn.

Transfer the tenderloin to a cutting board and cut into ¼-inch-thick slices.

To serve, top the tenderloin with the cabbage mixture and sprinkle the brown sugar. Serve with Applesauce (page 133).

PER SERVING: 182 Calories • 4g Fat (27% calories from fat) • 21g Protein • 14g Carbohydrates • 60mg Cholesterol • 102mg Sodium

Lamb Chops Braised with Tomatoes, Eggplant and Green Olives

EQUIPMENT: French chef's knife, cutting board, measuring cup and spoons, 10-inch wok, fine strainer and large covered sauté skillet or electric skillet

PREPARATION TIME: about 1 hour ○ Makes 6 servings

½ medium onion, diced

½ carrot, diced

½ stalk celery, diced

1 clove garlic, minced

1 teaspoon dried thyme

1 bay leaf, stem removed and crumbled

½ teaspoon freshly ground black pepper

1 tablespoon tomato paste

1 cup Low-Sodium Brown Veal or Beef Stock (page 219) or canned

2 teaspoons Low-Cholesterol Roux (page 190)

6 (¾- to 1-inch-thick) lamb chops

1 shallot, minced

½ cup Madeira

2 cups cubed eggplant

1 cup seeded and chopped plum tomatoes or canned whole tomatoes

6 green olives, thinly sliced

1 tablespoon chopped fresh parsley

In a hot, dry wok over medium-high, dry sauté the onion, carrot, celery and garlic until slightly browned, 3 to 5 minutes. Stir in the thyme, bay leaf and pepper. Add the tomato paste and cook, stirring until the paste turns reddish-brown in color, 3 to 4 minutes. Do not allow the residue that forms on the bottom of the pan to burn.

Slowly stir in the stock and roux. Cook, stirring, until the sauce begins to thicken slightly. Strain the sauce through a fine sieve and set aside.

In a hot, dry skillet over medium-high heat, place the chops. Sear until the chops release easily from the pan, 3 to 4 minutes. Using a flexible spatula, turn the chops and sear the other side for 4 to 5 minutes. Remove the chops to a warm platter and keep warm.

Add the shallot to the meat drippings and sauté until tender, 2 to 3 minutes, stirring occasionally.

Slowly stir in the Madeira and bring to a simmer. Stir in the reserved sauce, eggplant, tomatoes and olives. Return the chops to the skillet. Reduce the heat to medium-low, cover the pan, open the vent and simmer for 30 to 40 minutes.

To serve, top the chops with the tomato mixture and sprinkle with the parsley.

PER SERVING: 401 Calories • 32g Fat (71% calories from fat) • 22g Protein • 8g Carbohydrates • 85mg Cholesterol • 247mg Sodium (canned tomatoes add 50mg of Sodium per serving)

Grilled Marinated Tuna Steaks

EQUIPMENT: French chef's knife, butcher knife, cutting board, measuring spoons, large covered sauté skillet or electric skillet and food cutter (grating blade)

PREPARATION TIME: 15 minutes   ○   Makes 5 or 6 servings

1 medium Vidalia onion, diced

2 cloves garlic, minced

1 tablespoon steak sauce

1 tablespoon low-sodium soy sauce

2 teaspoons extra-virgin olive oil

5 sprigs fresh thyme or 2 teaspoons dried

1 bay leaf

5 sprigs fresh parsley

½ teaspoon freshly ground black pepper

Juice and peel of ½ large lemon

½ teaspoon hot pepper sauce

2 pounds tuna steaks, cut into 5 or 6 equal portions

Romaine lettuce leaves

1 tablespoon grated fresh ginger

To prepare the marinade, in a mixing bowl or large freezer bag, combine the onion, garlic, steak sauce, soy sauce, olive oil, thyme, bay leaf, parsley, pepper, lemon juice, lemon peel and hot sauce and mix well. Place the tuna steaks into the marinade, cover or seal the bag and refrigerate for at least 1 hour or up to 24 hours for improved flavor.

In a medium-hot dry skillet over medium-high heat, place the tuna. Sear until the tuna release easily from the skillet, 4 to 5 minutes. Turn the tuna and sear the other sides, 4 to 5 minutes. It is important not to overcook the tuna; it is best when served medium rare.

Transfer the tuna to a warm platter and keep warm. To the skillet, add the marinade and bring to a simmer. Cook until sauce thickens slightly.

To serve, place the steaks on a bed of Romaine lettuce and top with ginger. Spoon the sauce over the tuna. Serve with Broccoli Romano (page 139) or French Tarragon Potatoes (page 152).

PER SERVING: **258 Calories** • **9g Fat (33% calories from fat)** • **37g Protein** • **6g Carbohydrates** • **58mg Cholesterol** • **160mg Sodium**

Herb-Crusted Pork Chops

EQUIPMENT: Large covered sauté skillet or electric skillet, flexible spatula or pancake turner, measuring cup and spoons, butcher knife, French chef's knife and cutting board

PREPARATION TIME: 30 minutes ○ Makes 4 servings

4 (about 1½-inch-thick) pork loin chops, trimmed

1 tablespoon olive oil

3 tablespoons freshly ground pepper

2 tablespoons garlic powder

3 tablespoons Italian seasoning

¼ cup brewed coffee

½ cup Low-Sodium Brown Veal or Pork Stock (page 219)

1 teaspoon chopped fresh parsley

Brush each chop with a very light coating of the olive oil. Then press the pepper, garlic powder and Italian seasoning into each pork chop, covering the entire surface.

Place the chops in a medium-hot dry skillet over medium-high. Cover, open the vent and sear until the chops release easily from the skillet, 10 to 12 minutes. Using a flexible spatula, turn the chops, cover the pan and sear the other side, 10 to 12 minutes. Transfer the pork chops to a warm platter and keep warm.

Slowly stir in the coffee and stock. Bring to a simmer and cook until reduced by one-third.

To serve, spoon the gravy over the chops and sprinkle with the parsley.

PER SERVING: 274 Calories • 16g Fat (51% calories from fat) • 25g Protein
9g Carbohydrates • 71mg Cholesterol • 127mg Sodium

VARIATION

Substitute chicken, beef steak or veal cutlets for the pork chops.

Jambalaya with Scallops

EQUIPMENT: French chef's knife, cutting board, measuring cup and spoons and 6½–quart covered stockpot

PREPARATION TIME: 45 minutes ○ Makes 7 or 8 servings

1 large Spanish onion, diced

1 stalk celery, diced

1 clove garlic, minced

1 medium green bell pepper, diced

½ teaspoon dried thyme

2 bay leaves, stems removed and finely crushed

2 teaspoons chopped fresh parsley

½ teaspoon cayenne pepper

½ pound cleaned and peeled shrimp (optional)

½ pound bay scallops or 1 pound if not using shrimp

2 cups seeded and chopped plum tomatoes or canned whole tomatoes

2 cups Low-Sodium Chicken Stock (page 217) or canned

1 cup basmati or other long-grain rice

3 tablespoons chopped green onions

In a medium-hot dry stockpot over medium-high heat, dry sauté the onion, celery, garlic and bell pepper until slightly browned, 3 to 4 minutes. Stir in the thyme, bay leaf, parsley and cayenne.

To the stockpot, stir in the remaining ingredients, except the green onions, and mix well. Bring to a simmer and reduce the heat to medium-low. Cover the pan, close the vent and simmer for 25 to 30 minutes. Do not allow the jambalaya to boil.

To serve, top with the green onions.

PER SERVING, WITH SCALLOPS AND SHRIMP: 166 Calories •
1g Fat (6% calories from fat) • 16g Protein • 25g Carbohydrates •
52mg Cholesterol • 227mg Sodium (canned tomatoes add 90mg of Sodium per serving)

PER SERVING, WITH SCALLOPS: 161 Calories • 0.8g Fat (4% calories from fat) •
15g Protein • 25g Carbohydrates • 19mg Cholesterol • 231mg Sodium (canned tomatoes add 90mg of Sodium per serving)

Paella Valencia

EQUIPMENT: French chef's knife, cutting board, measuring cup and spoons, 1-quart saucepan and 13-inch gourmet skillet

PREPARATION TIME: 55 minutes ○ Makes 12 servings

3½ cups Low-Sodium Chicken Stock (page 217) or Low-Sodium Fish Stock (page 218)

12 saffron threads

1 Spanish onion, diced

1 green bell pepper, diced

3 cloves garlic, minced

1 cooked chorizo or hot Italian sausage link, cut into ¼-inch-thick slices (optional)

¾ cup Chardonnay or other dry white wine

1 boneless, skinless chicken breast half, cut into ¼-inch-thick slices

½ pound cleaned and peeled shrimp

½ pound bay scallops

½ pound cod, cut into strips

1 cup chopped seeded plum tomatoes

1 bay leaf

1 teaspoon dried thyme

1 teaspoon chopped fresh parsley

2 cups basmati or other long-grain rice

¾ cup frozen green peas

4 ounces pimientos, cut into 12 pieces

12 cherrystone clams

12 fresh asparagus spears, trimmed

12 lemon wedges

In the 1-quart pan, combine the chicken stock and saffron and bring to a simmer. Remove from the heat and set aside.

In a hot, dry skillet over medium heat, dry sauté the onion, pepper and garlic until slightly browned, 3 to 5 minutes, stirring occasionally. Add the sausage, if using, and cook, stirring, 2 to 3 minutes.

Slowly stir in ½ cup of the wine. Stir in the chicken, shrimp, scallops, cod and tomatoes. Simmer until partially cooked through, about 5 minutes, stirring occasionally. Stir in the stock with saffron and add the bay leaf, thyme, parsley, rice and peas. Mix well and bring to a simmer.

Reduce the heat to medium-low and garnish the top with the pimientos, clams and asparagus. Cover the pan, close the vent and allow the vapor seal to form, 3 to 5 minutes. After forming the seal, cook for about 35 to 40 minutes. If the rim between the cover and the pan spits moisture, the heat is too high. Don't peek. Removing the cover will destroy the vapor seal, lengthen the cooking time and may cause the rice to burn.

Serve with the lemon wedges.

PER SERVING: 231 Calories • 1.3g Fat (5% calories from fat) • 21g Protein • 34g Carbohydrates • 51mg Cholesterol • 249mg Sodium

PER SERVING WITH SAUSAGE: 254 Calories • 3.2g Fat (11% calories from fat) • 22g Protein • 34g Carbohydrates • 56mg Cholesterol • 311mg Sodium

Fish Poached in Court-Bouillon

EQUIPMENT: French chef's knife, cutting board, large covered sauté skillet or electric skillet and large slotted spatula

PREPARATION TIME: 25 minutes ○ Makes 4 or 5 servings

COURT-BOUILLON

1 medium onion, cut into ¼-inch-thick slices

1 medium green bell pepper, cut into ¼-inch-thick slices

1 lemon slice

1 bay leaf

1 sprig fresh thyme or ½ teaspoon dried

1 sprig fresh parsley with stem

4 cracked peppercorns

1 cup Chardonnay or other dry white wine

2 cups water or Low-Sodium Fish Stock (page 218)

FISH

2 pounds fish fillets without skin

2 to 3 tablespoons Light Hollandaise Sauce (page 199)

1 tablespoon chopped fresh parsley

4 or 5 lemon wedges

Make the court-bouillon for poaching: Place all the ingredients in the skillet and bring to a simmer over medium to medium-low heat, 10 to 12 minutes. Do not boil.

To cook the fish: Place the fish fillets in the simmering court-bouillon. Cover the pan, open the vent and gently poach the fillets until they turn from translucent to opaque, 8 to 10 minutes.

Remove the fillets to a warm serving platter. To serve, top with the Light Hollandaise Sauce and sprinkle with the parsley. Serve with the lemon wedges and cooked asparagus.

PER SERVING: 153 Calories • 1.3g Fat (8% calories from fat) • 33g Protein • 0.8g Carbohydrates • 82mg Cholesterol • 101mg Sodium

Fresh Salmon with Light Hollandaise Sauce and Dill

EQUIPMENT: French chef's knife or food cutter (slicing blade), cutting board and large covered sauté skillet

PREPARATION TIME: 20 minutes ○ Makes 4 servings

Court-Bouillon (page 122)

4 tablespoons Light Hollandaise Sauce (page 199)

4 (about 6-ounce) fresh salmon filets

1 tablespoon chopped fresh dill

Prepare the Court-Bouillon and Light Hollandaise Sauce.

Bring the Court-Bouillon to a slight boil and place the salmon in the liquid. Cover the pan, open the vent and cook just below the simmering point until the fish turns from translucent to opaque, 5 to 7 minutes.

Using a slotted serving spoon, place the salmon on individual serving plates. Top with the Light Hollandaise Sauce and sprinkle with the dill. Serve with Candied Carrots (page 142).

PER SERVING: 208 Calories • 6g Fat (28% calories from fat) • 36g Protein • 1g Carbohydrates • 97mg Cholesterol • 121mg Sodium

Seafood Étouffée

EQUIPMENT: French chef's knife, cutting board, measuring cup and spoons and large covered sauté skillet or electric skillet

PREPARATION TIME: 40 minutes ○ Makes 7 or 8 servings

1 medium onion, diced

1 medium green bell pepper, diced

3 cloves garlic, minced

1 teaspoon sweet paprika

⅛ teaspoon cayenne pepper

1 teaspoon dried thyme

1 medium bay leaf, stem removed and finely crushed

1 tablespoon chopped parsley

2½ cups Low-Sodium Chicken Stock (page 217) or Low-Sodium Fish Stock (page 218)

1 cup seeded chopped plum tomatoes or canned whole tomatoes

1 tablespoon Worcestershire sauce

1 cup basmati or other long-grain rice

½ pound bay scallops

½ pound white fish fillet or peeled and cleaned shrimp

½ cup chopped green onions

In a hot, dry skillet over medium heat, dry sauté the onion, bell pepper and garlic until slightly browned, 3 to 5 minutes, stirring occasionally. Stir in the paprika, cayenne, thyme, bay leaf and parsley.

Slowly stir in the stock. Stir in the tomatoes and Worcestershire sauce and bring to a simmer, 1 to 2 minutes. Stir in the rice and reduce to the heat to medium-low.

Add the scallops and fish fillets or shrimp. Cover the skillet and close the vent. When the cover spins freely on a cushion of water, the vapor seal has formed, 3 to 5 minutes. After forming the seal, cook for 25 to 30 minutes.

To serve, sprinkle with green onions.

PER SERVING, WITH FISH: 156 Calories   0.7g Fat (4% calories from fat)

16g Protein • 24g Carbohydrates • 22mg Cholesterol • 343mg Sodium

PER SERVING, WITH SHRIMP: 165 Calories • 1g Fat (5.4% calories from fat) •

17g Protein • 25g Carbohydrates • 52mg Cholesterol • 343mg Sodium

VARIATION

Cook the rice separately in 1½ cups of the stock. Spoon the Seafood Étouffée over the rice and sprinkle with the green onions.

Healthy
POTATOES AND VEGETABLES

Benefits of Waterless, Greaseless Cooking

For your good health, it's reassuring to know that all vegetables have a built-in natural supply of vital vitamins, minerals and digestive enzymes. Unfortunately, all the essential health-giving properties (dearly paid for at the supermarket) may quickly vanish in your kitchen. It can easily happen with old-fashioned cooking methods that require peeling and boiling, not to mention the health problems stemming from the need to use high-calorie fats and oils when sautéing.

NO NEED TO PEEL

With waterless, greaseless cooking, delicious vegetables can be prepared without sacrificing the wonders of nature. The first major breakthrough of this unique cooking method eliminates the need to strip away the flavor- and nutrient-rich skin. Peeling strips away natural vitamins and minerals located directly under the skin. For most vegetables, a gentle scrub is all that's needed before cooking. One more step to ensure that all of nature's goodness arrives "garden fresh" at your table.

LOWER HEAT

The second major breakthrough of the waterless, greaseless method eliminates the devastating damages caused by high-heat oil sautéing and boiling of vegetables. High heat destroys most of the health-giving, water- and fat-soluble minerals, along with the very delicate flavors and colors. The vegetable's most valuable nutritional advantages are often thrown out with the cooking oil or water.

With waterless, greaseless "flavor-sealing" covered utensils and heavy-duty construction, vegetables can be cooked with low heat, eliminating the need for boiling in water and sautéing in oil. With low heat, the vegetables are cooked "waterless" quickly and evenly in a vacuum below the boiling temperature, or "greaseless" without oil, and prepared in their own natural moisture. Using the vegetable's natural juices eliminates the need to add water or oil during cooking.

LESS OXIDATION

The third major breakthrough of waterless cooking is the elimination of harmful oxidation. Detrimental oxidation occurs when vegetables are boiled in uncovered utensils, pressure-cooked or microwaved, allowing a good share of the health-giving properties to evaporate.

The waterless feature of the cookware, with its unique vapor-sealing covers, locks vitamins, minerals and enzymes in the utensil. No steam is allowed to escape. Wonderful aromas remain inside the pan. Until the cover is removed, you won't know if it's broccoli or cabbage being prepared. The vegetables cook on low heat, cooking evenly in their natural moisture.

Cooking Vegetables the Waterless, Greaseless Way

SCRUB ROOT VEGETABLES

To clean root vegetables, scrub vigorously with a vegetable brush under cold running water and remove any surface blemishes with a paring knife. Do not peel.

Refresh Vegetables

All fresh vegetables, especially root vegetables, have a tendency to lose some of their natural moisture after harvesting. To add back some of the lost moisture, place the vegetables in the pan, fill the pan with water, add 1 tablespoon white distilled vinegar and soak for 10 to 15 minutes. Soaking also removes chemical sprays, preservatives and any other substances the vegetable may have come in contact with in transit and in storage. Pour the water off, rinse and cook according to the recipe.

Use the Right-size Pan

When cooking vegetables the waterless way, it's very important to use a pan that the vegetables nearly fill. This is an essential step in forming the vapor seal. The less vegetables in the pan, the more air, which can cause oxidation. In addition to oxidation, less-full pans will require a higher temperature setting to create a vapor seal, and more than likely, the vegetables will be scorched or burned.

Form the Vapor Seal

As the moist air inside the pan is heated, it expands and is forced out between the rim and the cover of the pan. Around the rim is a well, or reservoir, that collects the moisture. The covers are angled down to fit perfectly in line with the well. As the heated air continues to escape, the well is filled with moisture, forming the vapor seal. This usually takes 3 to 5 minutes.

Find the Right Temperature Setting

Whether you have an electric range with glass top, European or conventional burners, or a conventional or commercial gas range, waterless cookware takes all the guesswork out of cooking the waterless way.

Here are some simple tips:

- If the rim or well spits moisture, the temperature is too high.

- If the lid does not spin freely on a cushion of water after forming the seal, the temperature is too low.

Once you discover the proper setting, cooking the waterless way will be simple and easy. If you have a commercial gas range and you cannot achieve sufficient low temperatures for cooking vegetables the waterless, greaseless way, use a carbon steel trivet or flame tamer placed over the burner. You can also call your dealer and ask that they replace your commercial gas burners with those specifically and safely designed for the home kitchen.

REESTABLISH THE VAPOR SEAL

During the waterless cooking process, don't peek. Removing the cover will destroy the vapor seal, lengthen the cooking time and may cause the vegetables to burn. If you or another member of the family does lift the lid, cover the pan, close the vent and add 2 tablespoons water to the rim to reestablish the vapor seal. Add 3 to 5 minutes to the prescribed cooking time.

Cooking Fresh Vegetables

To cook, place the vegetables in a pan that they nearly fill. Rinse with cold water and pour the water off. The water that clings to the vegetables and its own natural moisture are sufficient for cooking the waterless way.

Cover the pan, close the vent and cook over medium-low heat. When the cover spins freely on a cushion of water, the vapor seal has formed. Cook according to the time chart (page 131). Don't peek. Removing the cover will destroy the vapor seal, lengthen the cooking time and may cause the vegetables to burn. If at first you are concerned about cooking without water, add 2 or 3 tablespoons of water to the pan after rinsing and cook as directed. As your confidence builds, you can lessen the amount of water used.

When finished cooking, test for doneness with a fork. If not done, cover the pan, close the vent and add 2 tablespoons of water to the rim to reestablish the vapor seal. Cook over low heat for 5 to 10 minutes.

Cooking Frozen Vegetables

Do not defrost. Place the frozen vegetables in the pan they most nearly fill. Rinse with cold water and pour the water off. The water that clings to the vegetable and its own natural moisture are sufficient for cooking the waterless way.

Cover the pan, close the vent and cook over medium-low heat. When the cover spins freely on a cushion of water, the vapor seal has formed. Cook according to the time chart (page 131). Don't peek. Removing the cover will destroy the vapor seal, lengthen the cooking time and may cause the vegetables to burn.

When cooking for one or two people, naturally the quantity of vegetables will be less. However, with waterless cooking more than one vegetable can be cooked in the same pan with no interchanging of flavors or colors. You can cook potatoes, sliced carrots and broccoli all in the same pan the waterless way. For example, using a 1- or 1¼-quart covered saucepan, place the potatoes in the pan, halved or whole, with the skin side to the surface of the pan, add two sliced carrots and top with the broccoli florets. Rinse the vegetables and pour the water off. Cook as directed above.

COOKING TIMES FOR APPLES AND VEGETABLES

VEGETABLE	COOKING TIME IN MINUTES*
Apples	10 to 15
Artichokes (whole)	30 to 45
Artichoke hearts	10 to 15
Asparagus	10 to 15
Beans, green (fresh, cut)	15 to 20
Beans, green (fresh, French cut)	10 to 15
Beans, green (frozen)	10 to 12
Beans, lima (fresh)	30 to 35
Beans, lima (frozen)	10 to 12
Beets (whole)	35 to 40
Broccoli	15 to 20
Brussels sprouts	15 to 20
Cabbage, shredded	10 to 15
Carrots, sliced	15 to 20
Cauliflower	10 to 15
Corn (fresh)	15 to 20
Corn (frozen)	10 to 12

VEGETABLE	COOKING TIME IN MINUTES*
Eggplant	5 to 8
Greens	10 to 12
Leeks	12 to 15
Mushrooms	5 to 10
Okra	15 to 20
Onions (whole)	15 to 20
Parsnips (sliced)	15 to 20
Peas (frozen)	5 to 7
Potatoes (quartered)	20 to 25
Potatoes (whole)	30 to 35
Potatoes, sweet	30 to 35
Spinach (frozen)	8 to 10
Spinach (fresh)	15 to 20
Squash, summer (yellow)	15 to 20
Squash, winter	25 to 30
Squash, zucchini	20 to 25
Tomatoes	10 to 15
Turnips and rutabagas	25 to 30

*After forming the vapor seal, which takes 3 to 5 minutes.

NOTE: To keep your vegetables hot and ready to serve, keep the cover on and the vent closed. The vegetables will stay hot in the pan for 20 to 25 minutes.

Applesauce

EQUIPMENT: **Vegetable brush, paring knife, French chef's knife, cutting board, food cutter (julienne blade), measuring spoons and 1-quart covered saucepan**
PREPARATION TIME: **20 minutes   o   Makes 7 or 8 servings**

6 medium red or green cooking apples

1 teaspoon sugar

½ teaspoon ground cinnamon

Under cold running water, scrub the apples with a vegetable brush and remove any surface blemishes with a paring knife. Do not peel. With a knife, cut each apple in half and remove the core and stem.

With a food cutter or a knife, chop the apples and fill the pan. The pan must be at least three-quarters full for the vapor seal to form. Apples have sufficient natural moisture for cooking the waterless way (see Note below). Cover the pan, close the vent and cook over medium-low heat. When the cover spins freely on a cushion of water, the vapor seal has formed, 3 to 5 minutes. After forming the seal, cook for 10 to 15 minutes. Don't peek. Removing the cover will destroy the vapor seal, lengthen the cooking time and may cause the apples to burn.

Remove from the heat. Stir in the sugar.

To serve, sprinkle with the cinnamon and serve warm or chilled.

PER SERVING: **63 Calories   •   0.4g Fat (5% calories from fat)   •   0.2g Protein   •   16.4g Carbohydrates   •   0mg Cholesterol   •   0mg Sodium**

NOTE: **If at first you are concerned about cooking without water, add 3 tablespoons of water to the pan after rinsing and repeat the steps as directed. As your confidence builds, you can lessen the amount of water used.**

Asparagus with Lemon Pepper

EQUIPMENT: French chef's knife, cutting board, 1½–quart covered saucepan, 7-inch gourmet skillet and whisk

PREPARATION TIME: 25 minutes ○ Makes 5 or 6 servings

1 bunch fresh asparagus spears, 1 to 1½ pounds

1 tablespoon Chardonnay or other dry white wine

2 teaspoons fresh lemon juice

2 tablespoons Light Béchamel Sauce (page 188)

½ teaspoon freshly ground black pepper

With a knife, trim the asparagus 1 to 2 inches from the base to remove the woody, fibrous part from the stem. Fill the pan with asparagus. The pan must be at least three-quarters full for the vapor seal to form. Rinse with cold water and pour the water off. The water that clings to the asparagus is sufficient for cooking the waterless way (see Note, page 3). Cover the pan, close the vent and cook over medium-low heat. When the cover spins freely on a cushion of water the vapor seal has formed, 3 to 5 minutes. After forming the seal, cook for 10 to 15 minutes. Don't peek. Removing the cover will destroy the vapor seal, lengthen the cooking time and may cause the asparagus to burn.

While the asparagus is cooking, in the gourmet skillet, combine the wine, lemon juice and béchamel sauce. Cook over medium-low heat, whisking, until the sauce thickens, about 5 minutes.

To serve, top the asparagus with the sauce and sprinkle with the pepper.

PER SERVING: 23 Calories • 0.3g Fat (10% calories from fat) • 1.9g Protein
4g Carbohydrates • 0mg Cholesterol • 4mg Sodium

Asparagus with Hollandaise Sauce

EQUIPMENT: French chef's knife, cutting board, 1½–quart covered saucepan, 10-inch wok or gourmet skillet, and whisk

PREPARATION TIME: 25 minutes   ○   Makes 5 or 6 servings

1 bunch fresh asparagus spears (1 to 1½ pounds)

Light Hollandaise or Classic Hollandaise Sauce (page 198)

Freshly ground black pepper

With a knife, trim the asparagus 1 to 2 inches from the base to remove the woody, fibrous part from the stem. Fill the pan with asparagus. The pan must be at least three-quarters full for the vapor seal to form. Rinse with cold water and pour the water off. The water that clings to the asparagus is sufficient for cooking the waterless way (see Note, page 3). Cover the pan, close the vent and cook over medium-low heat. When the cover spins freely on a cushion of water the vapor seal has formed, 3 to 5 minutes. After forming the seal, cook for 10 to 15 minutes. Don't peek. Removing the cover will destroy the vapor seal, lengthen the cooking time and may cause the asparagus to burn.

To serve, top the asparagus with the sauce and sprinkle with the pepper.

PER SERVING, WITH LIGHT HOLLANDAISE: 63 Calories • 1.4g Fat (15% calories from fat) • 4.5g Protein • 12.5g Carbohydrates • 35mg Cholesterol • 54mg Sodium

PER SERVING, WITH CLASSIC HOLLANDAISE WITH BUTTER: 162 Calories • 12g Fat (61% calories from fat) • 5g Protein • 12g Carbohydrates • 164mg Cholesterol • 15mg Sodium

PER SERVING, WITH CLASSIC HOLLANDAISE WITH MARGARINE: 158 Calories • 12g Fat (60% calories from fat) • 5g Protein • 12g Carbohydrates • 142mg Cholesterol • 15mg Sodium

Warm Green Bean Salad

EQUIPMENT: French chef's knife, cutting board, 1¼-quart covered saucepan, measuring spoons and mixing bowl

PREPARATION TIME: 25 minutes   ○   Makes 4 to 5 servings

1 pound fresh green beans, trimmed

3 tablespoons red wine vinegar

1 tablespoon dried oregano

1 tablespoon Dijon mustard

2 cloves garlic, minced

1 teaspoon olive oil (optional)

¼ teaspoon freshly ground black pepper

Fill the pan with green beans, rinse with cold water and pour the water off. The water that clings to the green beans is sufficient for cooking the waterless way (see Note, page 3). Cover the pan, close the vent and cook over medium-low heat. When the cover spins freely on a cushion of water, the vapor seal has formed, 3 to 5 minutes. After forming the seal, cook for 10 to 15 minutes. Don't peek. Removing the cover will destroy the vapor seal, lengthen the cooking time and may cause the green beans to burn.

Test the green beans for doneness with a fork. If not done, cover the pan, close the vent and add 2 tablespoons water to the rim to reestablish the vapor seal. Cook over low heat for 5 to 10 minutes.

While the green beans are cooking, combine the vinegar, oregano, mustard, garlic and olive oil, if using, in a small mixing bowl. Mix well and set aside.

Remove the beans from the heat and drain the excess moisture from the pan. Add the dressing to the pan and stir gently. Cover the pan and let set for 5 minutes, or until the dressing is warmed.

To serve, toss the green beans to combine all the ingredients. Sprinkle with the pepper and serve warm.

PER SERVING: 36 Calories   0.3g Fat (7% calories from fat)   2g Protein
8.2g Carbohydrates • 0mg Cholesterol •
43mg Sodium (olive oil adds 8 Calories and 1g Fat per serving)

Cold Green Bean Salad

Chill the dressing. Plunge the cooked green beans into an ice water bath for about 5 minutes. Remove the green beans to a strainer, drain well and dry. Garnish with dressing and serve.

Stovetop Baked Barbecue Beans

EQUIPMENT: **French chef's knife, cutting board, 2-quart covered saucepan and measuring cup and spoons**

PREPARATION TIME: **30 minutes** ○ **Makes 8 to 10 servings**

1 medium onion, diced

1 clove garlic, minced

¼ cup diced lean ham

1 tablespoon tomato paste

1 cup strong brewed coffee

¼ cup apple cider vinegar

½ cup packed light brown sugar

¼ teaspoon Dijon mustard

1 pinch red pepper flakes (optional)

4 cups cooked navy beans (page 30) or canned beans

In a hot, dry pan over medium heat, dry sauté the onion and garlic until slightly browned, about 5 minutes. Add the ham and sauté for 2 to 3 minutes, stirring occasionally.

Add the tomato paste and cook, stirring, until the paste turns reddish-brown in color, about 5 minutes. Do not allow the residue that forms on the bottom of the pan to burn.

Slowly stir in the coffee. Stir in the vinegar and simmer until reduced by half.

Stir in the remaining ingredients and reduce the heat to low. Cover the pan, close the vent and cook for about 15 minutes.

Serve as a side dish with barbecued beef, pork or chicken.

PER SERVING: 142 Calories • 0.6g Fat (4% calories from fat) • 7g Protein • 28g Carbohydrates • 2mg Cholesterol • 112mg Sodium (canned beans add 469mg Sodium per serving)

Broccoli Romano

EQUIPMENT: French chef's knife, cutting board, measuring spoons, food cutter (grating blade) and 2-quart covered saucepan

PREPARATION TIME: 25 minutes ○ Makes 5 or 6 servings

1 large head broccoli

6 lemon wedges

¼ teaspoon freshly ground black pepper

1 tablespoon freshly grated Romano cheese

Trim the broccoli stem just below the connecting branches to make the head fit inside the height of the pan. Place the broccoli in the pan, rinse with cold water and pour the water off. The water that clings to the vegetable is sufficient for cooking the waterless way (see Note, page 3). Cover the pan, close the vent and cook over medium-low heat. When the cover spins freely on a cushion of water, the vapor seal has formed, 3 to 5 minutes. After forming the vapor seal, cook for 10 to 15 minutes. Don't peek. Removing the cover will destroy the vapor seal, lengthen the cooking time and may cause the broccoli to burn.

Test for doneness. If not done, cover the pan, close the vent and add 2 tablespoons water to the rim to reestablish the vapor seal. Cook over low heat for 5 to 10 minutes.

To serve, squeeze lemon over each serving and sprinkle with the pepper and Romano cheese.

PER SERVING: 12 Calories • 0.4g Fat (17% calories from fat) • 1g Protein • 2.9g Carbohydrates • 1mg Cholesterol • 20mg Sodium

Cabbage Casserole

EQUIPMENT: French chef's knife, cutting board, measuring cups and spoons, 2-quart covered saucepan and food cutter (shredding blade)

PREPARATION TIME: 30 minutes ○ Makes 5 or 6 servings

1 medium onion, diced

1 clove garlic, minced

¼ pound ground turkey

¼ teaspoon dried thyme

¼ teaspoon dried oregano

½ cup diced seeded fresh plum tomatoes or canned whole tomatoes

1 teaspoon sugar

1 teaspoon white distilled vinegar

1 bay leaf

¼ cup cooked rice

½ head green cabbage, shredded

2 teaspoon chopped fresh parsley

In a hot, dry pan over medium heat, dry sauté the onion and garlic until slightly browned, about 5 minutes, stirring occasionally.

Add the turkey and cook, stirring to break up, until cooked through, about 5 minutes. Stir in the thyme, oregano, tomatoes, sugar, vinegar, bay leaf and rice. Add the cabbage. The pan must be at least three-quarters full for the vapor seal to form. Cover the pan, close the vent and cook over medium-low heat. When the cover spins freely over a cushion of water, the vapor seal has formed, 3 to 5 minutes. After forming the seal, cook for 10 to 15 minutes. Don't peek. Removing the cover will destroy the vapor seal, lengthen the cooking time and may cause the vegetables to burn.

To serve, discard the bay leaf and sprinkle with the parsley.

PER SERVING: 69 Calories • 1.8g Fat (23% calories from fat) • 4.8g Protein
9g Carbohydrates • 15mg Cholesterol • 125mg Sodium

Hot and Healthy Bacon Slaw

EQUIPMENT: **French chef's knife, cutting board, measuring cup and spoons, medium covered sauté skillet, measuring spoons and flexible spatula**

PREPARATION TIME: **30 minutes** o **Makes 4 or 5 servings**

2 slices bacon

4 cloves garlic, minced

¼ cup balsamic vinegar

½ head cabbage, shredded

½ teaspoon freshly ground black pepper

In a hot, dry pan over medium heat, cook the bacon until crisp. Remove the bacon to a paper towel and set aside. Remove the skillet from the heat and pour off the excess grease.

Reduce the heat to medium-low and return the skillet to the heat. Add the garlic and sauté in the bacon drippings for 2 to 3 minutes, stirring occasionally.

Stir in the balsamic vinegar. Fill the pan with the cabbage, cover the pan and close the vent. When the cover spins freely on a cushion of water, the vapor seal has formed, 3 to 5 minutes. After forming the seal, cook for 8 to 10 minutes. Don't peek. Removing the cover will destroy the vapor seal, lengthen the cooking time and may cause the cabbage to burn.

To serve, toss to combine. Crumble the bacon over the slaw and sprinkle with the pepper.

PER SERVING: **42 Calories** • **1.4g Fat (27% calories from fat)** • **2g Protein** • **6.5g Carbohydrates** • **2mg Cholesterol** • **57mg Sodium**

Candied Carrots

EQUIPMENT: Vegetable brush, paring knife, French chef's knife or food cutter (slicing or waffle cut blades), measuring spoons, and 1¼–quart covered saucepan

PREPARATION TIME: 40 minutes   ○   Makes 7 or 8 servings

1½ pounds carrots, unpeeled, cut into ¼-inch-thick rounds or grated

1 teaspoon sugar (optional)

1 tablespoon fresh lemon juice

¼ teaspoon ground cinnamon

Add the carrots to the pan and add enough water to fill the pan. Add the sugar, if using, and lemon juice and stir. Cover and let stand for 10 to 15 minutes. Pour the water off. The water that clings to the carrots is sufficient for cooking the waterless way (see Note, page 3). Cover the pan, close the vent and cook over medium-low heat. When the cover spins freely on a cushion of water, the vapor seal has formed, 3 to 5 minutes. After forming the vapor seal, cook for 15 to 20 minutes. Don't peek. Removing the cover will destroy the vapor seal, lengthen the cooking time and may cause the carrots to burn.

Test for doneness with a fork. If not done, cover the pan, close the vent and add 2 tablespoons water to the rim to reestablish the vapor seal. Cook over low heat for 5 to 10 minutes.

To serve, sprinkle the carrots with the cinnamon.

PER SERVING: 37 Calories   •   0.2g Fat (3.5% calories from fat)   •   0.8g Protein
9g Carbohydrates   •   0mg Cholesterol   •   27mg Sodium

Corn on the Cob

Enjoy nature's goodness with fresh corn's natural sugar and sodium; no salt or butter is needed.

EQUIPMENT: **Medium covered sauté skillet and tongs**

PREPARATION TIME: **20 minutes** o **Makes 4 servings**

4 ears of corn in the husks

To prepare the corn, remove the husks and silks. Rinse well. Place 5 or 6 clean husks in the bottom of the pan. This will prevent the natural sugars and starch of the corn from scorching on the cooking surface of the pan.

Place the ears of corn on the husks in the pan, rinse with cold water and pour the water off. The water that clings to the corn and husks is sufficient for cooking the waterless way (see Note, page 3). Cover the pan, close the vent and cook over medium-low heat. When the cover spins freely on a cushion of water, the vapor seal has formed, 3 to 5 minutes. After forming the seal, cook for 10 to 15 minutes. Don't peek. Removing the cover will destroy the vapor seal, lengthen the cooking time and may cause the corn to burn.

Test the corn for doneness with a fork. If not done, cover the pan, close the vent and add 2 tablespoons water to the rim to reestablish the vapor seal. Cook over low heat for 5 to 10 minutes.

PER SERVING: **120 Calories** • **1.6g Fat (11% calories from fat)** • **4.5g Protein** • **27g Carbohydrates** • **0mg Cholesterol** • **21mg Sodium**

VARIATION

If husks are not available, place a piece of paper towel in the bottom of the pan. Place the corn on the paper towel in the pan, rinse, pour the water off and cook according to the directions above.

Dad's Famous Cucumber and Onion Salad

Dad never cooked a lick, not even a hot dog at Mom's famous summer picnics. He did, however, create this wonderful, simple salad that has been a big hit in our family for more than fifty years.

EQUIPMENT: **French chef's knife or food cutter (slicing blade), cutting board and glass salad bowl**

PREPARATION TIME: **10 minutes o Makes 7 or 8 servings**

2 large cucumbers, unpeeled, cut into ¼-inch-thick slices

1 large white onion, cut into ¼-inch-thick slices

1 tablespoon sugar

½ tablespoon olive oil

½ cup distilled white vinegar

½ teaspoon freshly ground black pepper

1 teaspoon chopped fresh parsley

In a mixing bowl, combine all of the ingredients except pepper and parsley. Cover and chill for at least 1 hour before serving.

To serve, drain off the liquid and reserve. Place the cucumber and onion slices on individual salad plates. Top with 1 tablespoon of liquid and sprinkle with the pepper and parsley.

PER SERVING: **29 Calories • 1g Fat (27% calories from fat) • 0.7g Protein 5g Carbohydrates • 0mg Cholesterol • 70mg Sodium**

Tarragon Mushrooms with Lemon Sauce

EQUIPMENT: French chef's knife or food cutter (slicing blade), cutting board, 1-quart covered saucepan, measuring cup and spoons, 7-inch gourmet skillet and whisk

PREPARATION TIME: 25 minutes ◐ Makes 5 or 6 servings

8 ounces mushrooms

¼ cup Low-Sodium Chicken Stock (page 217) or canned

1 teaspoon fresh lemon juice

½ teaspoon arrowroot or 1 egg yolk

¼ teaspoons freshly ground black pepper

2 teaspoons chopped fresh tarragon

With a damp dishcloth or paper towel, wipe the mushrooms clean. With a knife or food cutter, cut the mushrooms into ½-inch-thick slices.

Fill the pan with the mushrooms, rinse with cold water and pour the water off. The water that clings to the mushrooms is sufficient for cooking the waterless way (see Note, page 3). Cover the pan, close the vent and cook over medium-low heat. When the cover spins freely on a cushion of water, the vapor seal has formed, 3 to 5 minutes. After forming the seal, cook for 5 to 10 minutes. Don't peek. Removing the cover will destroy the vapor seal, lengthen the cooking time and may cause the mushrooms to burn.

In a small gourmet skillet, combine the stock, lemon juice and arrowroot or egg yolk. Whisking vigorously, bring the mixture to a simmer over medium heat until the sauce thickens, about 5 minutes.

To serve, top the mushrooms with the sauce, sprinkle with the pepper and tarragon.

PER SERVING, WITH ARROWROOT: 2 Calories • 0g Fat (1.6% calories from fat) • 0.5g Protein • 0.4g Carbohydrates • 0mg Cholesterol • 22mg Sodium

PER SERVING, WITH EGG YOLK: 11 Calories • 0.9g Fat (61% calories from fat) • 0.9g Protein • 0.3g Carbohydrates • 35mg Cholesterol • 23mg Sodium

Mustard Greens, Italian Style

EQUIPMENT: **French chef's knife, cutting board, measuring cup and spoons, large covered sauté skillet and food cutter (grating blade)**
PREPARATION TIME: **20 minutes   O   Makes 4 or 5 servings**

1 medium onion, diced

4 cloves garlic, minced

½ teaspoon Italian seasoning

1½ pounds fresh mustard greens, washed, stems removed and chopped

3 tablespoons Low-Sodium Chicken Stock (page 217) or canned

2 tablespoons chopped prosciutto (optional)

2 teaspoons freshly grated Parmesan cheese

In a hot, dry skillet over medium heat, dry sauté the onion and garlic until slightly browned, about 5 minutes, stirring occasionally.

Reduce the heat to medium-low and allow the pan to cool slightly. Stir in the Italian seasoning and fill the skillet to the top with the wet mustard greens. Sprinkle with the stock, cover the pan and close the vent. When the cover spins freely on a cushion of water, the vapor seal has formed, 3 to 5 minutes. After forming the seal, cook for 12 to 15 minutes. Don't peek. Removing the cover will destroy the vapor seal, lengthen the cooking time and may cause the greens to burn.

To serve, toss the mustard greens to combine the ingredients. Sprinkle with prosciutto, if using, and the Parmesan cheese.

PER SERVING: 49 Calories   •   0.5g Fat (8% calories from fat)   •   4.8g Protein
8.8g Carbohydrates   •   1mg Cholesterol   •   176mg Sodium (prosciutto adds
10 Calories, 3mg Cholesterol and 150mg Sodium per serving)

Pearl Onions in Pepper Cream

EQUIPMENT: **Paring knife, measuring cup, 1-quart covered saucepan, French chef's knife, and cutting board, mixing bowl and potato masher or electric mixer**

PREPARATION TIME: **40 minutes   o   Makes 5 or 6 servings**

1 pound pearl onions, peeled

½ cup Light Béchamel Sauce (page 188)

1 tablespoon lowfat milk

¼ teaspoon freshly ground black pepper

1 teaspoon chopped fresh parsley or tarragon

Fill the saucepan with the onions, rinse with cold water and pour the water off. The water that clings to the onions is sufficient for cooking the waterless way (see Note, page 3). Cover the pan, close the vent and cook over low heat. When the cover spins freely on a cushion of water, the vapor seal has formed, 3 to 5 minutes. After forming the seal, cook for 15 to 20 minutes. Don't peek. Removing the cover will destroy the vapor seal, lengthen the cooking time and may cause the onions to burn.

Test the onions for doneness with a fork. They should be firm but cooked. If not done, cover the pan, close the vent and add 2 tablespoons water to the rim to reestablish the vapor seal. Cook over low heat for 5 minutes.

Remove from the heat and add the sauce, milk and pepper. Stir gently; cover the pan and let set for 5 minutes, or until the sauce is warmed. To serve, sprinkle with the parsley.

PER SERVING: 35 Calories   •   0.7g Fat (16% calories from fat)   •   1.4g Protein   •   6.1g Carbohydrates   •   1mg Cholesterol   •   192mg Sodium

VARIATION

Creamed Pearl Onions with Peas

Add ¼ cup of thawed frozen green peas with the sauce, milk and pepper.

PER SERVING: 39 Calories   •   0.7g Fat (16% calories from fat)   •   1.8g Protein   •   7g Carbohydrates   •   1mg Cholesterol   •   199mg Sodium

Parsnips and Cream

EQUIPMENT: **Measuring cup, 1-quart covered saucepan, French chef's knife, and cutting board, mixing bowl and potato masher or electric mixer**

PREPARATION TIME: **25 minutes** ○ **Makes 4 or 5 servings**

1 pound parsnips, coarsely chopped
½ cup Light Béchamel Sauce (page 188)
½ teaspoon freshly ground black pepper
½ teaspoon garlic powder
1 teaspoon chopped fresh parsley

Fill the saucepan to the top with the parsnips. Rinse with cold water and pour the water off. The water that clings to the vegetable is sufficient for cooking the waterless way (see Note, page 3). Cover the pan, close the vent and cook over low heat. When the cover spins freely on a cushion of water, the vapor seal has formed, 3 to 5 minutes. After forming the seal, cook for 20 to 25 minutes. Don't peek. Removing the cover will destroy the vapor seal, lengthen the cooking time and may cause the parsnips to burn.

Test the parsnips for doneness with a fork. If not done, cover the pan, close the vent and add 2 tablespoons water to the rim to reestablish the vapor seal. Cook over low heat for 5 minutes.

In a mixing bowl, combine the sauce, pepper and garlic with the parsnips. With an electric mixer, whip on medium speed until thick and creamy, about 3 minutes.

To serve, sprinkle with the parsley.

PER SERVING: **84 Calories** • **0.9g Fat (9% calories from fat)** • **2g Protein**
18g Carbohydrates • **1mg Cholesterol** • **21mg Sodium**

VARIATION

Carrots and Cream

Replace the parsnips with carrots, the garlic powder with cinnamon and the pepper with sugar.

PER SERVING: **55 Calories** • **0.8g Fat (12% calories from fat)** • **1.8g Protein**
11g Carbohydrates   **1mg Cholesterol**   **44mg Sodium**

Stovetop Baked Potatoes

EQUIPMENT: **Vegetable brush, paring knife, 1½-quart covered saucepan or medium covered sauté skillet and a measuring spoon.**

PREPARATION TIME: **40 minutes** O **Makes 4 servings**

4 medium russet potatoes

4 teaspoons sour cream

2 teaspoons chopped fresh chives

Under cold running water, scrub the potatoes with a vegetable brush and remove any surface blemishes with a paring knife. Do not peel.

Place the potatoes in the saucepan, rinse with cold water and pour the water off. The water that clings to the potatoes is sufficient for cooking the waterless way (see Note, page 3). Cover the pan, close the vent and cook over medium-low heat. When the cover spins freely on a cushion of water, the vapor seal has formed. After forming the seal, cook for 25 to 30 minutes. Don't peek. Removing the cover will destroy the vapor seal, lengthen the cooking time and may cause the potatoes to burn.

Test for doneness with a fork. If not done, cover the pan, close the vent and add 2 tablespoons water to the rim to reestablish the vapor seal. Cook over low heat for 5 to 10 minutes.

To serve, top the potatoes with the sour cream and sprinkle with the chives.

PER SERVING: **99 Calories** • **1 g Fat (10% calories from fat)** • **2.5g Protein** • **20g Carbohydrates** • **2mg Cholesterol** • **9mg Sodium**

TIP: **Unsalted butter or margarine adds about 100 calories and 11g fat per tablespoon.**

Stovetop au Gratin Potatoes

EQUIPMENT: Vegetable brush, paring knife, French chef's knife, cutting board, food cutter (grating, julienne and slicing blades), 1½– quart covered saucepan, measuring cup and spoons and mixing bowl

PREPARATION TIME: 35 minutes   ○   Makes 6 to 8 servings

¼ cup dry bread crumbs

½ teaspoon freshly ground black pepper

¼ cup freshly grated Parmesan cheese

¼ cup shredded cheddar cheese

2 medium russet potatoes

2 teaspoons chopped fresh parsley

In a mixing bowl, combine the bread crumbs, pepper and cheeses. Coat the inside of the pan with nonstick vegetable spray and sprinkle with some of the bread crumb mixture. Set the remaining bread crumb mixture aside.

Under cold running water, scrub the potatoes with a vegetable brush and remove any surface blemishes with a paring knife. Do not peel. With a French chef's knife or food cutter, cut into ¼-inch-thick slices. Rinse with cold water.

Cover the bottom of the pan with a layer of potatoes and sprinkle with some of the bread crumb mixture. Repeat the process until the pan is full. Top with the remaining bread crumb mixture. Cover the pan, close the vent and cook over medium-low heat. When the cover spins freely on a cushion of water, the vapor seal has formed, 3 to 5 minutes. After forming the seal, cook for 15 to 20 minutes. Don't peek. Removing the cover will destroy the vapor seal, lengthen the cooking time and may cause the potatoes to burn.

Test for doneness with a fork. If not done, cover the pan close the vent and add 2 tablespoons water to the rim to reestablish the vapor seal. Cook over low heat for 5 to 10 minutes.

To serve, place an inverted dinner plate over the open pan. Invert the pan and the plate together to transfer the potatoes onto the plate. Sprinkle with fresh parsley and cut into 6 or 8 equal servings.

PER SERVING: 69 Calories   2.2g Fat (28% calories from fat)   3g Protein

9.5g Carbohydrates   •   6mg Cholesterol   •   94mg Sodium

VARIATION

Au Gratin Potatoes with Supreme Sauce

Top the cooked potatoes with Supreme Sauce (page 193).

French Tarragon Potatoes

EQUIPMENT: Vegetable brush, paring knife, 2-quart covered saucepan, measuring spoons and small mixing bowl

PREPARATION TIME: 30 minutes ○ Makes 5 or 6 servings

12 small red potatoes, cut in half

1 tablespoon red wine vinegar

1 teaspoon Dijon mustard

2 tablespoons sour cream

1 tablespoons minced fresh tarragon

½ teaspoon freshly ground black pepper

Under cold running water, scrub the potatoes with a vegetable brush and remove any surface blemishes with a paring knife. Do not peel.

Place the potatoes in the pan, rinse with cold water and pour the water off. The water that clings to the potatoes is sufficient for cooking the waterless way (see Note, page 3). Cover the pan, close the vent and cook over medium-low heat. When the cover spins freely on a cushion of water, the vapor seal has formed, 3 to 5 minutes. After forming the seal, cook for 25 to 30 minutes. Don't peek. Removing the cover will destroy the vapor seal, lengthen the cooking time and may cause the potatoes to burn.

Test for doneness with a fork. If not done, cover the pan, close the vent and add 2 tablespoons water to the rim to reestablish the vapor seal. Cook over low heat for 5 to 10 minutes.

While the potatoes are cooking, combine the vinegar, mustard, sour cream and fresh tarragon in a mixing bowl. Mix well and set aside.

To serve, top the potatoes with the sour cream dressing and sprinkle with the pepper.

PER SERVING: 189 Calories • 1.3g Fat (5.9% calories from fat) • 4.9g Protein
40g Carbohydrates • 2mg Cholesterol • 27mg Sodium

Hash Brown Potatoes

EQUIPMENT: Vegetable brush, food cutter (shredding blade), measuring cup and spoons, large covered sauté skillet and flexible (pancake) turner

PREPARATION TIME: 20 minutes ○ Makes 4 or 5 servings

2 medium baking potatoes

2 egg whites or 1 egg

1 teaspoon all-purpose flour

½ medium onion, diced

¼ teaspoon freshly ground black pepper

¼ teaspoon sweet paprika

2 teaspoons chopped fresh parsley

1 teaspoon apple cider vinegar

1 tablespoon sour cream (optional)

Under cold running water, scrub the potatoes with a vegetable brush and remove any surface blemishes with a paring knife. Do not peel. Shred the potatoes.

In a mixing bowl, combine the shredded potatoes, egg white or egg, flour, onion, pepper and paprika. With your hands or a large serving spoon, form the potato mixture into 4 or 5 equal rounds.

Place the rounds in a hot, dry skillet over medium heat and press down with a flexible (pancake) turner.

Cover the pan, open the vent and cook until golden brown, 4 to 5 minutes. With the turner, flip the hash browns, cover the pan and brown the other side, 4 to 5 minutes.

To serve, sprinkle with the vinegar and parsley. Top with a dollop of sour cream, if using.

PER SERVING, WITH EGG WHITES: 59 Calories • 0.1g Fat (1.4% calories from fat) • 2.9g Protein • 12g Carbohydrates • 0mg Cholesterol • 81mg Sodium

PER SERVING, WITH EGG: 68 Calories • 1.1g Fat (14% calories from fat) • 2.7g Protein • 12g Carbohydrates • 43mg Cholesterol • 71mg Sodium

Home Fries

EQUIPMENT: **Vegetable brush, paring knife, French chef's knife, cutting board, medium covered sauté skillet, measuring spoons and flexible spatula**

PREPARATION TIME: **25 minutes**   **o**   **Makes 4 or 5 servings**

3 medium russet potatoes

½ medium onion, diced

2 slices bacon, diced

¼ teaspoon freshly ground black pepper

1 teaspoon chopped fresh parsley

Under cold running water, scrub the potatoes with a vegetable brush and remove any surface blemishes with a paring knife. Do not peel. With a knife, cut the potatoes into ½-inch cubes. Rinse in cold water.

In a hot, dry skillet over medium heat, dry sauté the potatoes, onion and bacon, covered, for 15 to 20 minutes, turning occasionally.

To serve, sprinkle with the pepper and parsley.

PER SERVING: **71 Calories**   •   **1.3g Fat (17% calories from fat)**   •   **2.3g Protein**
13g Carbohydrates   •   **2mg Cholesterol**   •   **99mg Sodium**

Pan-Roasted Potatoes

EQUIPMENT: Vegetable brush, paring knife, French chef's knife, cutting board, medium covered sauté skillet, measuring spoons and flexible spatula

PREPARATION TIME: 25 minutes   ○   Makes 4 or 5 servings

4 medium russet potatoes

½ teaspoon olive oil

¼ teaspoon garlic powder

¼ teaspoon sweet paprika

1 teaspoon chopped fresh parsley

Under cold running water, scrub the potatoes with a vegetable brush and remove any surface blemishes with a paring knife. Do not peel. With a knife, cut the potatoes in quarters lengthwise and rinse in cold water.

Place the potatoes, flesh side down, in a hot, dry skillet over medium heat. Cover the pan and close the vent. The potatoes will stick at first; when finished browning, they will release easily from the pan. Using a flexible spatula, turn the potatoes and brown, covered, on all sides, 6 to 7 minutes per side. Cover after each turning.

To serve, brush the potatoes with olive oil and sprinkle with the garlic powder, paprika and parsley.

PER SERVING: 72 Calories   •   0.1g Fat (1.3% calories from fat)   •   1.9g Protein   • 16g Carbohydrates   •   0mg Cholesterol   •   6mg Sodium

Mom's Famous Potato Salad

EQUIPMENT: **Vegetable brush, paring knife, 2-quart covered saucepan or medium covered sauté skillet, measuring spoon, French chef's knife, cutting board and large mixing bowl**

PREPARATION TIME: **1 hour 30 minutes   O   Makes 12 servings**

4 medium red potatoes

½ medium green bell pepper, diced

1 medium onion, diced

3 medium radishes, diced

1 stalk celery, diced

4 sweet pickles, diced

2 tablespoons pickle juice

¼ cup regular or nonfat mayonnaise

1 tablespoon sugar

1 tablespoon white distilled vinegar

Under cold running water, scrub the potatoes with a vegetable brush and remove any surface blemishes with a paring knife. Do not peel.

Place the potatoes in the pan, rinse with cold water and pour the water off. The water that clings to the potatoes is sufficient for cooking the waterless way (see Note, page 3). Cover the pan, close the vent and cook over medium-low heat. When the cover spins freely on a cushion of water, the vapor seal has formed, 3 to 5 minutes. After forming the seal, cook for 25 to 30 minutes. Don't peek. Removing the cover will destroy the vapor seal, lengthen the cooking time and may cause the potatoes to burn.

Test for doneness with a fork. If not done, cover the pan, close the vent and add 2 tablespoons water to the rim to reestablish the vapor seal. Cook over low heat for 5 to 10 minutes.

While the potatoes are cooling, in a mixing bowl, combine the remaining ingredients. When the potatoes have cooled sufficiently, cut in ½-inch cubes, add to the mixing bowl and stir gently. Cover and refrigerate for about 1 hour or up to 24 hours for a more intense flavor.

PER SERVING: 76 Calories   3.7g Fat (42% calories from fat)
1g Protein   •   10g Carbohydrates   •   3mg Cholesterol   •
125mg Sodium (with nonfat mayonnaise, 46 Calories, 1.2g Fat)

Parmesan Mashed Potatoes with Spinach

EQUIPMENT: Vegetable brush, measuring cup and spoons, 2-quart covered saucepan, French chef's knife, cutting board, mixing bowl and potato masher or electric mixer

PREPARATION TIME: 40 minutes ○ Makes 5 or 6 servings

3 medium red potatoes

2 cups fresh spinach, washed, stems removed and chopped

2 tablespoons Low-Sodium Chicken Stock (page 217) or lowfat milk

2 tablespoons sour cream

1 tablespoon freshly grated Parmesan cheese

2 tablespoons chopped fresh chives

Under cold running water, scrub the potatoes with a vegetable brush and remove any surface blemishes with a paring knife. Do not peel.

Place the potatoes in the bottom of the saucepan and fill the pan to the top with the spinach. Rinse with cold water and pour the water off. The water that clings to the vegetables is sufficient for cooking the waterless way (see Note, page 3). Cover the pan, close the vent and cook over medium-low heat. When the cover spins freely on a cushion of water, the vapor seal has formed, 3 to 5 minutes. After forming the seal, cook for 25 to 30 minutes. Don't peek. Removing the cover will destroy the vapor seal, lengthen the cooking time and may cause the potatoes to burn.

Test the potatoes for doneness with a fork. If not done, cover the pan, close the vent and add 2 tablespoons water to the rim to reestablish the vapor seal. Cook over low heat for 5 to 10 minutes.

In a large mixing bowl, combine the chicken stock or milk, sour cream and hot potatoes. With an electric mixer, whip on medium speed until thick and creamy, about 3 minutes. Stir in the hot spinach and serve.

To serve, top with the Parmesan cheese and sprinkle with the chives.

PER SERVING: 63 Calories • 1.4g Fat (19% calories from fat) • 2.5g Protein 11g Carbohydrates • 3mg Cholesterol • 47mg Sodium (39mg Sodium with lowfat milk)

Potato Pancakes

EQUIPMENT: Vegetable brush, paring knife, food cutter (shredding blade), mixing bowl, measuring spoons, French chef's knife, cutting board, large covered sauté skillet or electric skillet and a flexible (pancake) turner

PREPARATION TIME: 15 minutes   O   Makes 4 or 5 servings

2 medium red potatoes

1 medium shallot, minced

½ teaspoon fresh lime juice

1 egg or 2 egg whites

½ teaspoon freshly ground pepper

2 tablespoons all-purpose flour

2 tablespoons grated matzo crackers

4 teaspoons sour cream

1 teaspoon chopped fresh parsley

Under cold running water, scrub the potatoes with a vegetable brush and remove any surface blemishes with a paring knife. Do not peel. Grate the potatoes with the food cutter and shredding blade.

In a mixing bowl, combine the potatoes, shallots, lime juice, egg or egg whites, pepper, flour and crackers. With your hands or a large serving spoon, form the potato mixture into 4 or 5 equal rounds.

Place the rounds in a hot, dry skillet over medium heat and press down with a flexible (pancake) turner.

Cover the pan, open the vent and cook for 4 to 5 minutes or until golden brown. With the turner, flip the potato pancake, cover the pan and brown the other side, 4 to 5 minutes.

To serve, top with the sour cream and parsley.

PER SERVING, WITH WHOLE EGG: 96 Calories   •   2g Fat (19% calories from fat)   •   3.3g Protein   •   16g Carbohydrates   •   44mg Cholesterol   •   18mg Sodium

PER SERVING, WITH EGG WHITES: 88 Calories   •   1g Fat (10% calories from fat)   •   3.5g Protein   •   16g Carbohydrates   2mg Cholesterol   27mg Sodium

Punjabi Potatoes with Cauliflower

EQUIPMENT: Vegetable brush, paring knife, French chef's knife, cutting board, measuring spoons and medium covered sauté skillet

PREPARATION TIME: 35 minutes ○ Makes 4 or 5 servings

4 small red potatoes

1 medium onion, diced

1 teaspoon grated fresh ginger

½ cup diced, seeded plum tomatoes or canned whole tomatoes

3 tablespoons curry powder

½ head cauliflower, broken into florets

1 teaspoon chopped fresh parsley

Under cold running water, scrub the potatoes with a vegetable brush and remove any surface blemishes with a paring knife. Do not peel. With a knife, quarter the potatoes and set aside.

In a hot, dry pan over medium heat, dry sauté the onion until slightly browned, about 5 minutes, stirring occasionally. Stir in the ginger, tomatoes and curry powder and sauté 2 to 3 minutes. Remove from the heat.

Fill the pan with the potatoes and cauliflower. Reduce the heat to low, cover the pan and close the vent. When the cover spins freely on a cushion of water, the vapor seal has formed, 3 to 5 minutes. After forming the seal, cook for 20 to 25 minutes. Don't peek. Removing the cover will destroy the vapor seal, lengthen the cooking time and may cause the vegetables to burn.

Test the potatoes for doneness with a fork. If not done, cover the pan, close the vent and add 2 tablespoons water to the rim to reestablish the vapor seal. Cook over low heat 5 to 10 minutes.

To serve, sprinkle with the parsley.

PER SERVING: 102 Calories • 0.8g Fat (7% calories from fat) • 3.2g Protein
22g Carbohydrates • 0mg Cholesterol • 125mg Sodium

Stovetop Scalloped Potatoes

EQUIPMENT: Vegetable brush, paring knife, French chef's knife or food cutter (slicing blade), 1¼–quart covered saucepan and measuring cups and spoons

PREPARATION TIME: 35 minutes ○ Makes 6 to 8 servings

3 medium red potatoes

1 large Spanish onion, diced

2 slices lean bacon, diced

1 cup Light Béchamel Sauce (page 188)

1 bunch green onions, chopped

½ cup shredded low-sodium Swiss cheese

1 teaspoon chopped fresh parsley

Under cold running water, scrub the potatoes with a vegetable brush and remove any surface blemishes with a paring knife. Do not peel. With a knife or food cutter, slice and set aside.

In a hot, dry pan over medium heat, dry sauté the onion and bacon until slightly brown. Remove from heat and allow the pan to cool.

Add a layer of potatoes, 2 to 3 tablespoons of the sauce and some of the green onions and Swiss cheese. Repeat the layering process until the pan is filled to the top.

Cover the pan, close the vent and cook over medium-low heat. When the cover spins freely on a cushion of water, the vapor seal has formed, 3 to 5 minutes. After forming the seal, cook for 20 to 25 minutes. Don't peek. Removing the cover will destroy the vapor seal, lengthen the cooking time and may cause the potatoes to burn.

Test the potatoes for doneness with a fork. If not done, cover the pan, close the vent and add 2 tablespoons water to the rim to reestablish the vapor seal. Cook over low heat for 5 to 10 minutes.

To serve, sprinkle with the parsley.

PER SERVING: 91 Calories • 3.5g Fat (35% calories from fat) • 5g Protein • 10g Carbohydrates • 9mg Cholesterol • 112mg Sodium

Twice-Baked Potatoes

EQUIPMENT: Vegetable brush, paring knife, 1¼–quart covered saucepan, measuring spoons, French chef's knife, cutting board, 8-inch gourmet skillet, mixing bowl, electric mixer, large serving spoon and 6 small ramekins
PREPARATION TIME: 45 minutes ○ Makes 5 or 6 servings

4 medium red potatoes

2 slices bacon

1 medium onion, diced

1 clove garlic, minced

¼ teaspoon sweet paprika

3 tablespoons half-and-half or Light Béchamel Sauce (page 188)

2 teaspoons chopped fresh parsley

Under cold running water, scrub the potatoes with a vegetable brush and remove any surface blemishes with a paring knife. Do not peel.

Place the potatoes in the pan, rinse with cold water and pour the water off. The water that clings to the sweet potatoes is sufficient for cooking the waterless way (see Note, page 3). Cover the pan, close the vent and cook over medium-low heat. When the cover spins freely on a cushion of water, the vapor seal has formed, 3 to 5 minutes. After forming the seal, cook for 25 to 30 minutes. Don't peek. Removing the cover will destroy the vapor seal, lengthen the cooking time and may cause the potatoes to burn.

Test for doneness with a fork. If not done, cover the pan, close the vent and add 2 tablespoons water to the rim to reestablish the vapor seal. Cook over low heat for 5 to 10 minutes.

While the potatoes are cooking, fry the bacon in a hot, dry skillet over medium heat until crisp. Remove the bacon to a paper towel and set aside.

Pour off excess drippings and add the onion and garlic to the skillet. Sauté until slightly browned. Remove from the heat and set aside.

Test the potatoes for doneness with a fork. If not done, cover the pan, close the vent and add 2 tablespoons water to the rim to reestablish the vapor seal. Cook over low heat for 5 to 10 minutes.

In a large mixing bowl, combine the potatoes, onion, garlic, and half-and-half or sauce. With an electric mixer, whip on medium speed until thick and creamy, about 3 minutes.

With a serving spoon, place the whipped potato mixture in the ramekins and place under a preheated oven broiler until lightly browned, about 5 minutes.

To serve, crumble the bacon over each serving and sprinkle with the paprika and parsley.

PER SERVING, WITH HALF-AND-HALF: 87 Calories • 2g Fat (20% calories from fat) • 2.7g Protein • 15g Carbohydrates • 5mg Cholesterol • 133mg Sodium

PER SERVING, WITH LIGHT BÉCHAMEL SAUCE: 82 Calories • 1.3g Fat (15% calories from fat) • 2.7g Protein • 15g Carbohydrates • 2mg Cholesterol • 134mg Sodium

Warm and Creamy Parmesan Potatoes

EQUIPMENT: Vegetable brush, paring knife, 1¼-quart covered saucepan or medium covered sauté skillet, French chef's knife, cutting board, measuring spoon and mixing bowl

PREPARATION TIME: 35 minutes ○ Makes 7 or 8 servings

4 medium red potatoes, quartered

1 medium shallot, minced

1 teaspoon white distilled vinegar

½ teaspoon fresh lemon juice

1 teaspoon Italian seasoning

½ teaspoon Dijon mustard

3 tablespoons freshly grated Parmesan cheese

½ cup sour cream

¼ teaspoon freshly ground black pepper

2 teaspoons chopped fresh basil

Under cold running water, scrub the potatoes with a vegetable brush and remove any surface blemishes with a paring knife. Do not peel.

Place the potatoes in the pan, rinse with cold water and pour the water off. The water that clings to the potatoes is sufficient for cooking the waterless way (see Note, page 3). Cover the pan, close the vent and cook over medium-low heat. When the cover spins freely on a cushion of water, the vapor seal has formed, 3 to 5 minutes. After forming the seal, cook for 25 to 30 minutes. Don't peek. Removing the cover will destroy the vapor seal, lengthen the cooking time and may cause the potatoes to burn.

Test for doneness with a fork. If not done, cover the pan, close the vent and add 2 tablespoons water to the rim to reestablish the vapor seal. Cook over low heat for 5 to 10 minutes.

While the potatoes are cooking, combine the shallot, vinegar, lemon juice, Italian seasoning, mustard, Parmesan cheese and sour cream in a mixing bowl. Mix well and set aside.

Remove the potatoes from the heat. Add the dressing to the pan and stir gently. Cover the pan and let set for 5 minutes, or until the dressing is warmed.

To serve, sprinkle with pepper and basil.

PER SERVING: **87 Calories** • **3.7g Fat (37% calories from fat)** • **2.5g Protein** • **10g Carbohydrates** • **8mg Cholesterol** • **50mg Sodium**

VARIATION

Cover and refrigerate until chilled. Serve cold.

Sour Cream and Garlic Mashed Potatoes

EQUIPMENT: Vegetable brush, paring knife, 1¼–quart covered saucepan, measuring cups and spoons, mixing bowl and potato masher or electric mixer

PREPARATION TIME: 35 minutes   ○   Makes 5 or 6 servings

3 medium russet potatoes

½ teaspoon Italian seasoning

3 cloves garlic

2 tablespoons lowfat milk

2 tablespoons sour cream

½ teaspoon sweet paprika

1 tablespoon chopped fresh parsley

Under cold running water, scrub the potatoes with a vegetable brush and remove any surface blemishes with a paring knife. Do not peel. With the point of a paring knife, make an × in each potato and then turn the knife in a circular motion to bore a small hole. Place a small amount of the Italian seasoning in the hole and plug the hole with a clove of garlic.

Place the potatoes in the saucepan, with the garlic facing up, and add 3 tablespoons water. Cover the pan, close the vent and cook over medium-low heat. When the cover spins freely on a cushion of water, the vapor seal has formed, 3 to 5 minutes. After forming the seal, cook for 15 to 20 minutes. Don't peek. Removing the cover will destroy the vapor seal, lengthen the cooking time and may cause the potatoes to burn.

Test the potatoes for doneness with a fork. If not done, cover the pan, close the vent and add 2 tablespoons water to the rim to reestablish the vapor seal. Cook over low heat for 5 to 10 minutes.

In a large mixing bowl, combine the milk, sour cream, and hot potatoes with garlic. With an electric mixer, whip the potatoes on medium speed until thick and creamy, about 3 minutes.

To serve, sprinkle with the paprika and parsley.

PER SERVING: 75 Calories • 1.2g Fat (14% calories from fat) • 2g Protein • 15g Carbohydrates   2mg Cholesterol • 10mg Sodium

Ratatouille with Sausage and Beans

EQUIPMENT: 1-quart saucepan, paring knife, large mixing bowl, large slotted serving spoon, French chef's knife, cutting board, slotted serving spoon, vegetable brush and 3-quart covered saucepan

PREPARATION TIME: 30 minutes ○ Makes 7 or 8 servings

3 medium tomatoes

1 medium onion, diced

2 cloves garlic, minced

1 andouille or Italian sausage link, cut into ¼-inch-thick slices

½ medium green bell pepper, diced

½ medium red bell pepper, diced

½ small eggplant, diced

1 medium zucchini, diced

1 tablespoon chopped fresh basil

½ teaspoon dried thyme

1 teaspoon Italian seasoning

1 cup cooked white (cannellini) beans with liquid (page 30) or
    canned beans

To peel the tomatoes, bring a pan of water to a boil. With a paring knife, make an ✕ on the blossom end of each tomato. Place the tomatoes in the boiling water until the skin starts to curl at the ✕, 30 to 45 seconds. Remove the tomatoes to a mixing bowl filled with ice and water. Chill the tomatoes for 3 to 5 minutes.

With a paring knife, or your forefinger and thumb, peel off the tomato skin beginning at the ✕. With a knife, cut the tomatoes in half and scoop out the seeds with a teaspoon and discard. Dice the tomatoes and set aside.

In a hot, dry, 3-quart saucepan over medium heat, dry sauté the onion and garlic until slightly browned, stirring occasionally. Add the sausage and cook, stirring, until the sausage is cooked through, about 10 minutes. Add the remaining ingredients, mix well and reduce the heat to low. Cover the pan, close the vent and cook for about 15 minutes.

PER SERVING: 92 Calories • 3g Fat (27% calories from fat) • 5g Protein 12g Carbohydrates • 9mg Cholesterol • 206mg Sodium (canned beans add 147mg Sodium per serving)

Spinach, Italian Style

EQUIPMENT: French chef's knife, cutting board, measuring spoons, large covered sauté skillet, and food cutter (grating blade)

PREPARATION TIME: 20 minutes   ○   Makes 4 or 5 servings

1 medium onion, diced

3 cloves garlic, minced

½ teaspoon Italian seasoning

¼ teaspoon hot sauce

1½ pounds fresh spinach, washed, stems removed

2 tablespoons water or Low-Sodium Chicken Stock (page 217)

2 teaspoons freshly grated Parmesan cheese

2 tablespoons diced pimientos

In a hot, dry pan over medium heat, dry sauté the onion and garlic until slightly browned, about 5 minutes, stirring occasionally.

Reduce the heat to medium-low and allow the pan to cool slightly. Stir in the Italian seasoning and hot sauce. Fill the pan with spinach and sprinkle with the water, cover the pan and close the vent. When the cover spins freely on a cushion of water, the vapor seal has formed, 3 to 5 minutes. After forming the seal, cook for 10 to 15 minutes. Don't peek. Removing the cover will destroy the vapor seal, lengthen the cooking time and may cause the spinach to burn.

To serve, toss the spinach to combine all the ingredients. Sprinkle with the Parmesan cheese and top with the pimientos.

PER SERVING: 43 Calories   •   0.7g Fat (13% calories from fat)   •
5g Protein   •   7g Carbohydrates   •   1mg Cholesterol   •
231mg Sodium (chicken stock adds 13mg Sodium per serving)

Spinach with Cognac Cream

EQUIPMENT: **French chef's knife, cutting board, large covered sauté skillet, measuring cup and spoons**

PREPARATION TIME: **20 minutes** o **Makes 4 or 5 servings**

1½ pounds fresh spinach, washed and stems removed

½ cup Light Béchamel Sauce (page 188)

1 tablespoon cognac

¼ teaspoon freshly ground black pepper

Fill the pan to the top with the spinach, rinse with cold water and pour the water off. The water that clings to the vegetable is sufficient for cooking the waterless way (see Note, page 3). Cover the pan, close the vent and cook over low heat. When the cover spins freely on a cushion of water, the vapor seal has formed, 3 to 5 minutes. After forming the seal, cook for 10 to 15 minutes. Don't peek. Removing the cover will destroy the vapor seal, lengthen the cooking time and may cause the spinach to burn.

Remove from the heat and drain the excess liquid from the skillet. Combine the cognac with the béchamel sauce, mix well and add it to the spinach. Stir gently; cover the pan and let set for 5 minutes or until the sauce is warmed.

To serve, toss the spinach to combine the ingredients. Sprinkle with the pepper.

PER SERVING: **51 Calories** • **1.1g Fat (18% calories from fat)** • **4.7g Protein**
6.4g Carbohydrates • **1mg Cholesterol** • **119mg Sodium**

Yellow Squash Parmesan

EQUIPMENT: French chef's knife, cutting board, measuring cups and spoons, food cutter (grating and julienne blade), mixing bowl and medium covered sauté skillet

PREPARATION TIME: 30 minutes ○ Makes 4 or 5 servings

¼ cup Spaghetti Sauce (Salsa de Pomodoro) (page 204)

¼ cup Light Béchamel Sauce (page 188)

2 tablespoons lowfat milk

½ cup shredded part-skim mozzarella cheese

3 tablespoons freshly grated Parmesan cheese

4 or 5 yellow squash, cut crosswise into ¼-inch-thick slices

2 tablespoons chopped fresh basil

In a mixing bowl, combine the spaghetti sauce, béchamel sauce, milk and cheeses.

Rinse the yellow squash and place a layer of squash in the bottom of the pan. Cover the sliced squash with a thin layer of the sauce mixture and add another layer of yellow squash and a thin layer of sauce. Repeat the process until the pan is full to the top.

Cover the pan, close the vent and cook over medium-low heat. When the cover spins freely on a cushion of water, the vapor seal has formed, 3 to 5 minutes. After the seal is formed, cook for 20 to 25 minutes. Don't peek. Removing the cover will destroy the vapor seal, lengthen the cooking time and may cause the squash to burn.

To serve, sprinkle with the basil.

PER SERVING: 80 Calories • 3.5g Fat (37% calories from fat) • 6.3g Protein • 6.8g Carbohydrates • 9mg Cholesterol • 130mg Sodium

Butternut Cinnamon Squash

EQUIPMENT: Butcher knife, French chef's knife, cutting board, food cutter
(shredding blade), measuring spoons and 2-quart covered saucepan

PREPARATION TIME: 30 minutes ❂ Makes 5 or 6 servings

1 (about 2-pound) butternut squash

1 teaspoon ground cinnamon

1 tablespoon light brown sugar

½ teaspoon grated nutmeg

With a butcher knife, cut the squash in half lengthwise. Cut the halves into quarters and remove the seeds. Using a food cutter, placing the skin away from the blade, grate the squash.

Fill the pan with squash. The pan must be at least three-quarters full for the vapor seal to form (do not add water). Butternut squash has sufficient natural moisture for cooking the waterless way. Cover the pan, close the vent and cook over medium-low heat. When the cover spins freely over a cushion of water, the vapor seal has formed, 3 to 5 minutes. After forming the seal, cook for 15 to 20 minutes. Don't peek. Removing the cover will destroy the vapor seal, lengthen the cooking time and may cause the butternut squash to burn.

Test for doneness. If not done, cover the pan, close the vent and add 2 tablespoons water to the rim to reestablish the vapor seal. Cook over low heat for 5 to 10 minutes.

In a mixing bowl, combine the cooked squash with the cinnamon and brown sugar. With a potato masher or electric mixer, mash or whip the ingredients to a smooth consistency.

To serve, sprinkle with the nutmeg.

PER SERVING: 75 Calories • 0.2g Fat (2.4% calories from fat) • 1.5g Protein •
19g Carbohydrates • 0mg Cholesterol • 7mg Sodium

Squash with Strawberry Preserves

Combine 2 tablespoons strawberry preserves with ¼ teaspoon fresh lemon juice, and top each serving of squash with 1 teaspoon of the preserves.

PER SERVING: **16 Calories** • **0g Fat (0.7% calories from fat)** • **0g Protein** • **4.3g Carbohydrates** • **0mg Cholesterol** • **3mg Sodium**

Yellow Squash, Southern Style

EQUIPMENT: French chef's knife, cutting board, measuring cups and spoons, 1-quart covered saucepan, potato masher, 8- or 10-inch gourmet skillet and pot holder

PREPARATION TIME: 30 minutes   O   Makes 6 to 8 servings

6 medium summer squash, diced

½ medium onion, diced

1 tablespoon sugar

¼ teaspoon white pepper

¾ cup dry bread crumbs

1 teaspoon chopped fresh parsley

½ medium lemon, quartered

Fill the pan with the squash, rinse with cold water and pour the water off. The water that clings to the squash is sufficient for cooking the waterless way (see Note, page 3). Cover the pan, close the vent and cook over medium-low heat. When the cover spins freely on a cushion of water, the vapor seal has formed, 3 to 5 minutes. After forming the seal, cook for 10 to 15 minutes. Don't peek. Removing the cover will destroy the vapor seal, lengthen the cooking time and may cause the squash to burn.

Drain off the excess moisture. With a potato masher, coarsely mash the squash. Cover and set aside.

In a hot, dry gourmet skillet with metal handles, dry sauté the onion over medium heat until slightly browned, about 5 minutes, stirring occasionally. Remove from the heat. Add the squash to the onion, along with the sugar and pepper, and mix well.

Top the squash mixture with the bread crumbs and place under a preheated broiler for 3 to 5 minutes until the bread crumbs begin to brown. With a pot holder, remove the skillet to a trivet and serve.

To serve, sprinkle with the parsley and serve with the lemon wedges.

PER SERVING: 69 Calories   •   0.9g Fat (11% calories from fat)   •   2.4g Protein
14g Carbohydrates   0mg Cholesterol   107mg Sodium

Italian Vegetables

EQUIPMENT: **French chef's knife or food cutter (slicing blade), cutting board and 1-quart covered saucepan**

PREPARATION TIME: **20 minutes**   ○   **Makes 4 or 5 servings**

2 medium zucchini, cut into ¼-inch-thick slices

2 medium yellow squash, cut into ¼-inch-thick slices

1 medium onion, cut into ¼-inch-thick slices

3 medium plum tomatoes, cut into ¼-inch-thick slices

1 tablespoon Italian seasoning

1 teaspoon garlic powder

1 tablespoon freshly grated Parmesan cheese

1 tablespoon chopped fresh basil

Layer the vegetables in the saucepan and sprinkle Italian seasoning and garlic powder with each layer. Cover the pan, close the vent and cook over medium-low heat. When the cover spins freely on a cushion of water, the vapor seal has formed, 3 to 5 minutes. After forming the seal, cook 12 to 15 minutes. Don't peek. Removing the cover will destroy the vapor seal, lengthen the cooking time and may cause the vegetables to burn.

To serve, top with the Parmesan cheese and basil.

PER SERVING: **47 Calories**   •   **7g Fat (43% calories from fat)**   •   **11g Protein**   •   **9g Carbohydrates**   •   **20mg Cholesterol**   •   **266mg Sodium**

Eggnog Sweet Potatoes

EQUIPMENT: Vegetable brush, measuring cup and spoons, medium covered sauté pan, 10-inch stainless steel wok or 10-inch gourmet skillet and potato masher or electric mixer

PREPARATION TIME: 40 minutes ○ Makes 7 or 8 servings

4 medium sweet potatoes

½ cup whole milk

1 tablespoon sugar

2 egg whites or 1 egg

½ teaspoon vanilla extract

1 teaspoon grated nutmeg

Under cold running water, scrub the sweet potatoes with a vegetable brush and remove any surface blemishes with a paring knife. Do not peel.

Place the sweet potatoes in the pan, rinse with cold water and pour the water off. The water that clings to the sweet potatoes is sufficient for cooking the waterless way (see Note, page 3). Cover the pan, close the vent and cook over medium-low heat. When the cover spins freely on a cushion of water, the vapor seal has formed, 3 to 5 minutes. After forming the seal, cook for 25 to 30 minutes. Don't peek. Removing the cover will destroy the vapor seal, lengthen the cooking time and may cause the sweet potatoes to burn.

Test for doneness with a fork. If not done, cover the pan, close the vent and add 2 tablespoons water to the rim to reestablish the vapor seal. Cook over low heat for 5 to 10 minutes.

While the sweet potatoes are cooking, combine the milk, sugar, egg whites or egg and vanilla in the wok. Whisk vigorously until the mixture becomes light and creamy. Place the wok over a preheated medium-low electric burner or gas flame. Cook, whisking vigorously, until the eggnog triples in volume, 7 to 8 minutes.

To serve, quarter or cut the sweet potatoes into ½-inch-thick slices. Spoon the eggnog over the sweet potatoes and sprinkle with the nutmeg.

PER SERVING, WITH EGG WHITES: 90 Calories   0.8g Fat (8% calories from fat)   •
2.5g Protein   •   18g Carbohydrates   •   2mg Cholesterol   •   30mg Sodium

PER SERVING, WITH WHOLE EGG: 95 Calories   •   1.4g Fat (14% calories from fat)   •
2.5g Protein   •   18g Carbohydrates   •   29mg Cholesterol   •   24mg Sodium

Amaretto Sweet Potatoes

EQUIPMENT: **Vegetable brush, paring knife, 1½–quart covered saucepan, measuring cup and spoons, large mixing bowl, potato masher or electric mixer and 7-inch gourmet skillet**

PREPARATION TIME: **40 minutes**   ○   **Makes 5 or 6 servings**

3 medium sweet potatoes

2 tablespoons light brown sugar

½ cup lowfat milk

1 dash ground ginger

¼ teaspoon ground cloves

¼ teaspoon ground nutmeg

½ teaspoon ground cinnamon

AMARETTO CREAM SAUCE I

3 tablespoons amaretto

3 tablespoons Light Béchamel Sauce (page 188)

AMARETTO CREAM SAUCE II

3 tablespoons amaretto

1 tablespoon sour cream

2 tablespoons powdered sugar

Under cold running water, scrub the sweet potatoes with a vegetable brush and remove any surface blemishes with a paring knife. Do not peel.

Place the sweet potatoes in the pan, rinse with cold water and pour the water off. The water that clings to the potatoes is sufficient for cooking the waterless way (see Note, page 3). Cover the pan, close the vent and cook over medium-low heat. When the cover spins freely on a cushion of water, the vapor seal has formed, 3 to 5 minutes. After forming the seal, cook for 25 to 30 minutes. Don't peek. Removing the cover will destroy the vapor seal, lengthen the cooking time and may cause the potatoes to burn.

Test for doneness with a fork. If not done, cover the pan, close the vent and add 2 tablespoons water to the rim to reestablish the vapor seal. Cook over low heat for 5 to 10 minutes.

In a mixing bowl, combine the sweet potatoes with the brown sugar, milk, ginger, cloves and nutmeg. With a potato masher or electric mixer, mash or whip the ingredients to a smooth consistency.

Make Amaretto Cream Sauce I or II. To make Amaretto Cream Sauce I: In a small gourmet skillet combine the ingredients, mix well and simmer for about 3 minutes, stirring constantly as the sauce thickens. To make Amaretto Cream Sauce II: Combine all ingredients in a small bowl.

To serve, top the sweet potatoes with sauce and sprinkle with the cinnamon.

SWEET POTATOES, PER SERVING: 90 Calories • 0.5g Fat (4.7% calories from fat) • 1.8g Protein • 20g Carbohydrates • 1mg Cholesterol • 20mg Sodium

AMARETTO CREAM SAUCE I, PER SERVING: 25 Calories • 0.2g Fat (13% calories from fat) • 0.3g Protein • 2.7g Carbohydrates • 0mg Cholesterol • 4mg Sodium

AMARETTO CREAM SAUCE II, PER SERVING: 35 Calories • 0.5g Fat (19% calories from fat) • 0.1g Protein • 4.8g Carbohydrates • 1mg Cholesterol • 1mg Sodium

Candied Sweet Potatoes

EQUIPMENT: Vegetable brush, measuring cup and spoons, 1½–quart covered saucepan and potato masher or electric mixer

PREPARATION TIME: 35 minutes ○ Makes 5 or 6 servings

3 medium sweet potatoes

¼ cup fresh orange juice

1 teaspoon light brown sugar

¼ teaspoon ground cinnamon

3 tablespoons marshmallow cream

¼ teaspoon grated nutmeg

Under cold running water, scrub the sweet potatoes with a vegetable brush and remove any surface blemishes with a paring knife. Do not peel.

Place the sweet potatoes in the pan, rinse with cold water and pour the water off. The water that clings to the sweet potatoes is sufficient for cooking the waterless way (see Note, page 3). Cover the pan, close the vent and cook over medium-low heat. When the cover spins freely on a cushion of water, the vapor seal has formed, 3 to 5 minutes. After forming the seal, cook for 25 to 30 minutes. Don't peek. Removing the cover will destroy the vapor seal, lengthen the cooking time and may cause the sweet potatoes to burn.

Test for doneness with a fork. If not done, cover the pan, close the vent and add 2 tablespoons water to the rim to reestablish the vapor seal. Cook over low heat for 5 to 10 minutes.

In a mixing bowl, combine the sweet potatoes with the orange juice, brown sugar and cinnamon. With a potato masher or electric mixer, mash or whip the ingredients to a smooth consistency.

To serve, top the sweet potatoes with the marshmallow cream and sprinkle with the nutmeg.

PER SERVING: 103 Calories • 0.2g Fat (1.8% calories from fat) • 1.2g Protein
25g Carbohydrates • 0mg Cholesterol • 8mg Sodium

Pecan Sweet Potatoes

EQUIPMENT: Vegetable brush, paring knife, 1¼-quart covered saucepan or medium covered sauté skillet, measuring cups and spoons, mixing bowl and potato masher or electric mixer

PREPARATION TIME: 35 minutes ○ Makes 5 or 6 servings

3 medium sweet potatoes
½ cup fresh orange juice
1 tablespoon light brown sugar
¼ teaspoon ground cinnamon
¼ teaspoon grated nutmeg
¼ cup chopped pecans, roasted

Under cold running water, scrub the sweet potatoes with a vegetable brush and remove any surface blemishes with a paring knife. Do not peel. Cut into thick rounds.

Place the sweet potatoes in the pan, rinse with cold water and pour the water off. The water that clings to the sweet potatoes is sufficient for cooking the waterless way (see Note, page 3). Cover the pan, close the vent and cook over medium-low heat. When the cover spins freely on a cushion of water, the vapor seal has formed, 3 to 5 minutes. After forming the seal, cook for 25 to 30 minutes. Don't peek. Removing the cover will destroy the vapor seal, lengthen the cooking time and may cause the sweet potatoes to burn.

Test for doneness with a fork. If not done, cover the pan, close the vent and add 2 tablespoons water to the rim to reestablish the vapor seal. Cook over low heat for 5 to 10 minutes.

In a large mixing bowl, combine the orange juice, brown sugar, cinnamon and nutmeg. With an electric mixer, whip on medium speed until thick and creamy, about 3 minutes.

To serve, sprinkle with the pecans.

PER SERVING: 119 Calories • 3.3g Fat (24% calories from fat) • 1.7g Protein • 22g Carbohydrates • 0mg Cholesterol • 9mg Sodium.

Healthy SAUCES

A WORLD FAMOUS chef once said, "Each meal is an event that happens only once." Proper sauces are instruments to orchestrate the true melody of the meal. As melodramatic as this may sound, it is a fundamental truth that has survived changing tastes and food fads for centuries.

Sauces are unequivocally the heart and soul of memorable meals. Fortunately, there is nothing mysterious about making sauces. Let's start with the reasons we need them in the first place. Simply put, sauces provide any cook with the "magic" to create dishes with captivating flavors and eye dazzling textures. What more could any aspiring great home cook wish for?

As magical as sauces may appear, they do have limits. Rich sauces should be used sparingly, never exceeding more than one sauce in a meal. Also, sauces are not foolproof remedies to erase cooking mistakes. The best of sauces fall short when used to disguise a poorly flavored or improperly prepared dish. Sauces can stretch food budgets, adding appetite appeal to leftovers and savoir fare to economical dishes such as chicken. So add a new dimension to your meals with the magical world of sauces.

The key to preparing great sauces goes far beyond fantastic ingredients. Equipment designed specifically for the home cook and the application of classical methods are of equal importance.

In the next few pages you will learn how to prepare sauces in both the classic method, derived from low-sodium stocks, and the lighter versions. With appropriate and healthier alternatives, it's all covered in this chapter of *Healthy Meat and Potatoes*.

Classic White and Brown Sauces

Most of the sauces we use today are divided, like stocks, into two main categories: white and brown. Differences in flavors result when various ingredients are added to either a basic white or brown sauce.

WHITE SAUCES

For instance, what is termed by the French as a "roux" is the basis of many sauces. It is prepared by slowly cooking flour and butter in a pan. When milk and spices are added to a white roux, it becomes a béchamel, creating a mother sauce. When cheeses are added, the basic béchamel becomes Mornay Sauce, a splendid accompaniment for lobster, fish, chicken, vegetable dishes and poached eggs. When a roux is cooked with chicken or fish stock, it becomes Velouté Sauce. Add cream and sautéed mushrooms to the same velouté, it becomes a Supreme Sauce. This is a richer sauce frequently used with hot hors d'oeuvres, au gratin potatoes and vegetable dishes. Adding specific ingredients to a béchamel or velouté easily makes dozens of other white sauces as well.

BROWN SAUCES

Adding other ingredients to a basic roux also creates a whole pantheon of brown sauces. The "mother" of all brown sauces is called a *demi-glace*, created essentially by slowly simmering veal stock and the basic brown sauce together to a delicious thickened consistency. Different ingredients added to the demi-glace will change the taste and mission of the resulting sauce. Brown sauces are traditionally use to enhance the flavors of meat, fowl and game dishes.

Other Sauces

In addition to the classic and light versions of the French sauces, there are recipes for many of the other sauces, such as Spaghetti Sauce, Barbecue Sauce and even Cranberry Sauce, that we use to enhance our foods.

Bon Appétit!

Roux

You can tell by just looking at the word *roux* that its origin must be European. This most useful of all thickening agents was first created in France in the seventeenth century, although its name stems from the Latin word *russus,* meaning red. The name of the French chef who perfected this culinary breakthrough has been long lost in the dustbin of history. But much to his credit, for hundreds of years, roux has been a beloved servant of serious cooks the world over. What is the purpose of a roux? Very simply, it is used as a thickening agent, as are other ingredients such as cornstarch, arrowroot and flour.

To correctly pronounce *roux,* remember it rhymes with *too.* In this section, we will take the mystery (and any intimidation) out of preparing a roux in your kitchen. It is not the hush-hush provenance of master chefs, just the opposite. Once you learn how to make a roux, you will wonder how you ever managed to cook without this exciting culinary addition. More accolades to that anonymous Frenchman of the seventeenth century.

TO MAKE A GOOD ROUX

Cooks use two types of roux, a white (sometimes called blond) and medium or dark roux. The color is determined by how long the roux is cooked. Generally, white roux is used to create white sauces and dark roux to make brown sauces. Preparing dark roux takes a bit of skill to give it a brown color without burning. Personally, I have found that a white or blond roux is best suited for most applications, as it will not overpower any accompanying dish.

Using a properly shaped utensil makes a big difference in roux preparation. I recommend a 10-inch, 5- or 7-ply, greaseless, surgical stainless steel wok. With its sloped sides, the wok becomes a convenient mixing bowl. And its small cooking surface at the bottom, combined with overall heavy construction, helps control the wok's cooking temperature. Temperature control is critical in the creation of a delicate roux. For these reasons, a wok is much more dependable and easier to use than the large, commercially designed sauté pans or coated and cast-iron skillets, which affect both the taste and color of the roux; plus the cleanup is certainly much easier.

To prepare a good roux, use a stiff whisk or a large slotted serving spoon to stir together the butter (or margarine) and flour over medium heat. Cook the roux in the wok for about 5 minutes. When ready, it will often emit a pleasant, "baked cookie" aroma. At this point, remove the wok from the heat for about a minute, allowing the roux to briefly cool. After 1 minute, return the wok to the heat.

To Thicken a Sauce with Roux

While you make the roux, bring the liquid to be thickened, such as a stock or milk, to a simmer in another pot. After the roux is cooked and returned to the heat, pour in the hot liquid that has been simmering. Whisk as the ingredients are combined in the wok. Continue whisking until the evolving "sauce" comes to a simmer. Next, reduce the heat and slowly simmer the sauce in the wok for 20 to 30 minutes. Use a ladle to skim any impurities that form on the sauce's surface. Some cooks prefer to thicken the roux by simply adding the cold liquid to the hot roux. The secret is whisking thoroughly to prevent lumps from forming. Practice will tell which techniques work best for you.

There you have it—the simple gem that fine cooks the world over rely on! With a roux in your kitchen, the tastes of your sauces will rise to new heights. Cook away, and please try to be humble when the applause deafens. After all, that anonymous seventeenth-century Frenchman really deserves the credit!

Other Thickening Agents

The primary purpose of a roux is to thicken a dish and to provide some flavor. I recommend using a basic roux made from either butter or margarine as a thickening agent and to enhance the flavor. When dietary restrictions are of concern, use one of the following alternatives.

All-purpose Flour

PER TABLESPOON: 84 Calories • 1.2g Fat (2.5% calories from fat) • 0.9g Protein
6.0g Carbohydrates   0mg Cholesterol   0mg Sodium

ARROWROOT

PER TABLESPOON: 30 Calories • 0g Fat (0.3% calories from fat) • 0g Protein • 7.2g Carbohydrates • 0mg Cholesterol • 0mg Sodium

CORNSTARCH

PER TEASPOON: 30 Calories • 0g Fat (0% calories from fat) • 0g Protein • 7.2g Carbohydrates • 0mg Cholesterol • 0.9mg Sodium

Béchamel Sauce (White Sauce)

Béchamel is a creamy delicious white sauce prepared by incorporating roux with simmering milk or cream and seasoned with nutmeg or paprika, onion or onion powder and white pepper, stirred or whisked until the sauce thickens. It is best prepared in a medium, surgical stainless steel sauté skillet or (my preference) a 10-inch, 5- or 7-ply surgical stainless steel wok. The sauce can be refrigerated up to 3 days to use as needed.

EQUIPMENT: **Measuring cup and spoons, 10-inch stainless steel wok and large slotted serving spoon or whisk**

PREPARATION TIME: **15 minutes**   O **Makes about 1 cup (16 tablespoons)**

CLASSIC BÉCHAMEL SAUCE

1½ cups whole milk

¼ teaspoon onion powder

¼ teaspoon white pepper

¼ teaspoon grated nutmeg or paprika

1 tablespoon Classic Roux (page 190)

LIGHT BÉCHAMEL SAUCE

1½ cups lowfat milk

¼ teaspoon onion powder

¼ teaspoon white pepper

¼ teaspoon grated nutmeg or paprika

1 tablespoon Low-Cholesterol Roux (page 190)

For either sauce: In a medium-hot wok, bring the milk to a simmer. Do not boil. Add the remaining ingredients and simmer, stirring or whisking, until the sauce thickens, 5 to 10 minutes. Taste and adjust the seasoning.

Serve sparingly to enhance the flavors of appetizers, vegetables and entrees.

CLASSIC BÉCHAMEL PER TABLESPOON: **18 Calories** •

1.2g Fat (53% calories from fat)   **0.9g Protein** • **1.5g Carbohydrates**
3mg Cholesterol   **12mg Sodium**

LIGHT BÉCHAMEL PER TABLESPOON: 15 Calories   0.6g Fat (37% calories from fat)

0.9g Protein   •   1.5g Carbohydrates   •   0.9mg Cholesterol   •   12mg Sodium

VARIATION

To further enrich the Béchamel Sauce, add 1 beaten egg yolk to the finished sauce and whisk vigorously.

PER TABLESPOON: 24 Calories   •   1.5g Fat (57% calories from fat)   •   0.9g Protein   •

1.5g Carbohydrates   •   18mg Cholesterol   •   12mg Sodium

Roux

CLASSIC ROUX

1 stick (8 tablespoons) unsalted butter

1 cup all-purpose flour

LOW-CHOLESTEROL ROUX

1 stick (8 tablespoons) unsalted margarine

1 cup all-purpose flour

For either roux: In a wok over medium-low heat, gently melt the butter or margarine until slightly separated; simmer 1 or 2 minutes. Do not allow the butter to burn or turn brown in color. Stir in a little bit of flour at a time and cook, stirring occasionally. The roux is cooked through when it is light blond in color and has a slight aroma of baked cookies, 10 to 15 minutes. Cook, stirring constantly, about 15 to 20 minutes for a dark roux.

Roux can be wrapped in plastic wrap or stored in an airtight container in the refrigerator for up to 2 weeks, ready to use as needed.

CLASSIC ROUX, PER TABLESPOON: 111 Calories • 8.1g Fat (67% calories from fat)
1.2g Protein • 7.8g Carbohydrates • 21mg Cholesterol • 0.9mg Sodium

LOW-CHOLESTEROL ROUX, PER TABLESPOON: 105 Calories •
7.8g Fat (66% calories from fat) • 0.5g Protein • 8.1mg Carbohydrates
0mg Cholesterol • 0mg Sodium

Mornay Sauce

EQUIPMENT: Measuring cup and spoons, 8-inch gourmet skillet and whisk

PREPARATION TIME: 10 minutes ○ Makes about ½ cup

¼ cup Classic or Light Béchamel Sauce (page 188)

2 teaspoons Chardonnay or other dry white wine

2 tablespoons shredded Swiss cheese

1 tablespoon freshly grated Parmesan cheese

Combine all the ingredients in a hot 8-inch gourmet skillet over medium heat. Whisk until the sauce thickens, 5 to 7 minutes.

Serve sparingly to enhance the flavor of lobster, fish and vegetables.

CLASSIC MORNAY SAUCE PER TABLESPOON, WITH CLASSIC BÉCHAMEL SAUCE:
21 Calories • 1.5g Fat (58% calories from fat) • 1.2g Protein •
0.9g Carbohydrates • 6mg Cholesterol • 24mg Sodium (Béchamel Sauce with egg yolk adds 2mg cholesterol per serving)

LIGHT MORNAY SAUCE PER TABLESPOON, WITH LIGHT BÉCHAMEL SAUCE:
12 Calories • 0.6g Fat (40% calories from fat) • 0.9g Protein •
0.6g Carbohydrates • 0mg Cholesterol • 21mg Sodium

TIP: Use a low-sodium cheese to further reduce salt.

Velouté Sauce

In the French cuisine, a velouté is the mother sauce for a variety of exquisite stock-based white sauces. It's prepared by combining roux with chicken, fish, white pork or white veal stock (depending on the dish to be sauced) seasoned with spices and simmered, whisking, until the sauce thickens.

EQUIPMENT: Measuring cup and spoons, 10-inch stainless steel wok and whisk
PREPARATION TIME: 15 minutes ○ Makes about 1 cup (16 tablespoons)

1¼ cups Low-Sodium Chicken Stock (page 217), Low-Sodium Fish Stock (page 218) or
  Low-Sodium White Pork or Veal Stock (page 217) or canned
1 tablespoon Classic or Low-Cholesterol Roux (page 190)
Cayenne pepper to taste

In a medium-hot wok, bring the stock to a simmer. Add the roux and whisk until mixture thickens, 5 to 10 minutes. Season with cayenne.

Serve sparingly to enhance the flavors of vegetables and pan-broiled or roasted chicken.

CLASSIC VELOUTÉ SAUCE PER TABLESPOON, WITH CLASSIC ROUX: **6 Calories** • **0.3g Fat (37% calories from fat)** • **0.9g Protein** • **0.6g Carbohydrates** • **0.9mg Cholesterol** • **42mg Sodium**

LOW-CHOLESTEROL VELOUTÉ SAUCE PER TABLESPOON, WITH LOW-CHOLESTEROL ROUX: **6 Calories** • **0.3g Fat (36% calories from fat)** • **0.9g Protein** • **0.3g Carbohydrates** • **0mg Cholesterol** • **39mg Sodium**

VARIATION

To further enrich the Velouté Sauce, add 1 beaten egg yolk to the finished sauce and whisk vigorously.

Supreme Sauce

EQUIPMENT: Measuring cup and spoons, 10-inch stainless steel wok and whisk

PREPARATION TIME: 15 minutes   O Makes about ¾ cup (12 tablespoons)

¼ cup half-and-half or ¼ cup lowfat milk and ¼ teaspoon arrowroot or cornstarch

¼ cup cooked sliced mushrooms (optional)

1 pinch white pepper

½ cup Classic or Low-Cholesterol Velouté Sauce (page 192)

In a medium-hot 8-inch gourmet skillet, combine all ingredients. Simmer, whisking, until sauce reduces slightly and thickens, 3 to 5 minutes.

Serve sparingly, matching the flavor of the stock with that of the dish.

CLASSIC SUPREME SAUCE PER TABLESPOON, WITH HALF-AND-HALF: 9 Calories
0.9g Fat (60% calories from fat) • 0.6g Protein • 0.6g Carbohydrates •
3mg Cholesterol • 21mg Sodium

LIGHT SUPREME SAUCE PER TABLESPOON, WITH LOWFAT MILK AND LOW-CHOLESTEROL VELOUTÉ SAUCE: 6 Calories • 0.3g Fat (24% calories from fat) •
0.6g Protein • 0.9g Carbohydrates • 0mg Cholesterol • 21mg Sodium

VARIATION

To further enrich the sauce, add 1 beaten egg yolk and whisk vigorously.

PER TABLESPOON, WITH HALF-AND-HALF: 15 Calories •
1.2g Fat (65% calories from fat) • 0.9g Protein • 0.6g Carbohydrates •
21mg Cholesterol • 21mg Sodium

Brown Sauce
(Sauce Espagnole)

EQUIPMENT: **Measuring cup and spoons, large sauté skillet, large serving spoon and fine strainer**

PREPARATION TIME: **30 minutes**   ○   **Makes about 2 cups (32 tablespoons)**

1 small onion, diced

1 small carrot, minced

1 stalk celery, minced

1 tablespoon tomato paste

3 cups Low-Sodium Brown Veal Stock (page 219)

2 sprigs fresh parsley

½ teaspoon dried thyme

2 cracked peppercorns

1 small bay leaf

1 tablespoon Low-Cholesterol Roux (page 190)

In a hot, dry skillet over medium heat, dry sauté the onion, carrot and celery until slightly browned, 3 to 5 minutes, stirring occasionally. Add the tomato paste and cook, stirring until the paste turns reddish-brown in color, 3 to 5 minutes. Do not allow the residue that forms on the inside bottom of the pan to burn.

Slowly stir in the stock. Stir in the parsley, thyme, peppercorns, bay leaf and roux and mix well. Bring to a simmer and cook until reduced by about one-third, 10 to 15 minutes, stirring occasionally. Strain the sauce through a fine sieve.

PER TABLESPOON: **9 Calories** • **0.3g Fat (17% calories from fat)** • **1.2g Protein** • **1.5g Carbohydrates** • **0mg Cholesterol** • **51mg Sodium**

VARIATIONS

Prepare Brown Sauce with Low-Sodium Brown Beef or Pork Stock (page 220), depending on the menu.

Brown Gravy

In a hot 8-inch gourmet skillet over medium heat, combine ¼ teaspoon *each* of freshly ground black pepper and dried thyme with 1 cup Brown Sauce and simmer until gravy thickens, 5 to 10 minutes, stirring occasionally. Taste and adjust the seasonings and serve with meat dish or potatoes. Makes about ¾ cup.

PER TABLESPOON: 6 Calories • 0.09g Fat (20% calories from fat) • 0.3g Protein • 1.2g Carbohydrates • 0mg Cholesterol • 90mg Sodium

Demi-Glace (Rich Brown Sauce)

Different ingredients added to the demi-glace *will change the taste and mission of the resulting sauce. Brown sauces are traditionally used to enrich the flavors of meat, fowl and game dishes.*

EQUIPMENT: **Measuring cup, 10-inch stainless steel wok and large serving spoon**
PREPARATION TIME: **20 minutes**   o   **Makes about 1 cup (32 tablespoons)**

1 cup Low-Sodium Brown Veal Stock (page 219)
1 cup Brown Sauce (page 194)

In a hot wok over medium heat, simmer the stock until reduced by about half. Stir in the sauce and simmer until reduced by half again, 15 to 20 minutes, stirring occasionally.

PER TABLESPOON: 12 Calories   •   0.3g Fat (12% calories from fat)   •   1.8g Protein
0.9g Carbohydrates   •   0mg Cholesterol   •   198mg Sodium

Madeira Sauce

EQUIPMENT: Measuring cup, 8-inch gourmet skillet and whisk
PREPARATION TIME: 10 minutes   O   Makes about ½ cup

1 small shallot, minced

¼ cup Madeira or Marsala wine

½ cup Demi-Glace (page 196)

In a hot, dry skillet over medium heat, dry sauté the shallot until slightly browned, about 2 minutes.

Stir in the Madeira or Marsala and simmer until reduced by half. Stir in the Demi-Glace and simmer to desired consistency, about 5 minutes, stirring occasionally.

Serve hot over steak, veal or lamb chops.

PER TABLESPOON: 18 Calories • 0.9g Fat (5% calories from fat) • 0.6g Protein • 0.6g Carbohydrates • 0mg Cholesterol • 51mg Sodium

VARIATIONS

Marchand de Vin Sauce (Red Wine Sauce)

Substitute ¼ cup dry red wine for the Madeira and simmer until reduced by about half. Add 1 pinch *each* of dried thyme and freshly ground black pepper. Stir in the ½ cup Demi-Glace and simmer to desired consistency. Serve hot over steak, veal or lamb chops.

PER TABLESPOON: 9 Calories • 0.4g Fat (4.2% calories from fat) • 0.3g Protein • 0.6g Carbohydrates • 0mg Cholesterol • 72mg Sodium

Sweet and Sour Wine Sauce

Add 1 tablespoon blackberry or strawberry preserves and ½ teaspoon cider vinegar to Marchand de Vin Sauce.

PER TABLESPOON: 15 Calories • 5g Fat (34.5% calories from fat) • 0.3g Protein • 2.1g Carbohydrates   0mg Cholesterol   48mg Sodium

Hollandaise Sauce

EQUIPMENT: **Measuring cup and spoons, 1-quart saucepan, 10-inch wok and whisk**

PREPARATION TIME: **15 minutes** ○ **Makes about 10 tablespoons**

CLASSIC HOLLANDAISE SAUCE

2 tablespoons apple cider vinegar

2 tablespoons fresh lemon juice

2 tablespoons water

7 black peppercorns

1 small bay leaf

1 slice sweet onion

4 egg yolks

4 tablespoons unsalted butter or margarine, melted

LIGHT HOLLANDAISE SAUCE

2 tablespoons apple cider vinegar

2 tablespoons fresh lemon juice

2 tablespoons water

7 black peppercorns

1 small bay leaf

1 slice sweet onion

¼ cup Low-Sodium Chicken Stock (page 217) or canned

1 teaspoon arrowroot or cornstarch

1 egg yolk

For either sauce: In the wok, bring the vinegar, lemon juice, water, peppercorns, bay leaf and onion to a simmer and reduce by half. Remove from the heat and allow the reduction to cool.

Five minutes before you are ready to serve, and when the wok has cooled, remove the peppercorns, bay leaf and onion and discard, leaving the reduction in the wok.

To make Classic Hollandaise Sauce: Using the wok as a mixing bowl, add the egg yolks and whisk until the mixture doubles in volume. Place the wok over medium-low heat and add the melted butter, a little at a time, whisking vigorously, until the sauce doubles in volume and becomes light yet firm, 2 to 3 minutes. If your sauce is too thick, add 1 tablespoon water.

To make Light Hollandaise Sauce: Add the chicken stock, arrowroot or cornstarch and egg yolk and place the pan over medium-low heat and whisk vigorously until the sauce increases in volume and becomes light yet firm, 2 to 3 minutes.

Serve sparingly over poached eggs, broccoli, asparagus, fish, chicken or steak. Sprinkle with paprika.

CLASSIC HOLLANDAISE SAUCE PER TABLESPOON, WITH BUTTER: 87 Calories • 7.2g Fat (70% calories from fat) • 3g Protein • 5.1g Carbohydrates • 99mg Cholesterol • 9mg Sodium

CLASSIC HOLLANDAISE SAUCE PER TABLESPOON, WITH MARGARINE: 84 Calories • 6.9g Fat (69% calories from fat) • 3g Protein • 5.1g Carbohydrates • 84mg Cholesterol • 9mg Sodium

LIGHT HOLLANDAISE SAUCE PER TABLESPOON: 18 Calories • 0.6g Fat (20% calories from fat) • 1.5g Protein • 5.1g Carbohydrates • 21mg Cholesterol • 18mg Sodium

NOTE: The wok can be used as both a mixing bowl and a cooking pan. If you do not have a 5- or 7-ply 10-inch wok, cook in a double boiler over hot, not boiling, water.

Béarnaise Sauce

EQUIPMENT: Measuring cup and spoons, 1-quart saucepan, 10-inch wok and whisk

PREPARATION TIME: 15 minutes ○ Makes about 10 tablespoons

CLASSIC BÉARNAISE SAUCE

2 tablespoons red wine vinegar

2 tablespoons Chardonnay or other dry white wine

2 tablespoons water

1 medium shallot, finely minced

7 black peppercorns

4 sprigs fresh tarragon

4 tablespoons unsalted butter or margarine, melted

4 egg yolks

2 tablespoons chopped fresh tarragon leaves

LIGHT BÉARNAISE SAUCE

2 tablespoons red wine vinegar

2 tablespoons Chardonnay or other dry white wine

2 tablespoons water

1 medium shallot, finely minced

7 black peppercorns

4 sprigs fresh tarragon

1 egg yolk

¼ cup Low-Sodium Chicken Stock (page 217) or canned

1 teaspoon arrowroot or cornstarch

2 tablespoons chopped fresh tarragon leaves

For either sauce: In the wok, bring the vinegar, wine, water, shallot, peppercorns and tarragon sprigs to a simmer and cook until reduced by about half. Remove from the heat and allow the mixture to cool.

Five minutes before you are ready to serve, and when the wok has cooled, remove the peppercorns and tarragon sprigs and discard.

To make Classic Béarnaise Sauce: Using the wok as a mixing bowl, add the egg yolks to the reduction and whisk until the mixture doubles in volume, 2 to 3 minutes. Place the wok over a preheated, medium-low electric burner or flame. Adding the butter a little bit at a time, whisk vigorously until the sauce becomes light and creamy yet firm, 2 to 3 minutes. Stir in the chopped tarragon.

To make Light Béarnaise Sauce: Using the wok as a mixing bowl, add the egg yolk, chicken stock and arrowroot or cornstarch and whisk until the mixture increases in volume. Place the wok over medium-low heat and whisk vigorously until the sauce increases in volume and becomes light yet firm, 2 to 3 minutes. Stir in the chopped tarragon.

Adjust the seasoning and serve sparingly with steaks, especially a filet mignon.

CLASSIC BÉARNAISE SAUCE PER TABLESPOON, WITH BUTTER: 90 Calories • 7.2g Fat (73% calories from fat) • 1.8g Protein • 4.2g Carbohydrates • 99mg Cholesterol • 6mg Sodium

CLASSIC BÉARNAISE SAUCE PER TEASPOON, WITH MARGARINE: 84 Calories • 7.2 Fat (73% calories from fat) • 1.8g Protein • 4.2g Carbohydrates • 99mg Cholesterol • 6mg Sodium

LIGHT BÉARNAISE SAUCE PER TABLESPOON: 24 Calories • 0.6g Fat (22% calories from fat) • 1.2g Protein • 4.2g Carbohydrates • 21mg Cholesterol • 18mg Sodium

NOTE: The wok can be used as both a mixing bowl and a cooking pan. If you do not have a 5- or 7-ply 10-inch wok, cook in a double boiler over hot, not boiling, water.

Alfredo Sauce

EQUIPMENT: **Measuring cup and spoons, 10-inch stainless steel wok and slotted serving spoon**

PREPARATION TIME: **25 minutes**   O   **Makes about 1 cup**

CLASSIC ALFREDO SAUCE

½ cup half-and-half

½ cup Classic Béchamel Sauce (page 188)

1 tablespoon Chardonnay or other dry white wine

½ cup freshly grated Parmesan cheese, preferably Parmigiano-Reggiano

½ teaspoon anise seeds (optional)

LIGHT ALFREDO SAUCE

½ cup reduced-fat milk

½ cup Light Béchamel Sauce (page 188)

1 tablespoon Chardonnay or other dry white wine

½ cup freshly grated Parmesan cheese, preferably Parmigiano-Reggiano

½ teaspoon anise seeds (optional)

To make either sauce: In the wok over low heat, warm the half-and-half or milk until steam appears on the surface. Do not simmer or boil. Add the béchamel sauce and wine and stir in the cheese, a little at a time. Cook, stirring, until the sauce thickens, 15 to 20 minutes. Stir in the anise seeds, if using.

Serve over fettuccine or serve with vegetables and meat dishes.

CLASSIC ALFREDO SAUCE PER TABLESPOON: 84 Calories   •
6g Fat (65% calories from fat)   •   4.5g Protein   •   2.7g Carbohydrates   •
18mg Cholesterol   •   159mg Sodium

LIGHT ALFREDO SAUCE PER TABLESPOON: 63 Calories   •
3.3g Fat (49% calories from fat)   •   4.8g Protein   •   3g Carbohydrates   •
9mg Cholesterol   •   159mg Sodium

Mock Alfredo Sauce

EQUIPMENT: **Measuring cup and spoons, 10-inch stainless steel wok and slotted serving spoon**

PREPARATION TIME: **25 minutes** o Makes about 1 cup

½ cup whole milk

½ cup Low-Sodium Chicken Stock (page 217) or canned

2 teaspoons arrowroot or cornstarch

1 tablespoon Chardonnay or other dry white wine

½ cup freshly grated Parmesan cheese, preferably Parmigiano-Reggiano

½ teaspoon anise seeds (optional)

In the wok over low heat, warm the milk until steam appears on the surface. Do not simmer or boil. Combine the stock and arrowroot or cornstarch. Mix well and add the mixture to the milk. Stir in the cheese, a little at a time. Cook, stirring, until the sauce thickens, 15 to 20 minutes. Stir in the anise seeds, if using.

Serve over fettuccine or serve with vegetables and meat dishes.

PER TABLESPOON: **57 Calories** • **3g Fat (48% calories from fat)** • **5.1g Protein** • **2.4g Carbohydrates** • **9mg Cholesterol** • **201mg Sodium**

Spaghetti Sauce
(Salsa de Pomodoro)

Top pasta with this classic Italian gravy and sprinkle with freshly grated Parmesan cheese and fresh chopped basil. It can also be served with vegetables and meat dishes. The sauce can be frozen in airtight containers for up to 3 months.

EQUIPMENT: **French chef's knife, cutting board, blender or food processor, 12-quart covered stockpot and large serving spoon.**

PREPARATION TIME: **3 hours** ◐ **Makes 20 to 24 cups**

2 large onions, diced

6 cloves garlic, minced

3 tablespoons Italian seasoning

8 ounces tomato paste

10 cups seeded and chopped plum tomatoes or 3 (28-ounce) cans canned whole tomatoes

10 cups pureed plum tomatoes or 3 (28-ounce) cans tomato puree

10 cups water

¼ cup sugar

½ cup Chianti or other dry red wine

In a hot, dry stockpot over medium heat, dry sauté the onions and garlic until slightly browned, 3 to 5 minutes, stirring occasionally.

Stir in the Italian seasoning and allow it to release its flavor. Add the tomato paste and cook, stirring, until the paste turns reddish-brown in color, 3 to 5 minutes. Do not allow the residue that forms on the bottom of the pan to burn.

Add the tomatoes, tomato puree, water and sugar. Stir, cover the pan, open the vent and reduce the heat to medium-low. Simmer, about 2 hours, stirring occasionally. Stir in the wine; cover the pan, open the vent and simmer, about 1 hour, stirring occasionally.

PER ½ CUP: 41 Calories   .03g Fat (5% calories from fat)
1.5g Protein   •   9.4g Carbohydrates   •   0mg Cholesterol   •   42mg Sodium

VARIATION

If you prefer the flavor of olive oil in your sauce, stir in 1 or 2 tablespoons after you have finished browning the tomato paste. Olive oil, per tablespoon, has 119 calories and 14g fat.

Bordelaise Sauce

EQUIPMENT: **French chef's knife, cutting board, measuring cup and spoons, 10-inch wok, whisk and fine strainer**

PREPARATION TIME: **20 minutes**　**O**　**Makes about 1 cup (16 tablespoons)**

1 small onion, finely minced

½ medium carrot, diced

½ stalk celery, diced

1 clove garlic, minced

1 teaspoon chopped fresh parsley

½ teaspoon dried thyme

½ teaspoon freshly ground black pepper

1 small bay leaf

½ cup Bordeaux or other dry red wine

1¼ cups Low-Sodium Brown Veal or Beef Stock (page 219) or canned

1 teaspoon fresh lemon juice

1 tablespoon Low-Cholesterol Roux (page 190)

In a hot, dry wok over medium heat, dry sauté the onion, carrot, celery and garlic until slightly browned, 3 to 5 minutes, stirring occasionally. Stir in the parsley, thyme, pepper and bay leaf.

Slowly stir in the wine. Bring to a simmer and cook until reduced by half. Add the stock, lemon juice and roux and whisk vigorously to incorporate the roux into the sauce. Simmer to desired consistency. Season to taste and serve hot with filet mignon.

PER TABLESPOON: 16 Calories　•　0.4g Fat (25% calories from fat)　•　1.1g Protein
1.6g Carbohydrates　•　0mg Cholesterol　•　77mg Sodium

VARIATION

The sauce can be strained through a fine sieve and the vegetables discarded.

Classic Marinara with Port

EQUIPMENT: French chef's knife, cutting board, small mixing bowl, measuring cup and spoons, large sauté skillet and large serving spoon

PREPARATION TIME: 35 minutes ○ Makes 3 to 4 cups

1 large onion, diced

5 cloves garlic, minced

2 tablespoons tomato paste

1 cup port wine

3½ cups seeded and chopped plum tomatoes or 1 (28-ounce) can plum tomatoes

2 tablespoons dried oregano

1 teaspoon fresh lemon juice

In a hot, dry skillet over medium heat, dry sauté the onion and garlic until slightly browned, 3 to 5 minutes, stirring occasionally.

Add the tomato paste and cook, stirring, until the paste turns reddish-brown in color, 3 to 5 minutes. Do not allow the residue that forms on the bottom of the pan to burn.

Slowly stir in the port. Bring to a simmer and cook until reduced by half. Add the tomatoes, oregano and lemon juice. Reduce the heat to low, cover the pan, open the vent and simmer 20 to 25 minutes.

Serve over calamari, zucchini and yellow squash, veal Parmesan and pasta, or with Italian sausage, steak or chicken.

PER ½ CUP: 102 Calories • 0.6g Fat (8% calories from fat) •
1.7g Protein • 14g Carbohydrates • 0mg Cholesterol • 107mg Sodium

Pesto

EQUIPMENT: French chef's knife, cutting board and blender or food processor

PREPARATION TIME: 15 minutes ○ Makes about 8 teaspoons

20 to 25 large, fresh basil leaves

2 cloves garlic, peeled

2 tablespoons freshly grated Parmesan cheese

2 tablespoons Italian extra-virgin olive oil or Low-Sodium Chicken Stock (page 217) or canned

2 tablespoons chopped pine nuts (pignolia)

1 dash freshly ground black pepper

1 dash sweet paprika (optional)

Combine all the ingredients in a blender or food processor and pulse 15 to 20 times, until almost, but not quite, to a paste. Cover and refrigerate.

Serve as an accompaniment with melon, prosciutto, fish, steaks or chops.

PER TEASPOON, WITH OLIVE OIL: 57 Calories • 5.7g Fat (84% calories from fat) 1.5g Protein • 1g Carbohydrates • 1mg Cholesterol • 24mg Sodium

PER TEASPOON, WITH CHICKEN STOCK: 27 Calories • 2.3g Fat (66% calories from fat) • 1.7g Protein • 1g Carbohydrates • 1mg Cholesterol • 32mg Sodium

Cream of Pesto

EQUIPMENT: French chef's knife, cutting board and blender or food processor, 1½–quart saucepan and large serving spoon.

PREPARATION TIME: 30 minutes   O   Makes about 1 cup (16 tablespoons)

1 cup Light Béchamel Sauce (page 188)

Pesto (page 208)

Bring the béchamel sauce to almost a simmer over medium-low heat, about 5 minutes, stirring occasionally. Stir in the pesto. Serve over pasta, vegetables or pan-broiled chicken.

PER TABLESPOON, WITH OLIVE OIL: 47 Calories   •   4.2g Fat (77% calories from fat)   •   1.2g Protein   •   1.7g Carbohydrates   •   6mg Cholesterol   •   23mg Sodium

PER TABLESPOON, WITH CHICKEN STOCK: 33 Calories   •   2.5g Fat (66% calories from fat)   •   1.2g Protein   •   1.7g Carbohydrates   •   6mg Cholesterol   •   27mg Sodium

Barbecue Sauce

EQUIPMENT: **French chef's knife, cutting board, measuring cup and spoons and 2-quart covered saucepan**

PREPARATION TIME: **30 minutes** ○ **Makes about 2 cups**

2 medium sweet onions, diced

2 cloves garlic, minced

2 tablespoons tomato paste

2 cups strong brewed coffee

½ cup apple cider vinegar

2 tablespoons Worcestershire sauce

1½ cups packed light brown sugar

¼ teaspoon crushed red pepper

¼ teaspoon Dijon mustard

¼ teaspoon ground cinnamon (optional)

In a hot, dry saucepan over medium heat, dry sauté the onions and garlic until slightly browned, 3 to 5 minutes, stirring occasionally.

Add the tomato paste to the saucepan and cook, stirring, until the paste turns reddish-brown in color, 3 to 5 minutes. Do not allow the residue that forms on the bottom of the pan to burn.

Slowly stir in the coffee. Add the remaining ingredients and mix well. Reduce the heat to low. Cover the pan, open the vent and simmer, 20 to 25 minutes.

Serve with any recipe that calls for barbecue sauce.

PER TABLESPOON: 31 Calories • 0g Fat (0.8% calories from fat) • 0.2g Protein
8g Carbohydrates • 0mg Cholesterol • 16mg Sodium

VARIATION

For a smoky flavor, add 1 teaspoon liquid smoke, which adds 17mg Sodium.

Salsa

EQUIPMENT: French chef's knife, cutting board, 12-quart covered stockpot, blender or food processor and large serving spoon

PREPARATION TIME: 6 hours   ●   Makes about 3 quarts

STEP 1

1 large sweet onion, diced

2 medium green bell peppers, diced

2 stalks celery, diced

2 cloves garlic, minced

10 medium tomatoes, quartered, seeded and chopped

STEP 2

1 large sweet onion, quartered

2 medium green bell peppers, seeded and quartered

2 stalks celery

2 cloves garlic

10 medium tomatoes, quartered and seeded

Step 1: In a hot stockpot using no oil, dry sauté the onion, bell peppers, celery and garlic until slightly browned, 5 to 7 minutes, stirring occasionally. Add the tomatoes and bring to a simmer.

Step 2: In a blender or food processor, puree all the ingredients in batches. Add the pureed vegetables to the stockpot.

Cover the pan, open the vent and simmer for 5 to 6 hours, stirring occasionally. Do not allow salsa to boil.

To serve, chill before serving. Serve as a condiment or an appetizer with tortillas. It's delicious when simmered with browned chicken or pork and it's great with stuffed peppers. The salsa can be frozen up to 3 months.

PER TABLESPOON: 16 Calories   •   0.02g Fat (10% calories from fat)   •   0.7g Protein
3.7g Carbohydrates   0mg Cholesterol   9mg Sodium

Cranberry Sauce

EQUIPMENT: **Measuring spoons, strainer and 1-quart covered saucepan**

PREPARATION TIME: **25 minutes**   ❍   **Makes 7 or 8 servings**

1 pound fresh cranberries

1 tablespoon sugar

Juice of 1 lemon

In a strainer, rinse the cranberries under cold running water.

Fill the pan with cranberries. The pan must be at least three-quarters full for the vapor seal to form. Add no water, cranberries have sufficient natural moisture for cooking the waterless way (see Note, page 3). Cover the pan, close the vent and cook over medium-low heat. When the cover spins freely on a cushion of water, the vapor seal has formed, 3 to 5 minutes. After forming the seal, cook for 15 to 20 minutes. Don't peek. Removing the cover will destroy the vapor seal, lengthen the cooking time and may cause the cranberries to burn.

When finished cooking the cranberries, remove from the heat. To the pan, add the sugar and lemon juice and mix well.

The sauce can be served warm or chilled.

PER SERVING: 34 Calories   •   0.1g Fat (3% calories from fat)   •   0.2g Protein   •
9g Carbohydrates   •   0mg Cholesterol   •   1mg Sodium

Healthy
STOCKS

I ENCOURAGE THOSE who are just beginning to cook or are aspiring to be a great home cook to begin the learning process with stocks, sauces, soups and stews. They will not only give you a firm foundation in the basic techniques of food preparation and the chemistry of it all, but you will thoroughly enjoy the results.

In this chapter of *Healthy Meat and Potatoes* we will focus on the very foundation of all cuisines: the stocks. All experienced cooks rely on freshly made stocks to add delightful flavors to their appetizers, vegetables, entrees, soups and sauces. Making stocks began almost from the moment mankind discovered fire to cook his foods. Thus began an endless quest to improve the taste of our daily meals. But ancient man soon learned a basic truth that guided cooking throughout the ages. No matter how skillfully cooked, the natural juices of meats, poultry, game and fish are not enough to develop the tempting flavors we expect in our meals. That is where stocks take over. Good cooks learned that adding stocks during the cooking enhances the flavors of many dishes.

It's important to note that the preparation of stocks (like sauces, soups and stews) requires the use of some water. It is one of the few exceptions we will mention in this cookbook on waterless, greaseless cooking. Nevertheless, the even heat conductivity of waterless, greaseless cookware moves the heat across the bottom and up the sides of the pan, providing perfect heat control for the preparation of great stocks.

At first glance, stock preparation may appear to be a deeply held secret of professional chefs. This is far from true. Anyone can unlock the flavor-enhancing magic of stocks with easy-to-use preparation techniques and readily available ingredients. And the good news is that stocks are relatively inexpensive to prepare, produced with less expensive cuts of meat and their trimmings. A tall 6- or 7-quart covered stockpot and a strainer/steamer basket that fits down inside the stockpot are the basic tools needed to make stocks.

Stocks are classified into two main categories, *white* and *brown*. Each has specific roles to play in cooking, and will often be mentioned in the recipes contained in this cookbook.

White Stocks

We will begin our understanding with the preparation of white stocks. These are generally light in color and are used by cooks seeking to add delicate flavors to vegetables, poultry and fish. White stocks are made with a mix of raw poultry, fish, veal or pork, almost any kind of bones, aromatic vegetables and herbs, peppercorns and water. A key to creating the most effective stock is avoiding too much water in the mixture. A rule to follow is that the higher percentage of solid ingredients to water, the more flavorful the final stock.

Proper control of heat during cooking is essential when making stocks. Use the following heat control sequence when preparing a white stock. Put the steamer basket inside of the stockpot and place the meat in the basket. Fill the basket with water to about an inch below the larger perforated holes and bring the mixture to a boil over medium-high heat. Then, quickly reduce the heat setting to medium-low heat. That is the vital first step. The next step is to skim off the froth (fat and scum) that rises to the surface. This waste must be skimmed off to create a clear stock. It is very important not to accidentally allow the stock to return to a boil once the heat has been reduced. Reboiling will produce a cloudy stock with reduced flavor and may even burn the stock, turning it brackish in color. Once skimmed, aromatic vegetables and herbs are added to the brew. Perhaps the most important pivotal step to making effective stocks is simmering long enough to extract the maximum flavors from the ingredients. General cooking times are:

- ○ Fish stock for 30 to 45 minutes.

- ○ Chicken stock for about 3 hours.

- ○ Veal stock for up to 4 hours.

Brown Stocks

Brown stocks are made using essentially the same cooking methods except the bones, meat and aromatic vegetables are browned in a stockpot over medium heat. After browning, the meat, bones and vegetables are transferred to the steamer basket, and the basket is placed inside of the stockpot along with water, aromatic herbs and peppercorns. Again, the percentage of water to solid ingredients should be as low as possible. After the mixture is brought to a boil, the heat is immediately reduced to a simmer. Next, the froth is removed and skimmed off periodically as it rises to the top, and the stock is simmered for about 4 hours. Brown stocks are rich in color and essential in enhancing the flavors of soups, stews, game, red meats and brown sauces.

In the final process, and with both white and brown stocks, the basket is raised and the natural delicious juices are allowed to strain back into the stockpot. The basket contents, or *remouillage*, can be reserved and frozen as a starter for your next batch of stock. This is an excellent way to save money. The stock is then placed in the refrigerator and cooled sufficiently for the fat to coagulate on the surface. Once the fat is removed, you can either use the stock immediately or freeze it in quantities of 1 to 2 cups, ready to use as needed.

Following the above simple practices will provide a welcome supply of magical stocks to create exciting new tastes in your culinary travels. Your family and friends will applaud your efforts as never before. You can freeze any stock up to 3 months to be used when needed. Some cooks place their stock in ice cube trays and make handy, frozen cubes of stock. The results are stored in sealed plastic bags to prevent freezer burn.

Nothing compares to the flavor enhancements of stock prepared in your own home kitchen. Creating exciting sauces from stocks will give you a feeling of achievement, and your family and friends will be grateful with every exciting morsel prepared with homemade stocks.

N O T E: The recipes in this chapter have been created using the natural sodium provided by fresh vegetables and cooking methods that promote vitamin and mineral retention. They should not be confused with commercially manufactured stocks, broths, bouillons, or consommés, which most often contain preservatives, gums and a considerable amount of processed sodium (salt), none of which promote good health. When using commercially prepared products, be sure to read the label for the Nutrition Facts.

Low-Sodium Chicken Stock

EQUIPMENT: Butcher knife, French chef's knife, cutting board, 6½–quart
stockpot, 6-quart steamer basket, large serving spoon and 4-ounce ladle
PREPARATION TIME: 3 hours ○ Makes about 8 cups

3 to 4 pounds whole chicken, cut up, or 3 to 4 pounds necks and back

About 4 quarts water

2 onions, coarsely chopped

2 carrots, coarsely chopped

2 stalks celery with leaves, coarsely chopped

1 bay leaf

2 sprigs thyme or 1 teaspoon dried

4 sprigs parsley with stems

8 peppercorns, cracked

Place the steamer basket in the stockpot. Place the chicken in the basket and fill the pan with water to 1 inch below the large holes in the steamer basket. Bring to a boil over medium-high heat. With a large serving spoon, skim off the froth (fat and scum) that rises to the surface of the water and discard. Add the balance of the ingredients. Reduce the heat to low, cover the pan, open the vent and simmer for about 3 hours. Do not allow the stock to return to a boil.

To strain the stock, lift the steamer basket above the liquid level and press the juices out with a large serving spoon. The basket contents can be discarded or reserved and frozen as a starter for your next batch of stock.

To remove the fat, place the stock in the refrigerator. When it has cooled, the fat and debris will rise to the surface. Skim off and discard.

To store, package in 1-cup quantities and freeze up to 3 months.

VARIATIONS

Low-Sodium White Veal, Beef or Pork Stock

Replace the chicken with 3 to 4 pounds of meaty veal, beef or pork bones, meat and trimmings. Cook as directed.

Low-Sodium Fish Stock

EQUIPMENT: Filet knife, French chef's knife, cutting board, 6½–quart stockpot, 6-quart steamer basket, large serving spoon and 4-ounce ladle

PREPARATION TIME: 30 minutes ○ Makes about 8 cups

4 pounds whole cleaned fish, filets removed and reserved for another use

3 quarts water

2 onions, coarsely chopped

2 parsnips, coarsely chopped

2 stalks celery, coarsely chopped

1 bay leaf

2 sprigs fresh thyme or 1 teaspoon dried

4 sprigs fresh parsley with stems

1 slice orange peel

4 peppercorns, cracked

1 cup Chardonnay or other dry white wine

Place the fish in the steamer basket and add the water. Bring to a boil over medium-high heat. With a large serving spoon, skim off the froth (fat and scum) that rises to the surface and discard. Add the remaining ingredients. Reduce the heat to low, cover the pan, open the vent and simmer for 30 to 45 minutes. Do not allow the stock to return to a boil.

To strain the stock, lift the steamer basket above the liquid level and press the juices out with a large serving spoon. Discard the basket contents.

To remove the fat, place the stock in the refrigerator. When it has cooled, the fat and debris will rise to the surface. Skim off and discard.

To store, package in 1-cup quantities and freeze up to 1 month.

VARIATION

Shellfish Stock

Replace the fish with 3 to 4 pounds of lobster, clams or shrimp meat and trimmings. Cook as above.

Low-Sodium Brown Veal Stock

EQUIPMENT: Butcher knife, French chef's knife, cutting board, 6½–quart stockpot, 6-quart steamer/spaghetti basket, large serving spoon, 4-ounce ladle

PREPARATION TIME: 4 hours ○ Makes about 8 cups

3 to 4 pounds meaty veal bones, meat and trimmings

2 onions, coarsely chopped

2 carrots, coarsely chopped

2 stalks celery, coarsely chopped

2 tablespoons tomato paste

About 4 quarts water

1 bay leaf

2 sprigs fresh thyme or 1 teaspoon dried

4 sprigs fresh parsley with stems

8 peppercorns, cracked

In a hot, dry stockpot over medium heat, brown the bones, meat and trimmings thoroughly, about 10 minutes, turning occasionally. Remove the bones, meat and trimmings to a platter and set aside. Add the onions, carrots and celery. Sauté until slightly browned, about 5 minutes, stirring occasionally. Add the tomato paste and sauté until the paste turns reddish-brown in color, about 5 minutes. Do not allow the residue that forms on the bottom of the pan to burn.

Remove the stockpot from the heat and transfer all the ingredients to the steamer basket and place the basket inside the stockpot. Fill with water to just below the large holes. Over medium-high heat, bring the stock to a boil. With a large serving spoon, skim off the froth (fat and scum) that rises to the surface of the water and discard. Add the remaining ingredients. Reduce the heat to low, cover the pan, open the vent and simmer for about 5 hours. Do not allow the stock to return to a boil.

To strain the stock, lift the steamer basket above the liquid level and press the juices out with a large serving spoon. The basket contents can be discarded or reserved and frozen as a starter for your next batch of stock.

To remove the fat, place the stock in the refrigerator. When it has cooled, the fat and debris will rise to the surface. Skim off and discard.

To store, package in 1-cup quantities and freeze up to 3 months.

VARIATIONS

Low-Sodium Brown Beef or Pork Stock

Replace the veal with 3 to 4 pounds of meaty beef or pork bones, meat and trimmings. Cook as directed.

Low-Sodium Pan-Roasted Vegetable Stock

EQUIPMENT: French chef's knife, cutting board, 6½–quart stockpot, 6-quart steamer basket, large serving spoon and 4-ounce ladle

PREPARATION TIME: 1 hour o Makes about 8 cups

3 onions, chopped

6 carrots, chopped

6 stalks celery, chopped

3 cloves garlic, minced

2 tablespoons tomato paste

1 bay leaf

2 sprigs fresh thyme or 1 teaspoon dried

4 sprigs fresh parsley with stems

8 peppercorns, cracked

3 quarts water

In a hot, dry stockpot over medium heat, dry sauté the onions, carrots, celery and garlic until slightly browned, stirring occasionally. Add the tomato paste and cook, stirring, until the paste has turned reddish-brown in color, about 15 minutes.

Do not allow the residue that forms on the bottom of the pan to burn.

Remove the stockpot from the heat and transfer all the ingredients to the steamer basket and place the steamer basket inside the stockpot. Add the water and bring the stock to a boil. Reduce the heat to low, cover the pan, open the vent and simmer for about 1 hour, stirring occasionally.

To strain the stock, lift the steamer basket above the liquid level and press the juices out with a large serving spoon. Discard the basket contents.

To store, package in 1-cup quantities and freeze for up to 3 months.

Healthy DESSERTS

T HE ABILITY TO bake cakes on top of the stove, on low heat, demonstrates waterless, greaseless cookware's quality and capacity to evenly conduct heat. Although this is a relatively short chapter with only a few recipes, once you have baked on top of the stove, it will be very difficult to find a good reason to ever turn your oven on again.

Enjoy!

Amaretto Fruitcake

This fruitcake is baked on top of the stove. For maximum flavor, use a combination of apricots, apples, pineapple and cherries. You can also use the dried fruit and peel mixes that are available in your local grocery store during the holiday seasons.

EQUIPMENT: **Measuring cup and spoons, French chef's knife, cutting board, mixing bowl, 2-quart covered saucepan and serrated knife**
PREPARATION TIME: **50 minutes** ❍ **Makes 6 to 8 servings**

1 cup mixed dried fruit, finely chopped
¼ cup raisins
⅓ cup amaretto
1⅓ cups yellow cake mix or 1 (9-ounce) package Jiffy yellow cake mix
¼ teaspoon grated nutmeg
2 tablespoons almonds, finely chopped
2 eggs, lightly beaten
1 tablespoon dark corn syrup

In a mixing bowl, combine the dried fruit and raisins with the amaretto. Allow to stand for 20 to 30 minutes for the fruit to rehydrate. Add the remaining ingredients and mix well.

Coat the inside of the pan with nonstick vegetable spray and add the cake mixture. Cover the pan, close the vent and place over low heat. When the cover spins freely on a cushion of water, the vapor seal has formed. Do not peek. Bake for 25 to 30 minutes after the vapor seal has formed. Check for doneness; a toothpick inserted in the center should come out clean. If not done, cover the pan, close the vent and cook for 5 to 10 minutes more.

To release the cake from the pan, place the hot pan on a cold, damp dish towel for 2 to 3 minutes. Uncover the pan and place an inverted serving plate over the top. Invert the pan so that the cake falls onto the serving plate.

Slice the cake into 6 or 8 pieces with a serrated knife. Serve with mint chocolate chip ice cream, if desired. The cake can be served warm or cold.

PER SERVING: 247 Calories • 6g Fat (23% calories from fat) • 4g Protein
42g Carbohydrates   54mg Cholesterol   229mg Sodium

Blueberry and Spice Crumb Cake

EQUIPMENT: Mixing bowls, measuring cup and spoons, 2-quart covered saucepan, gourmet skillet

PREPARATION TIME: 40 minutes ○ Makes 8 to 10 servings

1⅓ cups spice cake mix or 1 (9-ounce) package Jiffy yellow cake mix

2 eggs

1 tablespoon light brown sugar

½ cup fresh blueberries

1 tablespoon unsalted butter, softened

3 tablespoons granulated sugar

3 tablespoons all-purpose flour

½ teaspoon vanilla extract

Combine the cake mix and eggs in a small mixing bowl and mix well.

Coat the inside of the pan with a vegetable spray and sprinkle the brown sugar in the bottom of the pan. Place the blueberries on top of the sugar and pour the cake mixture into the pan, smoothing the top with a spatula. Cover the pan, close the vent and cook on medium-low heat on top of the stove for 25 to 30 minutes. Do not peek.

Combine the butter, granulated sugar, flour and vanilla in a small mixing bowl. Sauté the butter, sugar and flour in a gourmet skillet until the mixture is cooked through and begins to crumble, about 7 minutes. Test for doneness with a fork.

To release the cake from the pan, place the hot pan on a cold, damp dishtowel for 2 to 3 minutes. Uncover the pan and place an inverted serving plate over the top of the pan. Invert the pan so that the cake falls onto the serving plate.

Top with the crumb mixture while the cake is still hot. Serve warm or at room temperature.

PER SERVING: 163 Calories • 5g Fat (27% calories from fat) • 3g Protein • 27g Carbohydrates • 46mg Cholesterol • 180mg Sodium

Carrot Cake with Vanilla Cream Icing

EQUIPMENT: **Food cutter (grating blades), mixing bowl, measuring cup and spoons and 2-quart covered saucepan or electric saucepan**

PREPARATION TIME: **35 minutes**   O   **Makes 10 servings**

3 medium carrots, unpeeled, grated

¾ cup packed light brown sugar

1 (8-oz.) can crushed pineapple with liquid

1 egg, lightly beaten

1⅓ cups spice cake mix or 1 (9-ounce) package Jiffy yellow cake mix

VANILLA CREAM ICING

4 ounces cream cheese, room temperature

1 tablespoon unsalted butter

1 teaspoon vanilla extract

1½ cups powdered sugar

TO SERVE

1 medium carrot, unpeeled, grated

1 tablespoon finely chopped dry-roasted pecans

Combine the carrots, brown sugar, crushed pineapple, egg and cake mix in a medium mixing bowl and mix well.

Coat the inside of the pan with nonstick vegetable spray and add the cake mixture to the pan. Cover the pan, close the vent and cook over medium-low heat on top of the stove for 25 to 30 minutes. Do not peek. Test for doneness with a fork. If the cake is not done, cover the pan and return to medium-low heat for 5 to 10 minutes more.

To release the cake from the pan, place the hot pan on a cold, damp dishtowel for 2 to 3 minutes. Uncover the pan and place an inverted serving plate over the top of the pan. Invert the pan so the cake falls onto the serving dish. Let cool.

Make the Vanilla Cream Icing: In a small mixing bowl, beat the cream cheese and butter with the vanilla and powdered sugar for about 3 minutes or until the mixture is smooth and creamy. Spread the icing over the cooled cake. Refrigerate until ready to serve.

To serve, top the cake with the carrot and pecans and cut into 10 pieces.

PER SERVING: 323 Calories • 7g Fat (calories from fat) • 3g Protein • 66g Carbohydrates • 37mg Cholesterol • 82mg Sodium

Bread Pudding with Brandy Sauce

EQUIPMENT: **Mixing bowl, medium covered sauté skillet, French chef's knife, cutting board and 1-quart covered saucepan**

PREPARATION TIME: 30 minutes ❍ Makes 7 or 8 servings

1 cup whole milk

2 eggs, lightly beaten

¼ cup powdered sugar

1 teaspoon vanilla extract

10 slices raisin bread, chopped

BRANDY SAUCE

4 tablespoons unsalted butter

½ cup powdered sugar

1 teaspoon vanilla extract

1 tablespoon brandy

TO SERVE

2 tablespoons finely chopped pecans

Combine the milk, eggs, ¼ cup of the sugar, vanilla and raisin bread in a medium mixing bowl and mix well. Coat the inside of the saucepan with nonstick vegetable spray and add the bread pudding mixture to the pan. Cover the pan, close the vent and cook on medium-low heat on top of the stove for 15 to 20 minutes. Do not peek.

Meanwhile, make the Brandy Sauce: Melt the butter in the skillet over medium-low heat; do not allow the butter to bubble or boil. Add the powdered sugar, vanilla and brandy to the skillet and mix well.

Uncover the pan and place an inverted serving plate over the top of the pan. Invert the pan so that the bread pudding releases onto the serving plate.

To serve, top the bread pudding with the warm Brandy Sauce and sprinkle with the pecans. Serve warm.

PER SERVING: **188 Calories** • **5g Fat (24% calories from fat)** • **5g Protein**
30g Carbohydrates   **58mg Cholesterol**   **158mg Sodium**

Dixie Instant Rice Pudding

The pudding can be decorated with whipped cream and a maraschino cherry.

EQUIPMENT: **Measuring cups and spoons and 2-quart covered saucepan**

PREPARATION TIME: **40 minutes** O **Makes 7 or 8 servings**

2 cups whole milk

½ cup powdered sugar

1 teaspoon vanilla extract

1 egg, lightly beaten

1½ cups instant rice

⅛ teaspoon ground cinnamon

⅛ teaspoon grated nutmeg

Combine the milk, sugar and vanilla in the saucepan. Simmer over medium heat for about 5 minutes, stirring occasionally.

Stir in the egg and cook, stirring, until the mixture thickens slightly, about 2 minutes. Add the instant rice, cover the pan and close the vent. Turn the heat off and let set for about 20 minutes. Do not peek.

To serve, sprinkle with cinnamon and nutmeg and serve warm or chilled.

PER SERVING: **144 Calories** • **3g Fat (17% calories from fat)** • **4g Protein** • **25g Carbohydrates** • **35mg Cholesterol** • **39mg Sodium**

Granny Smith Apple with Warm Tequila Sauce and Ice Cream

EQUIPMENT: French chef's knife, cutting board, measuring cup and spoons and large covered sauté skillet

PREPARATION TIME: 20 minutes ○ Makes 4 or 5 servings

1 medium Granny Smith apple, unpeeled, cored and cut into ¼-inch-thick slices

1 teaspoon fresh lime juice

¼ cup tequila

2 tablespoons light brown sugar

4 scoops vanilla ice cream

In a hot, dry skillet over medium heat, cook the apples with the cover on and the vent closed until slightly browned, 3 to 4 minutes on each side.

Sprinkle the apple with the lime juice. Add the tequila to the skillet and simmer to allow the alcohol to burn off, about 2 minutes.

To serve, spoon the apples, leaving the sauce in the skillet, into dessert dishes and sprinkle with the brown sugar. Top each serving with a scoop of ice cream. Spoon the sauce over the ice cream.

PER SERVING: 198 Calories • 7g Fat (38% calories from fat) • 2g Protein
24g Carbohydrates • 29mg Cholesterol • 55mg Sodium

Metric Conversion Charts

COMPARISON TO METRIC MEASURE

WHEN YOU KNOW	SYMBOL	MULTIPLY BY	TO FIND	SYMBOL
teaspoons	tsp.	5.0	milliliters	ml
tablespoons	tbsp.	15.0	milliliters	ml
fluid ounces	fl. oz.	30.0	milliliters	ml
cups	c	0.24	liters	l
pints	pt.	0.47	liters	l
quarts	qt.	0.95	liters	l
ounces	oz.	28.0	grams	g
pounds	lb.	0.45	kilograms	kg
Fahrenheit	F	5⁄9 (after subtracting 32)	Celsius	C

FAHRENHEIT TO CELSIUS

F	C
200–205	95
220–225	105
245–250	120
275	135
300–305	150
325–330	165
345–350	175
370–375	190
400–405	205
425–430	220
445–450	230
470–475	245
500	260

LIQUID MEASURE TO MILLILITERS

1⁄4 teaspoon	=	1.25 milliliters
1⁄2 teaspoon	=	2.5 milliliters
3⁄4 teaspoon	=	3.75 milliliters
1 teaspoon	=	5.0 milliliters
1 1⁄4 teaspoons	=	6.25 milliliters
1 1⁄2 teaspoons	=	7.5 milliliters
1 3⁄4 teaspoons	=	8.75 milliliters
2 teaspoons	=	10.0 milliliters
1 tablespoon	=	15.0 milliliters
2 tablespoons	=	30.0 milliliters

LIQUID MEASURE TO LITERS

1⁄4 cup	=	0.06 liters
1⁄2 cup	=	0.12 liters
3⁄4 cup	=	0.18 liters
1 cup	=	0.24 liters
1 1⁄4 cups	=	0.3 liters
1 1⁄2 cups	=	0.36 liters
2 cups	=	0.48 liters
2 1⁄2 cups	=	0.6 liters
3 cups	=	0.72 liters
3 1⁄2 cups	=	0.84 liters
4 cups	=	0.96 liters
4 1⁄2 cups	=	1.08 liters
5 cups	=	1.2 liters
5 1⁄2 cups	=	1.32 liters

Index

Alfredo Sauce, 202
Almonds
  Amaretto Fruitcake, 224
Amaretto Fruitcake, 224
Amaretto Sweet Potatoes, 178–179
Angelic Deviled Eggs, 9–10
Apples
  Applesauce, 133
  Braised Roast Pork Tenderloin with
    Cabbage and Apples, 112–113
  Granny Smith Apple with Warm
    Tequila Sauce and Ice Cream,
    230
  Stovetop Roast Stuffed Turkey,
    80–81
Artichokes
  Baked Artichoke Dip, 11
Asparagus
  Asparagus with Hollandaise Sauce,
    135

Asparagus with Lemon Pepper,
  134
Cream of Asparagus Soup, 42–43
Duck Orecchiette, 90–91
Paella Valencia, 120–121

Bacon
  Braised Roast Pork Tenderloin with
    Cabbage and Apples, 112–113
  Home Fries, 154
  Hot and Healthy Bacon Slaw, 141
  Stovetop Scalloped Potatoes, 161
  Twice-Baked Potatoes, 162–163
Baked Artichoke Dip, 11
Baked Potato Soup, 31
Bamboo shoots
  Sweet and Sour Sauce, 24–25
Barbecue Rosemary Chicken, 66–67
Barbecue Sauce, 210
Barb cued Turkey Meatballs, 12–13

Basil
  Bruschetta, 20
  Pesto, 208
Beans, dried
  Black Bean Chili, 32–33
  Homemade Beans, 30
  Minestrone, 54–55
  Pasta é Fagioli, 58
  Ratatouille with Sausage and
    Beans, 167–168
  Spanish Bean Soup, 59
  Stovetop Baked Barbecue Beans,
    138
  White Chili, 60
Beans, green
  Warm Green Bean Salad,
    136–137
Béarnaise Sauce, 200–201
Béchamel Sauce (White Sauce),
  188–189

Beef
  Beef Stew, 34
  Beef Stroganoff, 94–95
  Bourbon-Stuffed Filet Mignon,
    96–97
  Chateaubriand, 98–99
  Filet Mignon Bordelaise, 100
  Low-Sodium Brown Beef or Pork
    Stock, 220
  Low-Sodium White Veal, Beef or
    Pork Stock, 217
  Steak, how to cook the perfect,
    101
  Stuffed Peppers, 102–103
  Sweet Italian Meatballs, 108
Bell peppers
  Chicken Chow Mein, 70–71
  Court-Bouillon, 122
  Cuban Clam Chowder, 44–45
  Hungarian Goulash, 46–47
  Italian Turkey Soup, 49
  Jambalaya with Scallops, 119
  Mama's Sneaky Meatloaf, 84–85
  Manhattan Clam Chowder, 52–53
  Mom's Famous Potato Salad,
    156–157
  New Orleans–Style Seafood Filé
    Gumbo, 56–57
  Paella Valencia, 120–121
  Pasta é Fagioli, 58
  Ratatouille with Sausage and
    Beans, 167–168
  Salsa, 211
  Seafood Étouffée, 124–125
  Sloppy Gobblers, 82–83
  Stuffed Peppers, 102–103
Benefits of waterless, greaseless
    cooking, 127
Black Bean Chili, 32–33
Blue cheese
  Buffalo Chicken Wings, 16–17
Blueberry and Spice Crumb Cake,
    225
Bordelaise Sauce, 206
Bourbon
  Bourbon-Stuffed Filet Mignon,
    96–97
  Peking Duck in Bourbon Sauce,
    92–93
Braised Breast of Duck with
    Persimmons and Prunes, 89
Braised Roast Pork Tenderloin with
    Cabbage and Apples, 112–113
Brandy
  Brandy Sauce, 228
  Light Lobster Bisque, 50–51
Bread Pudding with Brandy Sauce,
    228

Broccoli
  Broccoli Hors d'Oeuvre, Italian
    Style, 14
  Broccoli Romano, 139
  Swiss Broccoli Soup, 61
Broiling, 5
Brown Gravy, 195
Brown Sauce (Sauce Espagnole), 194
Brown sauces, 184
Brown stocks, 215
Brunswick Stew, 35
Bruschetta, 20
Buffalo Chicken Wings, 16–17
Butternut Cinnamon Squash,
    172–173
Butternut Squash Soup, 36–37

Cabbage
  Braised Roast Pork Tenderloin with
    Cabbage and Apples, 112–113
  Cabbage Casserole, 140
  Hot and Healthy Bacon Slaw, 141
  Minestrone, 54–55
Cacciatore
  Chicken Cacciatore, 68–69
Cakes
  Amaretto Fruitcake, 224
  Blueberry and Spice Crumb Cake,
    225
  Carrot Cake with Vanilla Cream
    Icing, 226–227
Candied Carrots, 142
Candied Sweet Potatoes, 180
Capers
  Caribbean Crab Cake Dipping
    Sauce, 18–19
  Turkey Piccata, 88
Caribbean Crab Cake Dipping Sauce,
    18–19
Caribbean Crab Cakes, 18–19
Carrots
  Beef Stew, 34
  Brown Sauce (Sauce Espagnole), 194
  Brunswick Stew, 35
  Candied Carrots, 142
  Carrot Cake with Vanilla Cream
    Icing, 226–227
  Carrots and Cream, 148
  Chicken Cacciatore, 68–69
  Chicken Noodle Soup, 38–39
  Cream of Asparagus Soup, 42–43
  Hearty Chicken Stew, 48
  Light Lobster Bisque, 50–51
  Mama's Sneaky Meatloaf, 84–85
  Manhattan Clam Chowder, 52–53
  Minestrone, 54–55
  Osso Bucco with Gremolata,
    104–105

Pasta é Fagioli, 58
Spinach Dip, 26
Swiss Broccoli Soup, 61
Cauliflower
  Punjabi Potatoes with Cauliflower,
    160
Celery
  Angelic Deviled Eggs, 9–10
  Baked Potato Soup, 31
  Beef Stew, 34
  Brown Sauce (Sauce Espagnole), 194
  Brunswick Stew, 35
  Buffalo Chicken Wings, 16–17
  Butternut Squash Soup, 36–37
  Caribbean Crab Cakes, 18–19
Carrots
  Italian Turkey Soup, 49
  Chicken Cacciatore, 68–69
  Chicken Chow Mein, 70–71
  Chicken Noodle Soup, 38–39
  Cream of Asparagus Soup, 42–43
  Creamed Chicken and Basmati
    Rice, 74–75
  Garlic Roasted Stuffed Chicken
    with Port Marinara, 78–79
  Hearty Chicken Stew, 48
  Hungarian Goulash, 46–47
  Light Lobster Bisque, 50–51
  Mama's Sneaky Meatloaf, 84–85
  Manhattan Clam Chowder, 52–53
  Minestrone, 54–55
  Mom's Famous Potato Salad,
    156–157
  Osso Bucco with Gremolata,
    104–105
  Pasta é Fagioli, 58
  Salsa, 211
  Sloppy Gobblers, 82–83
  Spanish Bean Soup, 59
  Stuffed Peppers, 102–103
  White Chili, 60
Chateaubriand, 98–99
Cheese (see also Parmesan)
  Chicken Cordon Bleu, 72–73
  Mama's Sneaky Meatloaf, 84–85
  Momma LeAnnie's Stovetop
    Lasagna, 86–87
  Mornay Sauce, 191
  Stovetop au Gratin Potatoes,
    150–151
  Stovetop Scalloped Potatoes, 161
  Swiss Broccoli Soup, 61
  White Chili, 60
  Yellow Squash Parmesan, 171
Chicken
  Barbecue Rosemary Chicken, 66–67
  Brunswick Stew, 35
  Buffalo Chicken Wings, 16–17

Chicken Cacciatore, 68–69
Chicken Chow Mein, 70–71
Chicken Cordon Bleu, 72–73
Chicken Noodle Soup, 38–39
Creamed Chicken and Basmati Rice, 74–75
Creamed Saffron Chicken with Tortellini and Peas, 76–77
Garlic Roasted Stuffed Chicken with Port Marinara, 78–79
Hearty Chicken Stew, 48
Low-Sodium Chicken Stock, 217
Marinated Orange Rosemary Chicken, 65
Paella Valencia, 120–121
White Chili, 60
Chiles
  Baked Artichoke Dip, 11
  Black Bean Chili, 32–33
  Hot and Spicy Cornbread, 21
  Spinach Dip, 26
  White Chili, 60
Chili
  Black Bean Chili, 32–33
  White Chili, 60
Chow mein
  Chicken Chow Mein, 70–71
Chowder
  Cuban Clam Chowder, 44–45
  Manhattan Clam Chowder, 52–53
Clams
  Cuban Clam Chowder, 44–45
  Manhattan Clam Chowder, 52–53
  Paella Valencia, 120–121
Classic Marinara with Port, 207
Classic white and brown sauces, 184
Cleaning, 3
Cocktail Dipping Sauce, 18–19
Coffee
  Barbecued Turkey Meatballs, 12–13
  Barbecue Rosemary Chicken, 66–67
  Barbecue Sauce, 210
  Herb-Crusted Pork Chops, 118
  Orange Barbecue Pork Chops, 110
Cognac
  Spinach with Cognac Cream, 170
Cold Green Bean Salad, 137
Collard Greens Soup, 40–41
Cooking for one or two, 131
Cooking methods, 3–4
Cooking times for apples and vegetables, 131–132
Corn
  Brunswick Stew, 35
  Corn on the Cob, 143
  Hot and Spicy Cornbread, 21
Cornbread
  Hot and Spicy Cornbread, 21

Court-Bouillon, 122
Crabmeat
  Caribbean Crab Cakes, 18–19
  New Orleans–Style Seafood Filé Gumbo, 56–57
Cranberries
  Cranberry Sauce, 212
Cream cheese
  Vanilla Cream Icing, 226–227
Cream of Asparagus Soup, 42–43
Cream of Pesto, 209
Creamed Chicken and Basmati Rice, 74–75
Creamed Saffron Chicken with Tortellini and Peas, 76–77
Cuban Clam Chowder, 44–45
Cucumbers
  Dad's Famous Cucumber and Onion Salad, 144
Curry powder
  Punjabi Potatoes with Cauliflower, 160

Dad's Famous Cucumber and Onion Salad, 144
Demi-Glace (Rich Brown Sauce), 196
Dips
  Baked Artichoke Dip, 11
  Spinach Dip, 26
Dixie Instant Rice Pudding, 229
Duck
  Braised Breast of Duck with Persimmons and Prunes, 89
  Duck Orecchiette, 90–91
  Peking Duck in Bourbon Sauce, 92–93

Eggnog Sweet Potatoes, 176–177
Eggplant
  Lamb Chops Braised with Tomatoes, Eggplant and Green Olives, 114–115
  Ratatouille with Sausage and Beans, 167–168
Eggs
  Angelic Deviled Eggs, 9–10
Étouffée
  Seafood Étouffée, 124–125

Filet Mignon Bordelaise, 100
Fish
  Fish Poached in Court-Bouillon, 122
  Fresh Salmon with Light Hollandaise Sauce and Dill, 123
  Grilled Marinated Tuna Steaks, 116–117
  Low-Sodium Fish Stock, 218

Paella Valencia, 120–121
Seafood Étouffée, 124–125
Flavor, maximize, 4–5
French bread
  Bruschetta, 20
French Tarragon Potatoes, 152
Fresh Salmon with Light Hollandaise Sauce and Dill, 123
Fruitcake
  Amaretto Fruitcake, 224

Garlic
  Classic Marinara with Port, 207
  Garlic Roasted Stuffed Chicken with Port Marinara, 78–79
  Gremolata, 104–105
  Momma LeAnnie's Stovetop Lasagna, 86–87
  Orange Barbecue Pork Chops, 110
  Salsa, 211
  Sour Cream and Garlic Mashed Potatoes, 166
  Spinach, Italian Style, 169
Gin
  Braised Roast Pork Tenderloin with Cabbage and Apples, 112–113
Goulash
  Hungarian Goulash, 46–47
Granny Smith Apple with Warm Tequila Sauce and Ice Cream, 230
Gremolata, 104–105
Grilled Marinated Tuna Steaks, 116–117

Ham
  Chicken Cordon Bleu, 72–73
  Collard Greens Soup, 40–41
  Spanish Bean Soup, 59
  Stovetop Baked Barbecue Beans, 138
Hash Brown Potatoes, 153
Healthy Desserts, 223–230
Healthy Hors d'Oeuvres and Appetizers, 7–26
Healthy Meat and Other Entrees, 63–125
Healthy Potatoes and Vegetables, 127–181
Healthy Sauces, 183–212
Healthy Soups and Stews, 27–61
Healthy Stocks, 213–221
Hearty Chicken Stew, 48
Herb-Crusted Pork Chops, 118
Hollandaise Sauce, 198–199
Home Fries, 154
Homemade Beans, 30
Horseradish
  Baked Artichoke Dip, 11
  Cocktail Dipping Sauce, 18–19

Hot and Healthy Bacon Slaw, 141
Hot and Spicy Cornbread, 21
Hungarian Goulash, 46–47

Ice cream
    Granny Smith Apple with Warm
        Tequila Sauce and Ice Cream, 230
    Vanilla Cream Icing, 226–227
Introduction, xv–xvi
Italian Turkey Soup, 49
Italian Vegetables, 175

Jambalaya with Scallops, 119

Lamb
    Lamb Chops Braised with
        Tomatoes, Eggplant and Green
        Olives, 114–115
Lasagna
    Meatless Lasagna, 87
    Momma LeAnnie's Stovetop
        Lasagna, 86–87
    White Lasagna with Chicken and
        Spinach, 87
Lemon juice
    Cranberry Sauce, 212
Lemons
    Paella Valencia, 120–121
    Yellow Squash, Southern Style, 174
Lemon zest
    Gremolata, 104–105
Light Lobster Bisque, 50–51
Lima beans
    Brunswick Stew, 35
Lobster
    Light Lobster Bisque, 50–51
Low-Sodium Brown Beef or Pork
    Stock, 220
Low-Sodium Brown Veal Stock,
    219–220
Low-Sodium Chicken Stock, 217
Low-Sodium Fish Stock, 218
Low-Sodium Pan-Roasted Vegetable
    Stock, 221
Low-Sodium White Veal, Beef or Pork
    Stock, 217

Madeira Sauce, 197
Mama's Sneaky Meatloaf, 84–85
Manhattan Clam Chowder, 52–53
Maraschino cherries
    Sweet and Sour Sauce, 24–25
Marchand de Vin Sauce (Red Wine
    Sauce), 197
Marinated Orange Rosemary
    Chicken, 65
Marshmallow creme
    Candied Sweet Potatoes, 180

Meatballs
    Barbecued Turkey Meatballs, 12–13
    Sweet and Sour Meatballs, 24–25
    Sweet Italian Meatballs, 108
Meatloaf
    Mama's Sneaky Meatloaf, 84–85
Meats, Comparison of conventional
    and waterless, greaseless
    cooking of, 5–6
Minestrone, 54–55
Mock Alfredo Sauce, 203
Mom's Famous Potato Salad, 156–157
Momma LeAnnie's Stovetop Lasagna,
    86–87
Monterey Jack Cheese
    Spinach Dip, 26
Mornay Sauce, 191
Mushrooms
    Beef Stroganoff, 94–95
    Bourbon-Stuffed Filet Mignon,
        96–97
    Chateaubriand, 98–99
    Chicken Cacciatore, 68–69
    Creamed Chicken and Basmati
        Rice, 74–75
    Peking Duck in Bourbon Sauce,
        92–93
    Tarragon Mushrooms with Lemon
        Sauce, 145
Mustard Greens, Italian Style, 146

New Orleans–Style Seafood Filé
    Gumbo, 56–57
Noodles
    Beef Stroganoff, 94–95
    Chicken Chow Mein, 70–71
    Chicken Noodle Soup, 38–39
    Momma LeAnnie's Stovetop
        Lasagna, 86–87

Oats
    Barbecued Turkey Meatballs, 12–13
Okra
    New Orleans–Style Seafood Filé
        Gumbo, 56–57
Olive oil or butter, 5
Olives
    Angelic Deviled Eggs, 9–10
    Broccoli Hors d'Oeuvre, Italian
        Style, 14
    Lamb Chops Braised with
        Tomatoes, Eggplant and Green
        Olives, 114–115
Onions
    Baked Potato Soup, 31
    Barbecue Rosemary Chicken,
        66–67
    Barbecue Sauce, 210

Beef Stroganoff, 94–95
Black Bean Chili, 32–33
Bourbon-Stuffed Filet Mignon,
    96–97
Brown Sauce (Sauce Espagnole),
    194
Butternut Squash Soup, 36–37
Chateaubriand, 98–99
Chicken Cacciatore, 68–69
Chicken Chow Mein, 70–71
Chicken Noodle Soup, 38–39
Classic Marinara with Port, 207
Collard Greens Soup, 40–41
Court-Bouillon, 122
Cream of Asparagus Soup, 42–43
Creamed Chicken and Basmati
    Rice, 74–75
Creamed Pearl Onions with Peas,
    147
Cuban Clam Chowder, 44–45
Dad's Famous Cucumber and
    Onion Salad, 144
Grilled Marinated Tuna Steaks,
    116–117
Hearty Chicken Stew, 48
Home Fries, 154
Hungarian Goulash, 46–47
Italian Turkey Soup, 49
Italian Vegetables, 175
Jambalaya with Scallops, 119
Light Lobster Bisque, 50–51
Mama's Sneaky Meatloaf, 84–85
Manhattan Clam Chowder, 52–53
Minestrone, 54–55
Mom's Famous Potato Salad,
    156–157
Momma LeAnnie's Stovetop
    Lasagna, 86–87
Mustard Greens, Italian Style, 146
New Orleans–Style Seafood Filé
    Gumbo, 56–57
Osso Bucco with Gremolata,
    104–105
Paella Valencia, 120–121
Pasta é Fagioli, 58
Pearl Onions in Pepper Cream, 147
Peking Duck in Bourbon Sauce,
    92–93
Punjabi Potatoes with Cauliflower,
    160
Ratatouille with Sausage and
    Beans, 167–168
Roast Stuffed Veal, 106–107
Salsa, 211
Seafood Étouffée, 124–125
Sloppy Gobblers, 82–83
Spaghetti Sauce (Salsa de
    Pomodoro), 204–205

Spanish Bean Soup, 59
Spinach, Italian Style, 169
Stovetop Scalloped Potatoes, 161
Stuffed Peppers, 102–103
Sweet Italian Meatballs, 108
Swiss Broccoli Soup, 61
Twice-Baked Potatoes, 162–163
White Chili, 60
Yellow Squash, Southern Style, 174
Orange Barbecue Pork Chops, 110
Orange juice
    Braised Breast of Duck with
        Persimmons and Prunes, 89
    Candied Sweet Potatoes, 180
    Marinated Orange Rosemary
        Chicken, 65
    Pecan Sweet Potatoes, 181
    Roast Pork Chardonnay, 111
Orange marmalade
    Orange Barbecue Pork Chops, 110
Osso Bucco with Gremolata, 104–105

Paella Valencia, 120–121
Pan broiling and sautéing, 63–64
Pancakes
    Potato Pancakes, 159
Pan-Roasted Potatoes, 155
Parmesan cheese
    Baked Artichoke Dip, 11
    Béarnaise Sauce, 200–201
    Bruschetta, 20
    Chicken Cacciatore, 68–69
    Creamed Saffron Chicken with
        Tortellini and Peas, 76–77
    Minestrone, 54–55
    Mock Alfredo Sauce, 203
    Parmesan Mashed Potatoes and
        Spinach, 158
    Pasta é Fagioli, 58
    Pesto, 208
    Stuffed Zucchini Johnsonville, 22–23
    Sweet Italian Meatballs, 108
    Warm and Creamy Parmesan
        Potatoes, 164–165
Parsnips
    Baked Potato Soup, 31
    Braised Roast Pork Tenderloin with
        Cabbage and Apples, 112–113
    Creamed Chicken and Basmati Rice,
        74–75
    Parsnips and Cream, 148
    Roast Stuffed Veal, 106–107
    White Chili, 60
Pasta
    Chicken Cacciatore, 68–69
    Duck Orecchiette, 90–91
    Minestrone, 54–55
    Pasta é Fagioli, 58

Pearl Onions in Pepper Cream, 147
Peas
    Chicken Noodle Soup, 38–39
    Creamed Pearl Onions with Peas,
        147
    Creamed Saffron Chicken with
        Tortellini and Peas, 76–77
    Italian Turkey Soup, 49
    Paella Valencia, 120–121
    Saffron Sauce, 76–77
Pecans
    Bread Pudding with Brandy Sauce,
        228
    Pecan Sweet Potatoes, 181
Peking Duck in Bourbon Sauce, 92–93
Persimmons
    Braised Breast of Duck with
        Persimmons and Prunes, 89
Pesto
    Cream of Pesto, 209
    Pesto, 208
Piccata
    Turkey Piccata, 88
Pickles
    Mom's Famous Potato Salad,
        156–157
Pine nuts
    Pesto, 208
Pineapple
    Carrot Cake with Vanilla Cream
        Icing, 226–227
    Sweet and Sour Sauce, 24–25
Pork
    Black Bean Chili, 32–33
    Braised Roast Pork Tenderloin with
        Cabbage and Apples, 112–113
    Herb-Crusted Pork Chops, 118
    Low-Sodium Brown Beef or Pork
        Stock, 220
    Low-Sodium White Veal, Beef or
        Pork Stock, 217
    Orange Barbecue Pork Chops, 110
    Roast Pork Chardonnay, 111
Potatoes
    Baked Potato Soup, 31
    Beef Stew, 34
    Brunswick Stew, 35
    Collard Greens Soup, 40–41
    Cuban Clam Chowder, 44–45
    French Tarragon Potatoes, 152
    Hash Brown Potatoes, 153
    Hearty Chicken Stew, 48
    Home Fries, 154
    Mama's Sneaky Meatloaf, 84–85
    Manhattan Clam Chowder, 52–53
    Minestrone, 54–55
    Mom's Famous Potato Salad,
        156–157

Pan-Roasted Potatoes, 155
Parmesan Mashed Potatoes and
    Spinach, 158
Potato Pancakes, 159
Punjabi Potatoes with Cauliflower,
    160
Roast Stuffed Veal, 106–107
Sour Cream and Garlic Mashed
    Potatoes, 166
Spanish Bean Soup, 59
Stovetop au Gratin Potatoes,
    150–151
Stovetop Baked Potatoes, 149
Stovetop Scalloped Potatoes,
    161
Twice-Baked Potatoes, 162–163
Warm and Creamy Parmesan
    Potatoes, 164–165
Prunes
    Braised Breast of Duck with
        Persimmons and Prunes, 89
Puddings
    Bread Pudding with Brandy Sauce,
        228
    Dixie Instant Rice Pudding, 229
Punjabi Potatoes with Cauliflower,
    160

Radishes
    Mom's Famous Potato Salad,
        156–157
Raisins
    Amaretto Fruitcake, 224
    Ratatouille with Sausage and Beans,
        167–168
Rice
    Cabbage Casserole, 140
    Chicken Chow Mein, 70–71
    Creamed Chicken and Basmati Rice,
        74–75
    Dixie Instant Rice Pudding, 229
    Jambalaya with Scallops, 119
    New Orleans–Style Seafood Filé
        Gumbo, 56–57
    Paella Valencia, 120–121
    Stuffed Peppers, 102–103
Ricotta cheese
    Momma LeAnnie's Stovetop
        Lasagna, 86–87
    Roast Stuffed Veal, 106–107
Roast Pork Chardonnay, 111
Roast Stuffed Veal, 106–107
Roasting, 6, 64
Rosemary
    Barbecue Rosemary Chicken,
        66–67
    Marinated Orange Rosemary
        Chicken, 65

Roux (about), 185–186
Roux, 190

Saffron
  Paella Valencia, 120–121
  Saffron Sauce, 76–77
Salads
  Cold Green Bean Salad, 136–137
  Dad's Famous Cucumber and
    Onion Salad, 144
  Mom's Famous Potato Salad,
    156–157
  Warm Green Bean Salad,
    136–137
Salsa, 211
Sauces
  Alfredo Sauce, 202
  Barbecue Sauce, 210
  Béarnaise Sauce, 200–201
  Béchamel Sauce (White Sauce),
    188–189
  Bordelaise Sauce, 206
  Brandy Sauce, 228
  Brown Sauce (Sauce Espagnole),
    194
  Caribbean Crab Cake Dipping
    Sauce, 18–19
  Classic Marinara with Port, 207
  Cocktail Dipping Sauce, 18–19
  Cranberry Sauce, 212
  Demi-Glace (Rich Brown Sauce),
    196
  Hollandaise Sauce, 198–199
  Madeira Sauce, 197
  Marchand de Vin Sauce (Red Wine
    Sauce), 197
  Mock Alfredo Sauce, 203
  Mornay Sauce, 191
  Saffron Sauce, 76–77
  Spaghetti Sauce (Salsa de
    Pomodoro), 204–205
  Supreme Sauce, 193
  Sweet and Sour Sauce, 24–25
  Sweet and Sour Wine Sauce, 197
  Velouté Sauce, 192
Sausage
  Black Bean Chili, 32–33
  Collard Greens Soup, 40–41
  Cuban Clam Chowder, 44–45
  Hungarian Goulash, 46–47
  Manhattan Clam Chowder, 52–53
  New Orleans–Style Seafood Filé
    Gumbo, 56–57
  Paella Valencia, 120–121
  Ratatouille with Sausage and
    Beans, 167–168
  Sloppy Gobblers, 82–83
  Spanish Bean Soup, 59

Stuffed Zucchini Johnsonville,
  22–23
Sweet and Sour Meatballs, 24–25
Sautéing
  Dry sautéing, 3
  Wet sauteing, 3
  Sautéing (meat), 5–6
  Sautéing without fat, 3–4
Scallops
  Seafood Étouffée, 124–125
  Jambalaya with Scallops, 119
  New Orleans–Style Seafood Filé
    Gumbo, 56–57
  Paella Valencia, 120–121
Seafood Étouffée, 124–125
Shallots
  Bruschetta, 20
  Caribbean Crab Cakes, 18–19
  Garlic Roasted Stuffed Chicken
    with Port Marinara, 78–79
  Potato Pancakes, 159
  Veal Chops in Red Wine Sauce, 109
  Warm and Creamy Parmesan
    Potatoes, 164–165
Shellfish Stock, 218
Shrimp
  Jambalaya with Scallops, 119
  Paella Valencia, 120–121
Slaw
  Hot and Healthy Bacon Slaw, 141
Sloppy Gobblers, 82–83
Sodium and salt, 28
Sour cream
  Beef Stroganoff, 94–95
  Buffalo Chicken Wings, 16–17
  Caribbean Crab Cake Dipping
    Sauce, 18–19
  Sour Cream and Garlic Mashed
    Potatoes, 166
  Warm and Creamy Parmesan
    Potatoes, 164–165
Spaghetti Sauce (Salsa de
  Pomodoro), 204
Spanish Bean Soup, 59
Spinach
  Parmesan Mashed Potatoes and
    Spinach, 158
  Roast Stuffed Veal, 106–107
  Spinach Dip, 26
  Spinach with Cognac Cream, 170
  Spinach, Italian Style, 169
Squash (see also zucchini)
  Butternut Cinnamon Squash,
    172–173
  Butternut Squash Soup, 36–37
  Italian Vegetables, 175
  Yellow Squash Parmesan, 171
  Yellow Squash, Southern Style, 174

Steak, how to cook the perfect, 101
Stews
  Beef Stew, 34
  Brunswick Stew, 35
  Hearty Chicken Stew, 48
Stocks
  Low-Sodium Brown Beef or Pork
    Stock, 220
  Low-Sodium Brown Veal Stock,
    219–220
  Low-Sodium Chicken Stock, 217
  Low-Sodium Fish Stock, 218
  Low-Sodium Pan–Roasted
    Vegetable Stock, 221
  Low-Sodium White Veal, Beef or
    Pork Stock, 217
  Shellfish Stock, 218
Stovetop au Gratin Potatoes, 150–151
Stovetop Baked Barbecue Beans, 138
Stovetop Baked Potatoes, 149
Stovetop Roast Stuffed Turkey, 80–81
Stovetop Scalloped Potatoes, 161
Stroganoff
  Beef Stroganoff, 94–95
Stuffed Peppers, 102–103
Stuffed Zucchini Johnsonville, 22–23
Supreme Sauce, 193
Sweet and Sour Meatballs, 24–25
Sweet and Sour Wine Sauce, 197
Sweet Italian Meatballs, 108
Sweet potatoes
  Amaretto Sweet Potatoes, 178–179
  Candied Sweet Potatoes, 180
  Eggnog Sweet Potatoes, 176–177
  Pecan Sweet Potatoes, 181
Swiss Broccoli Soup, 61

Tarragon
  French Tarragon Potatoes, 152
  Tarragon Mushrooms with Lemon
    Sauce, 145
Temperature setting, find the right,
  129–130
Tequila
  Granny Smith Apple with Warm
    Tequila Sauce and Ice Cream,
    230
Thickening agents, 186–187
Tomato paste
  Barbecue Rosemary Chicken, 66–67
  Barbecue Sauce, 210
  Brown Sauce (Sauce Espagnole), 194
  Classic Marinara with Port, 207
  Garlic Roasted Stuffed Chicken
    with Port Marinara, 78–79
  Orange Barbecue Pork Chops, 110
  Osso Bucco with Gremolata,
    104–105

Spaghetti Sauce (Salsa de
Pomodoro), 204–205
Tomato puree
Light Lobster Bisque, 50–51
Tomatoes
Broccoli Hors d'Oeuvre, Italian Style,
14
Brunswick Stew, 35
Bruschetta, 20
Cabbage Casserole, 140
Chicken Cacciatore, 68–69
Classic Marinara with Port, 207
Cuban Clam Chowder, 44–45
Duck Orecchiette, 90–91
Garlic Roasted Stuffed Chicken with
Port Marinara, 78–79
Hungarian Goulash, 46–47
Italian Vegetables, 175
Jambalaya with Scallops, 119
Lamb Chops Braised with Tomatoes,
Eggplant and Green Olives,
114–115
Manhattan Clam Chowder, 52–53
Minestrone, 54–55
New Orleans–Style Seafood Filé
Gumbo, 56–57
Paella Valencia, 120–121
Punjabi Potatoes with Cauliflower,
160
Ratatouille with Sausage and Beans,
167–168
Salsa, 211
Seafood Étouffée, 124–125
Spaghetti Sauce (Salsa de
Pomodoro), 204–205
Stuffed Peppers, 102–103
Tortellini
Creamed Saffron Chicken with
Tortellini and Peas, 76–77
Italian Turkey Soup, 49
Turkey
Barbecued Turkey Meatballs, 12–13
Cabbage Casserole, 140
Hungarian Goulash, 46–47

Italian Turkey Soup, 49
Mama's Sneaky Meatloaf, 84–85
Momma LeAnnie's Stovetop
Lasagna, 86–87
Sloppy Gobblers, 82–83
Stovetop Roast Stuffed Turkey, 80–81
Sweet and Sour Meatballs, 24–25
Turkey Piccata, 88
Twice-Baked Potatoes, 162–163

Vanilla Cream Icing, 226–227
Vapor seal, form the, 129
Vapor seal, reestablish the, 130
Veal
Low-Sodium Brown Veal Stock,
219–220
Osso Bucco with Gremolata,
104–105
Roast Stuffed Veal, 106–107
Sweet Italian Meatballs, 108
Veal Chops in Red Wine Sauce, 109
Vegetable cooking, waterless, 3
Vegetable juice cocktail
Manhattan Clam Chowder, 52–53
Vegetables the waterless, greaseless
way, cooking, 128
Vegetables, cooking fresh, 130
Vegetables, cooking frozen, 130
Vegetables
Low-Sodium Pan-Roasted Vegetable
Stock, 221
Velouté Sauce, 192

Warm and Creamy Parmesan Potatoes,
164–165
Water chestnuts
Chicken Chow Mein, 70–71
Waterless, Greaseless Cooking, 1–6
Waterless, greaseless cookware, 2–3
White Chili, 60
White sauces, 184
White stocks, 214–215
Wine
Black Bean Chili, 32–33

Bordelaise Sauce, 206
Chateaubriand, 98–99
Chicken Cacciatore, 68–69
Chicken Cordon Bleu, 72–73
Classic Marinara with Port,
207
Collard Greens Soup, 40–41
Court-Bouillon, 122
Creamed Chicken and Basmati Rice,
74–75
Garlic Roasted Stuffed Chicken with
Port Marinara, 78–79
Lamb Chops Braised with Tomatoes,
Eggplant and Green Olives,
114–115
Light Lobster Bisque, 50–51
Madeira Sauce, 197
Marchand de Vin Sauce (Red Wine
Sauce), 197
Minestrone, 54–55
Osso Bucco with Gremolata,
104–105
Paella Valencia, 120–121
Roast Pork Chardonnay, 111
Spaghetti Sauce (Salsa de
Pomodoro), 204–205
Spanish Bean Soup, 59
Stovetop Roast Stuffed Turkey,
80–81
Sweet and Sour Wine Sauce, 197
Sweet Italian Meatballs, 108
Turkey Piccata, 88
Veal Chops in Red Wine Sauce,
109

Yellow Squash Parmesan, 171
Yellow Squash, Southern Style, 174

Zucchini
Italian Vegetables, 175
Minestrone, 54–55
Ratatouille with Sausage and Beans,
167–168
Stuffed Zucchini Johnsonville, 22–23

About the Author

Charles Knight has enjoyed a diverse career in food, marketing and writing. He attributes his early interest in cooking, which started during high school, to the rich flavors of his diverse ethnic neighborhood. It later led him to attend Peter Kump's Cooking School in New York to sharpen his culinary skills. His career in cookware began as a part-time job selling pots and pans, became a full-time job and finally he created his own business with waterless, greaseless cookware. In 1983 he started Health Craft, which is now a multimillion dollar operation, as a family business with his wife, LeAnn.

Knight is a cookbook author and a popular television and radio chef as well as a successful entrepreneur. He lives with his family in Tampa.

CLASSROOM
BULLETIN
BOARDS

With Learning Activities
For Preschool Children

by Cathy Allen Falk

Unless otherwise indicated, all Scriptures quoted from the *International Children's Bible, New Century Version,* copyright © 1986, 1988 by Word Publishing, Dallas, Texas 75039. Used by permission.

Scripture quotations marked NIV are from the HOLY BIBLE: NEW INTERNATIONAL VERSION®. Copyright © 1973, 1978, 1984 by International Bible Society. Used by permission of Zondervan Publishing House. All rights reserved.

The "NIV" and "New International Version" trademarks are registered in the United States Patent and Trademark Office by International Bible Society. Use of either trademark requires the permission of International Bible Society.

Illustrated by Kathryn Hutton
Edited by Karen Brewer

The Standard Publishing Company, Cincinnati, Ohio
A division of Standex International Corporation
© 1994 by The Standard Publishing Company
All rights reserved
Printed in the United States of America

01 00 99 98 97 96 95 94   5 4 3 2 1

Library of Congress Cataloging-in-Publication Data

Falk, Cathy Allen.
    Classroom bulletin boards : with learning activities for preschool
children / by Cathy Allen Falk.
        p.   cm.
    ISBN 0-7847-0222-5
    1. Christian education--Bulletin boards. 2. Christian education
of preschool children. I. Title.
BV1535.25.F35 1994
268'.432--dc20   94-17197
                                            CIP

Contents

Psalm 9:1   Praise to God..4

Matthew 28:7   Spring Is Full of God's Good Gifts 6

Acts 4:20   Come With Me..8

1 Peter 5:7   God Cares About Me.................................10

2 Timothy 4:5   Good News!..12

Genesis 2:18   God Gives Us Families 14

John 13:34   Jesus Loves Us 16

2 Timothy 3:15   We Learn From the Bible........................18

John 15:14   A Friend Is Someone Special 20

1 John 3:22   Our Hands Can Help the Love of Jesus Grow............22

Psalm 105:1   God Hears My Prayers............................24

Proverbs 4:26   Pleasing God 26

John 3:16   The Best Present 28

Acts 17:24   God Made Everything..............................30

Hebrews 12:28   Thank You God......................................32

Exodus 23:25   Worship God 34

Ephesians 4:32   Friends 36

Ecclesiastes 12:13   God's Word 38

Luke 2:11   A Savior Has Been Born 40

2 Timothy 2:24   I Can Help 42

Revelation 1:18   Jesus Is Alive! 44

2 Timothy 2:19   God Knows My Name..............................46

Psalm 100:2   Let Us Worship 48

1 Peter 2:21   Following Jesus 50

Psalm 106:3   Happy Are Those Who Do Right................52

Deuteronomy 6:18   I Will Do Right 54

1 John 4:8   God Loves Me...56

2 Thessalonians 1:3 It Is Right to Thank God.........................58

Mark 10:16   Our Friend Jesus...................................60

1 Peter 5:7   I Am Important to God 62

How to Use the Transparency Patterns

It's Easy!

(**1**) Remove the two transparencies from the book.

(**2**) Select a pattern.

(**3**) The best part is that with a transparency, any size object can be made. If you have a small bulletin board, make the object small. If you have a large board, make the object large. The transparency can also be reversed to change the direction and look of objects.

(**4**) Cover the bulletin board and trace objects directly onto the background, or trace objects onto mounted paper. Then remove and cut out.

(**5**) Add color as desired. Be creative! Use markers, crayons, paints, colored pencils, and fabric. Add a little color or a lot.

(**6**) Save your creations and use them again and again!

Praise to God

I will praise you, Lord, with all my heart.
I will tell all the miracles you have done wonders. Psalm 9:1

Materials:

Background:	white paper
Border:	wide red or red print ribbon
Lettering:	black
Hearts:	hearts made by children in the art activity
	lace

Directions: Cover the board and mount the ribbon border around its edge. Add the caption.
   Randomly attach hearts made by children in the art activity. Add lace around some edges to add interest.

Art—*Collages*

Materials:
  heart transparency pattern (optional)
  pink and red paper
  magazines

Cut several large hearts from paper. (Trace from the transparency pattern if desired.)
Ask children to tear pictures from magazines which show things for which we can give God thanks and praise. Allow children to glue the pictures in a random manner to the paper hearts. Add to the bulletin board. (Edges may need to be trimmed after children glue and before mounting.)

Circle Time—*Wings of Praise*

Materials:
  gift wrap ribbon
  crepe paper
  black marker
  safety pins

Cut a 30" piece of ribbon and four 24" strips of crepe paper for each child. Staple one end of a crepe paper strip three inches from each end of the ribbon. Then staple one end of a crepe paper strip eight inches from each end of the ribbon.

Talk about what it means to praise God. Then say to the children, "Can you name some of the things for which we can praise God?" Print the children's responses on the strips of crepe paper.

Attach each ribbon to a child's clothing by pinning it at the neck, each wrist, and each elbow. (For children wearing short sleeves, make the ends of the ribbon long enough to tie to the children's wrists.)

While it is great fun to run with arms outstretched and let the streamers fly, you may wish to lead the children in a more structured activity. Join hands and with arms stretched wide, circle and sing "Praise Him, All Ye Little Children."

> Praise Him, praise Him, all ye little children;
> God is love, God is love;
> Praise Him, praise Him all ye little children,
> God is love, God is love.

For variety, lead the children through a series of motions while singing the song. Space children far enough apart to avoid bumping into each other. Raise hands overhead each time you sing the word "praise" and lower them on the word "Him". For the phrase "all ye little children," spin around with arms stretched wide. Point upward while singing the word "God." Place both hands over the heart on the word "love."

Spring Is Full of God's Good Gifts

He (Jesus) has risen from the dead. Matthew 28:7 (NIV)

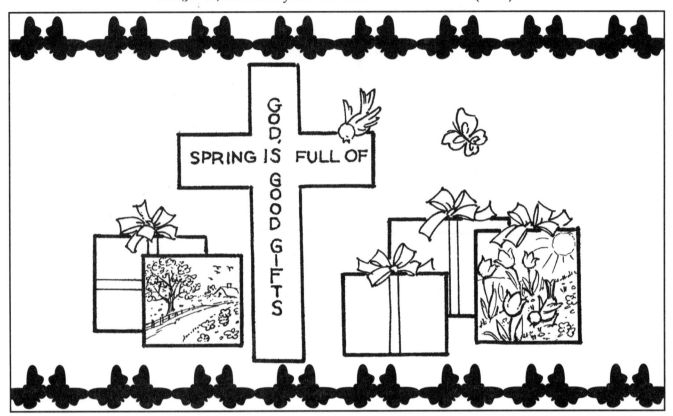

Materials:

Transparency Pattern:	cross with bird
Background:	yellow paper
Border:	butterfly pattern below, pink printed wrapping paper
	white chenille wires
Cross:	blue paper, dark blue marker
Gifts:	large pictures of spring
	colored plastic wrap
	assorted ribbon

Directions: Cover the board. Use the pattern here to cut a butterfly border. Fan-fold 3" high strips of paper into 3" wide rectangles. Place the butterfly pattern on top of the folded paper, making sure broken lines of the pattern touch folded paper edges. Cut out the butterfly and unfold. Glue two 2" chenille wires to the center of each butterfly for a body with antlers.

Trace and cut out the cross with bird. Add lettering and bird details with a marker. Mount to the center of the board. Cut spring pictures into rectangles or mount on rectangular paper. Cover each with plastic wrap. Add ribbons and bows to create "gifts," being careful not to hide the spring pictures. Mount gifts around the cross.

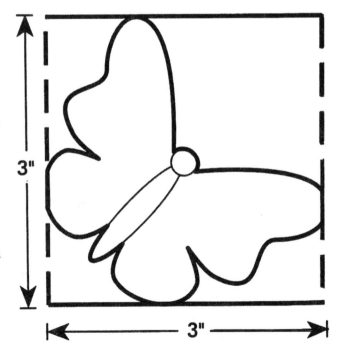

Table Game—*Spring Sorting Sticks*

Materials:
   spring stickers
   craft sticks or recycled Popsicle sticks
   6 ounce frozen juice cans
   Con-Tact paper

Attach two stickers, back-to-back, to one end of a craft stick. Place the same stickers on several different sticks. Use a variety of stickers that represent spring to make many different sets of sticks so children will have several to sort.

Cover the juice cans with Con-Tact paper. Place one sticker of each design on a different can.

Discuss the picture on each sticker telling the children how it relates to the season. Let the children put each stick into its matching can.

Circle Time—*Guess Who We Are!*

Lead the children through a series of pantomimes which represent various aspects of spring. Be fluttering butterflies, growing flowers, splattering raindrops, the shining sun, hatching chicks, a robin looking for worms, or blowing breezes.

After children understand which motions to do for each idea, choose one child to leave the circle momentarily. Help the remaining children decide which aspect of spring they would like to act out.

When the child returns, all the other children act out the selected movement without any sound. The returning child guesses what the children are acting out.

Active Play—*Butterfly Relay*

Materials:
   tissue paper
   clothes pins

Fan-fold a 10" square piece of tissue paper and slip the center into a clothes pin to make a butterfly. Make one butterfly for each team.

Form teams of equal numbers. Designate a start and finish line. Give the first child of each team a butterfly. The teacher should stand at the finish line.

At the teacher's signal, the first child on each team walks, runs, gallops, or slides to the finish line. Each child should recite the Bible words such as "He has risen from the dead" to the teacher. Each child then returns to the starting line and gives the butterfly to the next child in line and the game continues.

Come With Me

We cannot keep quiet. We must speak about what we have seen and heard. Acts 4:20

Materials:

Transparency Pattern:	church building
Background:	yellow paper
Border:	paper doll pattern below
Church:	white paper, rectangular sponges, gray tempera paint
	permanent black marker
	two paper fasteners, class photo
Windows:	black paper, assorted colors of paper

Directions: Trace the church building. Let children sponge paint "bricks" onto the building. Let dry and cut out.

Trace and cut out two windows from black paper. Cover with glue and let children tear pieces of colored paper to scatter on the glue. Add the windows to the church building.

Cut the doors up the center and across the top. Fold doors open at the hinged sides. Add paper fastener door knobs.

Use the pattern here to cut a paper doll border. Fan-fold 2 3/4" high strips of paper into 2 3/8" wide rectangles. Place the doll pattern on top of the folded paper, making sure broken lines of the pattern touch folded paper edges. Cut out the doll and unfold. (Enlarge if desired.)

Cover the board and add the doll border around its edge. Mount the church in the center of the board on top of a class photo that will show when the church doors are opened.

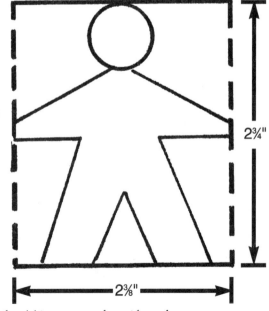

Cooking—*Stained Glass Window Cookies*

Materials:
  sugar cookie dough (homemade or refrigerator dough)
  10-15 lollipops or clear hard candies
  freezer-strength plastic bag
  mallet
  baking sheets
  aluminum foil

Remove the wrappers from the lollipops. Place the lollipops in a plastic bag and close. Crush by hitting the bag with a mallet. Open the bag and remove sticks.

Give children a small amount of dough, and ask them to roll the dough into "ropes" about 1/4" thick. Help children form the dough into a window shape on baking sheets lined with aluminum foil. Place strips of dough inside the window to form cross bars in the window. Pinch the dough joints together. Sprinkle crushed lollipops in the openings. Note the location of each child's cookie on the baking sheet. Bake at 375° for 7-9 minutes.

For Very Young Children: Shape cookies in advance. Store in refrigerator until ready to use. Let children help crush the candy and then sprinkle it into the openings of the cookie.

Active Play—*Come With Me to My Church*

This game may be played either indoors or out. Designate one area as the church building. Choose one child as the leader. The other children may be sitting or standing around the play area. The leader walks around touching each child on the shoulder, saying, "Come with me to my church." One-by-one the children fall in line following the leader. When all the children have joined in the line, the leader takes them to the area you have designated as the church building. All children join hands, circle, and chant the following:

> My church is a happy place.
> My church is fun.
> Here we learn about Jesus,
> God's only Son.

Choose a new leader and repeat.

God Cares About Me

He cares for you. 1 Peter 5:7

Materials:

Background:	pink paper
Border:	hearts made by children in the art activity
Lettering:	black marker
Mirror:	duct tape
	small lightweight mirror

Directions: Cover the board. Mount hearts made by the children in the art activity around its edge for a border. Use the easy dotted letters illustrated above to write the caption with a marker directly onto the background. Tape the mirror under the caption low enough for the children to see themselves. Write the children's names around the mirror.

Art—*Heart Art*

Materials:
    marbles
    thick red, pink, and lavender tempera paint in shallow containers
    6" white paper hearts (cut by freehand or traced from the transparency pattern)
    square cake pans or boxes
    newspapers

Put 2-3 marbles in each color of paint. Place one paper heart in a cake pan. Spoon one color of the paint-covered marbles into the pan. Allow a child to tilt the pan to make the wet marbles roll across the heart. Remove the first marbles and puts in marbles from a different color. Encourage children to say "God loves me!" as they complete their heart designs.

Remove painted heart from cake pan and lay on newspapers to dry. As the paint is drying, talk with the children about how many hearts they printed. Explain that the amount of love God has for them is even greater than the number of hearts they see.

Active Play—*Let's Go Fishing*

Materials:
    fish pattern
    assorted paper
    paper clips
    28" piece of string
    empty cardboard gift wrap tube
    small U-shaped or a circle magnet

Make several colorful copies of the fish in a photocopy machine. (Enlarge if desired.) Give one fish to each child. Ask the children to draw self-portraits on the back of the fish. Collect the fish and attach a paper clip to each.

Make a fishing pole by tying one end of the string through a small hole you have punched in the end of the cardboard tube. Tie the other end to the magnet.

Place fish, portrait sides down, on the floor in the middle of the circle of children. Let children take turns "fishing." After each catch, identify whose picture is on the fish. Then ask, "Does God care for _____ ?" and name the child pictured. Assure children that God cares for each one of them.

Good News!

Do the work of telling the Good News. 2 Timothy 4:5

Materials:

Transparency Pattern:	children
Background:	white paper
Border:	assorted colors of balloons
	crepe paper streamers
	mylar stars
Lettering:	orange
Children:	white paper, assorted markers

Directions: Cover the board. Trace and cut out the children. Add color as desired. Mount in the center and add the caption above their heads.

Add balloons, streamers, and mylar stars to each top corner.

Active Play—*Spreading the Good News*

This game is played like the reverse of Freeze Tag. Begin with all the children scattered about the room or play yard. Instruct children not to move until someone comes to them and speaks. One child is the missionary. The missionary goes to a child and says, "I have good news. Jesus loves you." After being spoken to, a child is no longer frozen. The second child joins the first, and now there are two missionaries. Each child approaches another child and tells the good news. Those two children become missionaries and now there are four to spread the news. Continue until all children are free to move. Then form a line and march about, follow-the-leader style. Pretend to cross an ocean and arrive in a new country. Scatter the children, designate one as the missionary, and repeat the game.

Circle Time—*Packing a Missionary's Suitcase*

Materials:
   grocery bag
   various objects
   empty suitcase
   cardboard box

Collect a variety of items and put them all in a grocery bag. Choose items that a missionary would take such as a Bible, Christian books, stationery, medical supplies, teaching aids, etc. Also include items a missionary would not or could not take—food, a plant, an electrical appliance. (Be careful to use the real item. Children are very concrete at this age. If you include a toy car, hoping the children will understand missionaries may not be able to ship a real automobile, children may leave with the impression that missionaries do not take toys.)

Seat children in a circle. Take one item out of the grocery bag. Tell the children what it is and pass it around the circle. Each child should repeat the name of the item as they pass it on. When the item returns to the teacher ask, "Would missionaries pack this in their suitcase?" Let all the children answer. Next, ask one child to take the item and put it in the suitcase if the answer is yes and in the box if the answer is no.

Song—*Missionary Song*

Sing to the tune of "A-Hunting We Will Go:"

   To Africa we'll go, To Africa we'll go,
   We'll tell everyone of Jesus' love
   To Africa we'll go.

Create additional verses by changing the destination (e.g., to the city we will go or to Russia we will go).

God Gives Us Families

The Lord God said, "It is not good for the man to be alone." Genesis 2:18

Materials:

Background:	light green
Border and Streets:	gray crepe paper
Lettering:	dark blue
Houses:	houses made by children in the art activity

Directions: Cover the board and mount the crepe paper border around its edge. Mount houses made by the children in the art activity in rows. Add crepe paper "streets" between house rows and divide houses into "blocks" with crepe paper. Add the caption in one or two "blocks."

Art—*This Is Where My Family Lives*

Materials:
  house transparency pattern
  heavy white paper
  crayons

Trace and cut out a house for each child using the transparency pattern or enlarge and copy the house in a photocopy machine. Have each child color a house to look like his or hers. Discuss with the children that families live in many different kinds of houses. Stress the fact that God loves everyone no matter what kind of house a family lives in. Post the houses on the bulletin board.

Song—*My Family*

Sing to the tune of "The Muffin Man:"

  Oh, do you know the mem-bers of,
  My fam-i-ly, my fam-i-ly?
  Lis-ten ve-ry care-ful-ly,
  I'll name them now for you.

After everyone sings the song, call on one child to name the members of his or her immediate family. Be prepared to prompt children if necessary. Repeat the song until each child has had a turn. Be sensitive to and affirming of different family structures.

Finger Play—*Families*

Some families are large.
  (Stretch arms wide.)

Some families are small.
  (Bring hands close together.)

No matter the size,
  (Shake head no and hold palms up.)

God loves them all!
  (Point up then make a sweeping gesture out.)

Jesus Loves Us

You must love each other as I have loved you. John 13:34

Materials:

Transparency Pattern:	Jesus with heart
	heart (optional)
Background:	light blue
Border:	border strips made by children in the art activity
Lettering:	dark blue
Jesus:	white and red paper
	black and brown markers
Small Hearts:	pink paper
	pink yarn

Directions: Cover the board. Mount the border around its edge.

Trace and cut out Jesus from white paper. Add details with a black marker and color hair with a brown marker. Trace and cut out the heart from red paper. Attach the red heart to Jesus' chest, leaving the top of the heart unattached to make a pocket.

Cut out a small heart by freehand for each child, or use the transparency to trace and cut out several small hearts. Write each child's name on a heart. Attach a piece of yarn to each heart and hang heart strings randomly on each side of Jesus. Encourage each child to put the heart with his name on it inside Jesus' pocket upon arrival each day. (Be sure each piece of yarn is long enough to do this.)

Art—*Heart Art*

Materials:
  sponges
  clip clothes pins
  red, pink, and lavender thick tempera paint
  3 shallow containers for paint
  wide roll of adding machine tape
  newspapers

Cut the sponges into various sized hearts. (Wet sponges cut easily with large scissors.) Attach a clothes pin to each sponge. Put one color of paint into each container.

Let 2-3 children paint at a time. Place a strip of adding machine tape on newspaper for each child. Demonstrate holding the clothes pins and printing the hearts. Encourage children to use different sized sponges and different colors of paint. Suggest to the children that each time they make a heart print they say to themselves, "Jesus loves me!"

Cooking—*Cookie to Share*

Materials:
  12" pizza pan
  margarine
  refrigerator sugar cookie dough
  powdered sugar
  toothpick
  small red candies or chocolate chips

Have children grease the pizza pan with margarine. Allow refrigerator dough to come to room temperature and then have the children pat it evenly into the pan. If dough is sticky, children may dust their hands with powdered sugar.

Use a toothpick to draw a heart into the dough. Let children place candies or chocolate chips on the heart outline. Bake at 350° for ten minutes. Cut and share. Tell children that sharing is one way of showing Jesus' love to others.

Song—*Jesus Knows My Name*

Sing to the tune of "The Farmer in the Dell:"

  Jesus knows my name, Jesus knows your name
  Jesus knows your name is (child holding beanbag responds).
  Jesus knows our names.

Sit in a circle and pass a beanbag while singing this song. At the phrase, "He knows your name is . . . ." the child with the beanbag holds it and says his own name.

We Learn From the Bible

The Scriptures are able to make you wise. 2 Timothy 3:15

Materials:

Transparency Pattern:	Bible
Background:	tan paper
Border:	wide red ribbon
Lettering:	dark blue
Bible:	white paper
	black marker
	wide red ribbon
	cardboard tubes from wrapping paper or paper towels
	long pins
Children:	self-portraits drawn by children

Directions: Cover the board and attach the ribbon border around its edge.

Trace and cut out the Bible. Color the Bible cover, draw in pages, and letter "The Bible" with a marker. Add a wide ribbon as a bookmark. To give the Bible a 3-D look when mounting, use long pins to secure cardboard tubes under each side of the Bible near the center.

Attach self-portraits drawn by the children around the Bible.

Table Game—*B-I-B-L-E Sandpaper Rubbing*

Materials:
  B-I-B-L-E transparency pattern
  coarse sandpaper
  tagboard
  white paper
  crayons

This activity will help children recognize the word "Bible." Enlarge the B-I-B-L-E transparency pattern in a photocopy machine. Use the photocopy to cut the letters from coarse sandpaper. Glue the letters to tagboard. You may want to make more than one set.

Show children how to place a piece of paper on top of the letters and rub across the sandpaper with the side of a crayon. (Taping the paper down will help hold it in place.) The letters "B-I-B-L-E" will appear.

Song—*The Bible is the Word of God*

Sing to the Tune of "Mary Had a Little Lamb:"

  The Bible is the Word of God, Word of God, Word of God.
  The Bible is the Word of God . . .

    Verse 1—It tells us of God's love.
    Verse 2—It will never change.
    Verse 3—A very special book.
    Verse 4—Written long ago.

Finger Play—*The Bible*

  The Bible is the Word of God *(Form imaginary book with both hands.)*
  Sent from Heav'n above. *(Point upward.)*
  It shows us how to live our lives, *(Point to self then others.)*
  And tells us of his love. *(Place both hands on heart.)*

Circle Time—*I Can Say Bible Words*

Materials:
  tape recorder and tape

Tape record children individually reciting a Bible verse. (You may need to say the words quietly with a shy child.) Play the recording back to the group. Let children guess who is speaking.

A Friend Is Someone Special

You are my friends if you do what I command you. John 15:14

Materials:

Transparency Pattern: Jesus with children
Background: light yellow
Border: cloud pattern
    white paper
    grass pattern
    green paper
Jesus with Children: white paper
    assorted markers

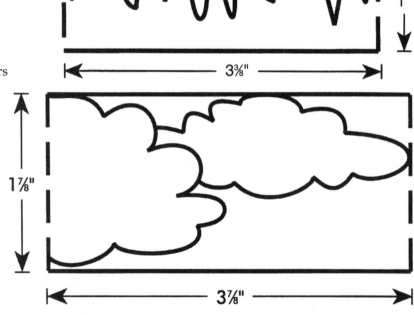

Directions: Cover the board. Use the pattern here to cut a cloud border. Fan-fold 1 7/8" high strips of white paper into 3 7/8" wide rectangles. Place the cloud pattern on top of the folded paper, making sure broken lines of the pattern touch folded paper edges. Cut out the clouds and unfold. Repeat with the grass pattern and green paper, using the measurements provided. Mount the clouds across the top and the grass across the bottom.

     Trace and cut out Jesus with the children. Add color as desired and mount.

Pattern reprinted from *Borders Made Easy*.

Active Game—*Friendship Beanbag Toss*

Material:
  heart transparency pattern
  red paper
  magazines and old Sunday school materials
  beanbag
  masking tape

Trace and cut out 3-5 hearts. Look in magazines and old Sunday school materials for pictures of children who are being friends to others. Mount one picture on each heart. Talk about the pictures with the children.

To play the game, tape the hearts on the floor, spacing them a few feet apart. Mark the place the children are to stand by placing a masking tape X on the floor. (Make the game more challenging by placing a series of Xs further from the hearts.) As you hand the beanbag to each child, ask, "How can you be a friend?" Help the child answer the question by telling about the picture on the heart that the beanbag lands closest to.

Song—*Jesus Wants to Be My Friend*

Sing to the tune of "Mary Had a Little Lamb:"

  Jesus wants to be my friend, be my friend, be my friend.
  Jesus wants to be my friend because he loves me so.

  Jesus wants to be my friend, be my friend, be my friend.
  Jesus wants to be my friend; He listens when I pray.

  Jesus wants to be my friend, be my friend, be my friend.
  Jesus wants to be my friend; He knows just how I feel.

Ask the children how they know that Jesus is their friend? Use the children's responses as additional verses in the song.

  I know that Jesus is my friend, is my friend, is my friend.
  I know that Jesus is my friend, because . . . .

Our Hands Can Help the Love of Jesus Grow

Do what pleases him (God). 1 John 3:22

Materials:

Transparency Pattern:	house (optional)
Background:	light green and light blue paper
Flowers:	dark green marker, assorted colors of tempera paint, paintbrush
Rainbow:	red, orange, yellow, green, blue, indigo, and violet tempera paints (top to bottom order)
Trees:	medium green paper
House:	white paper, black marker
Sun:	yellow paper

Directions: Cover the board with green paper on the bottom half of the board and blue paper on the top half. Cut a ragged edge or tear the top edge of the green paper for an interesting effect.

Draw stems and leaves across the bottom edge of the green paper with a marker. Use a paint brush to paint one hand of each child. (This will work best if done one child at a time.) Instruct each child to press his painted hand onto a stem, making a flower with petals. (Or print hands on separate paper, dry, cut out, and mount.)

Paint a rainbow in the color order above across the blue background. Anchor the rainbow with trees and a house cut by freehand or by using the transparency pattern.

Cut a large sun by freehand and add to the upper right corner.

Active Play—*Who Will Help Me?*

Lead the children in pantomiming a series of helping motions. Ask, "Who will help me ___?", completing the question with a job that the children can act out. For example, "Who will help me pick strawberries?" The children all respond, "We will help you pick strawberries." Then stoop to pretend to pick berries. Include tasks such as these:

rock the baby	wash the car
pull the wagon	carry these sacks
rake the leaves	stir this batter
hammer this nail	shake this rug
sweep the sidewalk	paint the wall
push open the door	wash the window
walk the dog	dig a hole
dust the furniture	put the groceries away
wash the dishes	vacuum the carpet

End the game by thanking the children for their help. Say, "It makes God happy when you help others."

Finger Play—*Helping Hands*

Here are hands that can help you do *(Raise hands.)*
Many thing if you ask me to. *(Point away and then to self.)*
I can dust or feed the cat. *(Pet imaginary cat.)*
I can sweep or get your hat. *(Pat head.)*
There are many things these hands can do. *(Raise hands.)*
Ask me please, and I'll help you. *(Point to self than point away.)*

Circle Time—*Riddles*

Describe people that young children can help. For each person, name a simple way children can help. Let children respond by naming the individual you are thinking of. For example:

This is someone who uses a pacifier.
When she drops it, I can pick it up.
(baby)

This is someone who cares for me.
When she is cleaning, I can help by picking up my toys.
(Mom)

This is my mom's mom.
When she needs her glasses, I can bring them to her.
(Grandma)

God Hears My Prayers

Give thanks to the Lord, and pray to him. Psalm 105:1

Materials:

Background:	blue
Border:	plastic tableware, Plasti-Tak
Lettering:	yellow
Place Settings:	4 colorful paper napkins
	plates and cups made by children in the table activity

Directions: Cover the board. Attach plastic tableware with Plasti-Tak around the edge for a border. Mount lettering in the upper left corner.

Open four paper napkins and arrange them in the leftover space. Mount a paper plate from the table activity to each napkin. Use a thumbtack on the inside of each cup to tack to each napkin. Add plastic tableware as desired.

Table Game—*Give Thanks*

Materials:

4 large paper plates   assorted magazines
4 clear plastic cups   assorted paper

Divide the children into four groups and assign each group breakfast, lunch, dinner, or snack time. Give each group a paper plate, a plastic cup, and assorted magazines.

Guide children to tear out pictures of things they would like to eat for their meal or snack. Glue pictures to the plate. Fill the cup with wadded paper the color of their chosen drink.

Post the plates and cups on the bulletin board. Talk about each meal and how God gives us many wonderful things to eat. End with a snack and a prayer of thanksgiving.

Hint: This activity will work best if a teacher guides each group.

Active Game—*Harvest Basket*

Materials:

fruit patterns
assorted heavy paper
hole punch
yarn
small basket

First, enlarge the fruit patterns to actual size in a photocopy machine. Trace and cut out one fruit for each child or photocopy the fruit onto heavy colored paper and cut out. Turn the paper fruit into necklaces by punching two holes near the top and threading yarn through the holes.

With children standing in a circle, hold a small basket containing several copies of each fruit. Say, "What food is in my thanksgiving basket?" Pull out one picture. All the children wearing that necklace trade places in the circle. Be sure everyone finds a place and no one is ever "out." Call the names of all the fruit one by one in random order. Children will have fun waiting for their fruit to be called and finding a new place. Remind the children that food is only one thing for which we can thank God. When we pray we can thank God for many things. We can also pray to God and ask for his help or pray to say we are sorry for something we have down that is wrong.

Pleasing God

Be careful what you do.
Always do what is right. Proverbs 4:26

Materials:

Transparency Patterns:	four hearts, pointing hand
Background:	blue
Border:	wide red, white, and blue ribbon
Lettering:	red
Hearts:	white paper, permanent black marker, crayons
Pointing Hand:	skin-tone paper, brown marker

Directions: Cover the board and attach the ribbon border around its edge. Trace and cut out the pointing hand and mount in the center of the board. Arch the caption over the hand.

Trace and cut out the four hearts. Ask older children to color the pictures. Attach a heart at each corner of the board.

Art—*A Smile Is a Frown Turned Upside Down*

Materials:
  7" white paper plate
  7 1/2" x 1" strip of tagboard
  stapler
  red paper
  red glitter

Lay the strip of tagboard down the middle of the back of a paper plate. Staple each end of the strip even with the edges of the paper plate so that the strip gaps, leaving room for a young child to insert his hand. Cut a "smile" by freehand from red paper that is approximately 4" long. Let the child add red glitter. Glue the smile to the center of the paper plate. Help fit the child's hand in the strip on the back of the plate. Show how to turn the paper plate upside down so the smile becomes a frown.

Circle Time—*Pleasing God Makes Me Smile*

Materials:
  paper plate smiles made in the art activity

Play this game with the children seated in a circle and the paper plate "smile" fitted on their hands. Prepare a list of actions that either would or would not be pleasing to God. Read one item and wait for the children to respond. If they think God would be pleased, they should hold the paper plate so that it is a smile. If it is something that would not please God, children should turn the plate upside down and show a frown.

Try these statements. It pleases God when I . . .

help others.	do not obey my parents.
ask a new neighbor to play.	go to church.
say I'm sorry.	give money to help others.
am a good friend.	tell others about Jesus.
listen to Bible stories.	visit a lonely person.
say mean words.	argue with my brothers.
say angry words.	thank him for my food.
pray.	share.
am kind to others.	sing songs of praise.

The Best Present

For God loved the world so much that he gave his only Son. John 3:16

Materials:

Background:	white paper
Tree:	green tissue paper
	corrugated cardboard
Gifts:	cardboard
	assorted Christmas wrapping paper
	assorted ribbons
	large picture of baby Jesus
Gift Tag:	white paper
	black marker

Directions: Cover the board. Cut several Christmas tree layers by freehand from tissue paper. Cut a rectangle from the corrugated cardboard for a tree trunk. Mount the trunk on the left side and top with overlapped tree layers. Decorate the tree if desired.

Cut cardboard into rectangular shapes. Wrap the cardboard rectangles with Christmas paper. Add ribbon to decorate like gifts. Mount by stacking the gifts to the right of the tree.

Cut a piece of cardboard slightly larger than the picture of baby Jesus. Score the cardboard 2" from the top, being careful not to cut through the cardboard. Wrap this gift with the scoring on the back and add ribbon.

Mount the picture of baby Jesus on top of the stack of gifts. Securely attach the 2" scored edge of cardboard to the top of the picture, covering Jesus. Cut a gift tag by freehand and write "To you, From God." Tie onto the gift with Jesus' picture hidden beneath. Children may lift the gift to see Jesus.

Art—*Christmas Candle Gift*

Materials:
  clean baby food jars
  Christmas pictures cut from old greeting cards
  clear glitter
  votive candle

Glue a small Christmas picture to the outside of a baby food jar. Paint the picture and the entire jar, including the lip, with thinned glue. Sprinkle clear glitter over wet glue and allow to dry. Place a small votive candle inside. Give the Christmas candle as a gift.

Active Play—*Present Pass*

Materials:
  6 empty boxes
  Christmas gift wrap in 2 designs
  picture of Jesus

Wrap three boxes in one gift wrap design and three in the other. Place presents under the class Christmas tree or in a central location. Divide the group into two teams and assign each a gift wrap design.

Each team sits in a circle. Designate a leader for each team. On the command, "Go!," the leader of each team goes to the tree and picks up one gift. The leader returns to the team and passes the present around the circle. As soon as the leader has given the present to the first person, he or she returns to the tree, picks up another present, starts that present around the circle, and then gets the third. The last child in the circle returns each present under the tree as quickly as possible.

Say to the children: "We've just had a race to see who could pass the presents the fastest. If we aren't careful, Christmas becomes a race to see who gets the most presents. Christmas is really about one gift. The gift God gave to the world, his one and only Son." Show the picture of Jesus.

Circle Time—*Gifts for Jesus*

Materials:
  small paper hearts
  small gift box (optional)

Lead the children in a discussion of why we give presents at Christmas time and to whom. Ask children what they could give to Jesus to show their love. Write each child's answer on a heart. The hearts can be put in a box and placed under a tree or displayed on the bulletin board as ornaments for the tree.

God Made Everything

He is the God who made the whole world and everything in it. Acts 17:24

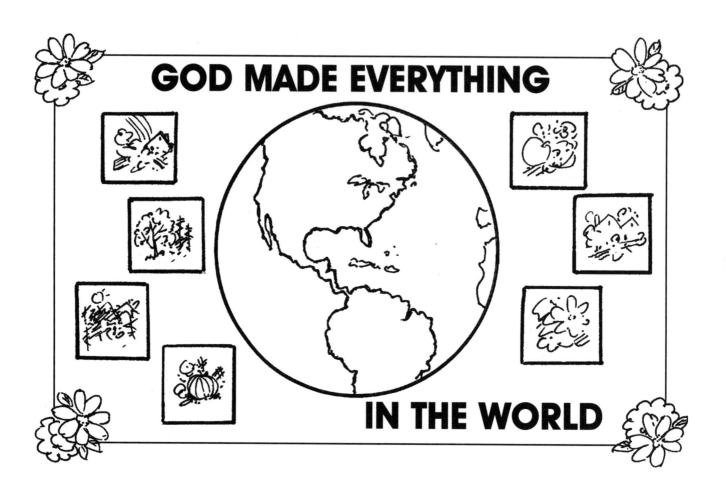

Materials:

Transparency Pattern:	world
Background:	white paper
Corner Border:	silk flowers
Lettering:	orange
World:	white paper, black permanent marker
	green and blue tempera paint, plastic grocery bags
Collages:	collage made by children in the arts activity

Directions: Cover the board and add silk flowers to the four corners.

Trace the world with a permanent marker. Paint water blue and land green. Cut out the world along with another circle the same size. Staple the two circles together around the outer edge, leaving about eight inches open. Stuff with plastic grocery bags and staple completely closed. Mount the 3-D world in the center of the board. Add the caption above and below the world. Arrange collages in the space available.

Art—*Creation Collage*

Materials:
magazines, catalogs, or old Sunday school materials
paper

Help children understand the difference between things God created and man-made objects. Have them cut or tear pictures of God's creations from magazines, catalogs, or old Sunday school materials. Help each child glue pictures onto a piece of paper in a random fashion overlapping one another and completely covering the paper. Place the children's collages around the world on the bulletin board.

Table Game—*Circle Sort*

Materials:
several frozen juice can lids
small pictures or stickers
4 shoe boxes
4 colors of paper with matching markers

Cover each box with a different color of paper. Label each box with a picture—1) food, 2) animals, 3) people, 4) nature. Glue a small picture or place a sticker on each metal lid using the same categories. Lay the lids, picture sides up, on the table. Lead the children to sort lids into the correct boxes. To make the game self-correcting, mark the back of each lid with a corresponding colored marker.

Active Game—*God Gives Us So Many Things*

This game is a variation of "London Bridge." Have the children stand and form a circle. Choose two children to form a bridge. One child stands inside the circle and the other child stands outside the circle. The two children stand facing each other and raise their joined hands to form a bridge. All the other children walk slowly in the circle, passing under the bridge.
Sing the following words to the tune of "London Bridge."
God has ma-de many things, many things, many things.
God has ma-de many things. We thank you now our God.

On the last word, the two children forming the bridge drop their hands and capture a child between them. The rest of the children stop circling and everyone sings:
Can you na-me just one thing, just one thing, just one thing?
Can you na-me just one thing that our Go-d made?

The captured child (with the help of the other children if necessary) names one thing God created and is released. The children repeat the game by circling through the bridge and singing the first verse again.

Thank You God

Let us be thankful. Hebrews 12:28

Materials:

Transparency Patterns:	praying girl with four thought balloons
Background:	light blue paper
Border:	dark blue scalloped
Lettering:	dark blue
Praying Girl:	white paper
	assorted colored markers
	lace and ribbon (optional)
Thought Balloons:	white paper
	permanent black marker
	crayons

Directions: Cover the board and mount the border around its edge. Add the caption to the bottom center of the board.

Trace and cut out the praying girl. Color as desired. Add interest by attaching a ribbon hair bow and collar lace instead of tracing these items.

Trace the thought balloons with a permanent marker. Let older children color the pictures. Mount the thought balloons around the girl. Cut graduating circles of white paper to mount between the girl and each thought balloon.

Circle Time—*What is Missing?*

Have children sit in a half-circle. In the middle, place 3-5 items for which we can be thankful. You might include an apple, a toy, mittens, a photograph of a family, and a Bible. Name each item and remind the children that it is right to thank God for each one. Ask the children to close their eyes. Remove one thing. Let the children take turns identifying what is missing. Return the missing item to the center of the circle and lead the children in saying, "Thank you God for (the item)." Allow children to take turns removing items.

Song—*We Are Thankful*

Sing to the tune of "Frère Jacques:"

We are thankful, we are thankful;
For our food, for our food.
God is good to u-s, God is good to u-s.
Thank you God! Thank you God!

Encourage children to think of other gifts from God for which they are thankful to create additional verses.

Finger Play—*Counting God's Gifts*

Sometimes when it's Thanksgiving, I trace around my hand,
   (*Use pointer of right hand to trace around the spread fingers of the left.*)

Making a pretty turkey with feathers that are grand.
   (*Flutter fingers. *)

But instead of drawing turkeys, this year what I will do
   (*Touch temple with pointer finger.*)

Is count on these fingers the gifts God gave to me and to you.
   (*Touch each finger, then point to self and another person.*)

Circle Time—*Who Can Tell Me What God Made?*

Find single pictures of things God made. Cover the majority of each picture with a plain piece of paper, letting a significant portion of the picture show (e.g., the fin of a fish, the trunk of a tree, the arm of a person). Say, "I'm holding a picture of something God made. Who can tell me what it is? . . . Yes, it's a fish. God made fish." Help the children think of something good about each of God's creations.

Worship God

Worship the Lord your God. Exodus 23:25

Materials:

Transparency Pattern:	music notes
	Bible
Background:	white
Lettering:	black and red letters
	red paper
Music Staff:	yardstick
	black yarn
	black marker
Praying Hands:	skin-tone paper, brown marker
Bibles:	white paper, black marker, red ribbon

Directions: Cover the board. Cut a red heart by freehand about the size of the black letters spelling "We God." Mount the heart between the two words in the top center of the board. Mount the left hand red captions dividing the remaining space into thirds.

Use a yardstick to draw the music staff onto the background with a light pencil line. Cover the lines with yarn. Using a marker, draw in hollow notes with smile faces.

Trace hands of children to make praying hands. Let older children cut out their own hands and mount in a row.

Trace and cut out the Bibles. Color the cover with a marker. Instead of tracing the ribbons add ribbon for interest. Mount Bibles in a row. Optional: If Bibles are large enough, older children could draw a Bible story picture on the pages.

Active Play—*Worship God*

Materials:
  beanbag

Lead the children to stand in a circle. Choose one child to stand in the center with a beanbag. The child tosses the beanbag to a child in the circle. That child catches (or picks up) the beanbag and runs around the outside of the circle. While the child is running, skipping, or galloping, the other children chant:

> I'm on my way to church today, to worship God, to sing and pray!
> I'm on my way to church today, to worship God, to sing and pray!

The child who tosses the bag becomes part of the circle and the child catching the bag then tosses it.

Circle Time—*Musical Instruments*

Music is an important part of worship. The Bible tells us to "Make a joyful noise unto the Lord" (Psalm 100:1, KJV) and a rhythm band certainly falls into that category. Instruments are simple to make.

Rhythm Sticks:	Cut 1/4" dowel rods into equal lengths.
Sandpaper Blocks:	Cover pairs of wooden rectangles with coarse sandpaper. Nail or glue a spool on the back for a handle.
Maracas:	Put dry beans, pebbles, or unpopped corn into small cans with removable plastic lids. Seal with masking tape.
Jingle Bells:	Sew several bells to an elastic band which fits around the child's wrist.
Drums:	Open both ends of a coffee can or shortening can. Cover each end with a plastic lid. Seal with masking tape.

Table Game—*Sewing Cards*

Materials:
  worship transparency patterns: cross, music note, heart, open Bible
  clean Styrofoam meat trays
  large nail or dull pencil
  shoe strings

Enlarge worship transparency patterns in a photocopy machine and cut out. Place a pattern on a Styrofoam meat tray. Trace the pattern into the tray with a nail or dull pencil, and then punch holes at regular intervals around the etching. Knot a shoe string and pull it up through one hole in the tray, down through the next hole, etc. Children will enjoy "sewing" the worship objects.

Friends

Be kind and loving to each other. Ephesians 4:32

Materials:

Transparency Pattern:	FRIENDS
	heart
Background:	black or dark blue
Hearts:	assorted colors of paper
FRIENDS:	white paper

Directions: Cover the board. Trace and cut out several hearts of various sizes and colors by using the transparency pattern. Mount hearts randomly across the whole board.

Trace and cut out the letters F-R-I-E-N-D-S. Write the name of each child somewhere on the letters as illustrated above. Older children may be able to write their own names.

Periodically ask children to find their names on the board. Remind them what the big word says.

Art—*Friends Make Us Happy Magnet*

Materials:
  frozen juice can lid
  red and yellow tissue paper cut into 2" squares
  black permanent marker
  magnetic strip

Draw a happy face (two bold eyes and a bright smile) on the juice can lid with a permanent marker. Dot glue on the eyes and mouth. Show the child how to crumple red tissue paper squares into wads and place them in the glue. When complete, cover the background with glue and yellow tissue paper wads. Cut a small magnetic strip to adhere to the back when dry.

Cooking—*Friendship Fruit Salad*

Materials:
  fresh or canned fruit   plastic serrated knives
  can opener   cutting board
  large bowl   plastic cups and spoons
  serving spoon

Send a note home or mail a postcard asking each child to bring a piece of fresh fruit or a can of fruit next week. Explain that you will make a Friendship Fruit Salad to demonstrate how friends share and cooperate.

Have children wash their hands. Demonstrate the proper way to cut. Warn the children that even though these knives are plastic, they are sharp. Supervise the children as they cut the fruit. Combine all of the fruit in a large bowl. Serve as a snack.

Active Play—*Cooperation Relay*

Materials:
  bed pillow for each team
  masking tape

Divide the children into teams of equal number. Place strips of masking tape on the floor to mark the starting point for each team as well as the turn around point. (If played outdoors, mark with beanbags.)

Pair the members of each team. The first pair of each team is handed a bed pillow. They hold the ends of the pillow, move across the floor to the turn around point, and return to their teams. They pass the pillow to the next pair and the relay continues until each pair has had a turn. Vary the way the children move to fit the developmental level of your group. For instance, they may walk, run, skip, gallop, hop, walk backwards, or walk on tip toes.

God's Word

Honor God and obey his commands.
This is the most important thing people can do. Ecclesiastes 12:13

Materials:

Transparency Pattern:	BIBLE
Background:	white
Border:	any purchased border
BIBLE:	black paper
	old Sunday school materials

Directions: Cover the board and add a border across the top and bottom. Trace and cut out the letters B-I-B-L-E from the transparency pattern. Lay each letter on the floor and assign a group of children to each letter. Let children tear out Bible story pictures from old take-home papers or visuals and glue them onto the letters. As children work, talk about the important things God tells us in this special book. Mount the letters in order across the board. (Hint: Letters may need to be trimmed after little hands glue on pictures.)

Art—*Bible Book Mark*

Materials:
  heart transparency pattern (optional)
  white tagboard
  black permanent marker
  newspapers
  thin tempera paint
  plastic straw
  hole punch
  yarn

Trace and cut out a 2" heart using the transparency pattern or enlarge and copy the heart in a photocopy machine. Print on the words, "Honor God's Word."

Place the heart on newspaper. Put a couple of drops of paint on the heart. Show the child how to blow through the straw to scatter the paint across the heart. As the child paints, read the words printed on the heart. Ask the child to repeat the words.

When dry, punch a hole near the bottom of the heart. Cut yarn into two 12" pieces. Fold in half and insert the fold through the hole in the heart. Pull the four ends through the yarn loop and pull tightly.

The bookmark may be a gift for Mother's Day or Father's Day.

Active Play—*B-I-B-L-E Relay*

Materials:
  B-I-B-L-E transparency pattern
  2 colors of flannel
  2 flannel boards
  masking tape

Enlarge the transparency pattern in a photocopy machine. Use the photocopy to cut out B-I-B-L-E from two colors of felt. Place a strip of masking tape on the floor to mark the starting point for each team. Place flannel boards a fair distance away.

Divide children into five member teams. Have them stand in a row behind the starting line. Give each child one letter. (Extra children may be the spelling "inspectors" or make smaller teams and have children run more than once.)

For young children, pass out the letters in the correct order. Scramble the letters for older children and let them put the letters in the proper order. At the signal, the first member of each team moves to the flannel board and puts on his letter. When the first member returns to the starting line the next player may go. The relay continues until each team has spelled the word Bible. For variety, change the way the children move each time you play the game. They can walk, crawl, slide, or gallop.

A Savior Has Been Born

Today your Savior was born in David's town.
He is Christ, the Lord. Luke 2:11

Materials:

Transparency Patterns:	angel and shepherd scene
	star (optional)
Background:	dark blue paper, white chalk
Lettering:	gold foil
Sheep with Shepherds:	white paper, assorted markers or paint, cotton
Angel:	white paper, assorted markers or paint
Stars:	gold foil wrapping paper or gold star stickers

Directions: Cover the board. Trace the hillside line with chalk using the transparency, or draw by freehand. Trace and cut out the shepherds and sheep. Add color as desired and glue cotton onto sheep. Mount onto the right hill.

Trace and cut out the angel. Add color as desired and mount to the left hill.

Mount the caption in the sky. Add stars traced from the transparency and cut out, or adhere star stickers to the sky.

Active Play—*The Shepherds and the Angels*

Choose one child to be the angel; the other children will be shepherds. The angel squats in the center of the circling shepherds. The shepherds hold hands, walk, and sing the following words to the tune of "Ring Around the Rosy:"

Shepherds on the hillside, watching the-ir she-ep,
An-gels ap-pear, shepherds fall down.

The angel stands up on the word "appear" and the shepherds fall face down on the word "fall." When the song is complete, the angel says, "Don't be afraid. I bring good news. Jesus is born." (Let the angel state this in his own words.)

Then lead the children around the room to the place where baby Jesus has been laid (a wrapped doll). As the children follow in single file, they all sing these words (also to the tune of "Ring Around the Rosy"):

Let's go to Bethlehem, and se-e th-e ba-by.
Hur-ry, hur-ry, let's see the King.

Lead the children in a discussion about how the shepherds might have felt.

Circle Time—*Beanbag Toss*

Children sit in a circle passing a beanbag. The group repeats the phrase, "The shepherds were watching their sheep, baa-baa-baa." The child holding the beanbag on the third "baa" answers a question which reviews the Christmas story such as Who appeared in the sky to the shepherds? or Where did the shepherds find the baby?

Finger Play—*The Shepherd's Story*

While shepherds watched their sheep one night, angels filled the sky.
(Hold one hand above eyes, then point upward.)

"Do not be afraid," the angels said, "And we will tell you why.
(Wag finger no, then point away from self.)

We bring good news of greatest joy, to people everywhere.
(Spread both arms wide.)

Go to Bethlehem and you will find, a new born Savior there."
(Fold arms as if holding a baby.)

The shepherds did as they were told, and hurried right away.
(Run in place.)

They found the babe and worshiped him, that joyful Christmas day.
(Fold hands as if in prayer.)

I Can Help

Be kind to everyone. 2 Timothy 2:24

Materials:

Transparency Pattern:	children
Background:	tan paper
Border:	wide yellow ribbon
Lettering:	black marker
Children:	white paper, assorted markers or paint
Hands:	assorted tempera paint, paint brush

Directions: Cover the board and attach the ribbon border around its edge. Trace and cut out the children. Add color as desired. Mount on the right side of the board.

Use the simple illustrated method of lines and dots to letter the caption with a marker. With a paint brush, paint one hand on each child. (This will work best if done one child at a time.) Press hands around the caption. (Or print hands on separate paper, dry, cut out, and mount.)

Finger Play—*It Pleases God*

It pleases God when I am kind, *(Point upward.)*
And when I help and share. *(Pretend to give object away.)*
It pleases God when I show love *(Place both hands on heart.)*
To people everywhere! *(Stretch arms wide.)*

Circle Time—*Helping Others*

Materials:
magazine pictures of several people in need of help

Hold up each picture individually and ask, "How might you help this person?" Let children volunteer their ideas. Remind them that Jesus wants us to love everyone. Helping others is one way to show you love them. Discuss others ways to show love.

Song—*It Pleases God*

Sing to the tune of "Mulberry Bush:"

It pleases God whenever we share,
Whenever we share, whenever we share.
It pleases God whenever we share.
It pleases him so much.

> Verse 2—It pleases God whenever we help.
> Verse 3—It pleases God when we go to church.
> Verse 4—It pleases God whenever we're kind.
> Verse 5—It pleases God whenever we pray.

Because we love God, we want to please him,
We want to please him, we want to please him.
Because we love God we want to please him.
We love him more each day.

Jesus Is Alive!

*(Jesus said,) "I am the One who lives. I was dead, but look:
I am alive forever and ever!"* Revelation 1:18

Materials:

Transparency Patterns:	Jesus, flowers
Background:	light green
Lettering:	white
Jesus:	white paper, assorted markers or paint
Flowers:	assorted paper, assorted markers

Directions: Cover the board. Trace and cut out Jesus. Add color as desired. Mount Jesus in the center of the board.

Trace and cut out several flowers in assorted sizes and colors. Curl edges to make flowers 3-D.
Overlap flowers across the bottom of the board to make a flower garden. Add the caption at the top.

Art—*Crushed Eggshell Mosaics*

Materials:
cross transparency pattern
tagboard
eggshells, washed and dried
egg dye kit

Enlarge the cross transparency pattern in a photocopy machine. Use the photocopy to trace a cross onto tagboard. Before class use a variety of colors to dye the empty egg shells. Allow to dry. Break shells into pieces.
Cover the cross with glue and allow the child to glue on shell pieces.

Active Play—*Egg Roll*

Materials:
hard-boiled eggs or plastic eggs with clay inside
masking tape
spoons

Explain that it is believed this custom was started to commemorate the rolling of the stone away from Jesus' tomb.
To roll eggs inside, use masking tape to mark the beginning and end of the path. Outside use a yardstick or a length of yarn to mark the start and finish. Children use spoons to roll eggs along a path. All the children can roll at once or in teams. It is not necessary to have a winner.

Circle Time—*Praise Him*

Sing "Praise Him."

Praise Him. Praise Him.
Praise Him in the morning, Praise Him at the noontime.
Praise Him. Praise Him,
Praise Him when the sun goes down.

Add this second verse.

Praise Him. Praise Him.
Praise Him in the springtime, Praise Him at Easter time.
Praise Him. Praise Him,
Praise Him th-e whole year long.

God Knows My Name

The Lord knows those who belong to him. 2 Timothy 2:19

Materials:

Transparency Pattern:	heart (optional)
Background:	white
Lettering:	red
Flowers:	green marker
	red, pink, and green paper
	heart-shaped paper doilies (optional)
	a photograph of each child
Butterflies:	red and pink paper
	tan chenille wire

Directions: Cover the board and mount the caption across the top.

Use a marker to make flower stems across the bottom of the board. Cut several green hearts of different sizes. Curl edges and attach randomly to the stems. Cut several sizes of hearts from red and pink paper for flowers. Layer colors with heart-shaped paper doilies to make various flower styles. Attach flowers to stems. Mount each child's picture onto a heart flower.

Use two layered hearts to make butterflies. Fold hearts in half and glue two chenille wires to the center folds to create bodies with antlers. Attach the 3-D butterflies above the flowers.

Note: All hearts can be made by freehand or by using the transparency pattern to enlarge and copy hearts in a photocopy machine.

Active Play—*Name Search*

Materials:
  3" x 5" index cards, two per child
  assorted markers

Prepare two name cards for each child. Write the phrase "God knows _____," along with the child's name. For younger children, write each child's name in a different color (e.g., Jon in blue, Erin in red). Hide one card of each pair around the room. Give each child one card with the instruction to search for the matching one which you have hidden. Caution children not to pick up any card except their own. As children bring the name cards to you, read the phrase aloud. When repeating the game, let children take turns hiding the names.

Active Play—*Follow the Name Road*

Materials:
  paper
  assorted markers

Cut the paper into irregular stepping-stone shapes. Write a child's name on each stone, using each name more than once. (It would be helpful to write each child's name with a different color for color identification too.) Place the stones on the floor making a large circular path.

Play this game with a small group of children. Tell the children that God knows each of our names, and we want to know the names of everyone in our class. Ask each child to stand on a stone with his name on it. Determine which direction players will walk and who moves first. The teacher taps one child and the first child to move says the name of the child tapped. If the child correctly names the other child, he or she advances to the closest stone with that child's name. (Two children may be on the same stone.) The teacher will need to help read the names on the stones. Continue the game until each child has had several turns.

Active Play—*Toss the Name Ball*

Materials:
  inflatable beach ball
  permanent marker

Inflate the beach ball. Write the words, "God knows my name" on the ball. Write each child's name (as well as the teacher's) on the ball, saying the name out loud as you do so. Stand in a circle. The child holding the ball calls out one person's name and then tosses the ball to that person. Children can only toss the ball to those whose names they know.

Let Us Worship

Serve the Lord with joy. Come before him with singing. Psalm 100:2

Materials:

Transparency Pattern:	singing children
	music notes (optional)
Background:	white
Lettering:	purple
Children:	white paper
	assorted markers or paints
Notes:	black marker

Directions: Cover the board. Trace and cut out the singing children. Add color as desired. Mount the children across the bottom of the board and the caption across the top. Draw notes by freehand with a marker or trace the transparency pattern.

Song—*Come Let Us Worship the Lord*

Sing to the tune of "Itsy Bitsy Spider:"

Come, let us worship Jesus Christ our Lord.
Come, let us worship Jesus Christ our Lord.
Come, let us worship Jesus Christ our Lord.
Let us praise him for his goodness and for his loving care.

Circle Time—*Praise Him*

Have a special praise time. Ask the children to respond to your sentences with "Praise God!" Instruct them to speak softly on their first response and get louder each time.

Teacher:	God is so good.
Children:	Praise to God!
Teacher:	God can do anything.
Children:	Praise to God!
Teacher:	God loves you and God loves me.
Children:	Praise to God!
Teacher:	Let's thank God.
Everyone:	Thank you God!

This time instruct children to respond with "Let's praise the Lord."

Teacher:	God made mountains, butterflies and trees.
Children:	Let's praise the Lord!
Teacher:	God gave us flowers, rainbows and the seas.
Children:	Let's praise the Lord!
Teacher:	God has given us many things.
Everyone:	Praise to God!

Song—*Now It's Time to Talk to God*

Sing to the tune of "Jacob's Ladder:"

Now it's time to talk to God. Now it's time to talk to God.
Now it's time to talk to God. Children let us pray.

Use this song to prepare children for prayer time.

Following Jesus

You should follow in his steps. 1 Peter 2:21 (NIV)

Materials:

Transparency Pattern:	walking Jesus
Background:	tan
Lettering:	red
Jesus:	white paper
	assorted markers
Footprints:	large black ink pad

Directions: Cover the board. Trace and cut out Jesus. Add color as desired. Mount Jesus to the left side of the board.

Create footprints by pressing the bottom of your fist onto an ink pad, and then printing it onto the background paper. (Right fists make right feet and left fists make left feet.) Add five toes to each with fingerprints. (This may be an activity children can do with proper guidance.)

Add the caption across the top right, replacing O's with footprints.

Circle Time—*I Can Learn Bible Words*

Materials:
  beanbag

Ask children to sit in a circle. Recite a Bible verse or shortened phrase and ask the children to repeat it after you. Repeat the words as many times as necessary until most of the children can say them with the group. Pass a beanbag around the circle. Tell the children when the beanbag reaches them they are to say only one word of the Bible verse. The first person says the first word of the verse, the second the next, and so forth. Repeat the phrase as the beanbag travels around the circle several times increasing the speed a little each time.

Explain to children that when we learn what the Bible says we learn what Jesus taught and we know better how to live our lives.

Art—*Follow the Leader*

Materials:
  white cardstock paper
  walking Jesus transparency pattern
  paper doll pattern—page 8
  assorted crayons or markers
  empty cardboard toilet paper rolls

Photocopy the walking Jesus transparency pattern to be approximately 6" tall. Color and cut out. Glue the cutout to the side of a cardboard toilet paper roll so that Jesus stands.

Photocopy a paper doll pattern from page 8 for each child, enlarging the doll to approximately 6" tall. Cut out and let children color. Glue each to the side of a cardboard toilet paper roll to stand.

Talk about what following Jesus means—doing what Jesus says and did. Allow the children to play "Follow the Leader" with the dolls. Demonstrate an action with the Jesus doll and let the children follow with their dolls (i.e., sharing, giving, praising God). Add the dolls to a play center.

For Very Young Children: Draw in facial features as you talk with each child. Allow children to scribble color their dolls. Coloring dolls before cutting them out will be easiest.

Happy Are Those Who Do Right

Happy are those people who are fair,
who do what is right at all times. Psalm 106:3

Materials:

Transparency Pattern:	circle of faces
Background:	tan
Border:	orange scalloped
Lettering:	orange letters or orange marker
Circle of Faces:	assorted permanent markers

Directions: Cover the board and mount the border around its edge. Trace the circle of faces with a black marker directly onto the background. Add a bit of color by coloring the children's hair a variety of colors.

Add the caption to the center by mounting letters or tracing from the transparency with a marker.

Circle Time—*Do Right and Be Happy*

The Bible tells us that those who want to do right are happy (Matthew 5:6). Describe situations and allow the children to point to faces on the board describing the situation. This can be done one at a time or several children at once. For example:

Alicia picked up her toys when her daddy asked.	smiling face
Joe gave one of his cookies to his sister.	smiling face
Mother asked Kevin to eat his breakfast but Kevin said, "No!"	sad face

Point to faces on the bulletin board during other activities to emphasize obeying and disobeying.

Circle Time—*Whom Should I Obey?*

Materials:
heart transparency pattern
red paper
black marker
magazine pictures of a mother, a father, a grandmother, and a grandfather
beanbag

Trace and cut out a large heart using the transparency pattern. Divide the heart into four sections with a marker. Glue one picture to each section—a mother, a father, a grandmother, and a grandfather. Talk with the children about the pictures and identify each.

Place the heart on the floor and make a circle of children around the heart. Let children take turns tossing the beanbag on the heart. Ask the child who tossed it, "Whom will you obey?" The child responds by naming the picture the beanbag landed on—mother, father, grandmother, or grandfather. Take turns tossing the bag.

Active Play—"*Teacher May I?*"

Play "Teacher May I?" like "Mother May I?"
Stand 12-18 feet from the children. Because young children have trouble waiting for their turn, modify the game so that all the children move at once. One child asks, "Teacher, may we take two steps?" Respond with "Yes, you may take two steps" or "No, you may not take two steps." If the answer is yes, all the children take two steps. If the answer is no, children must stay where they are. A second child gets to repeat the question, this time changing the number of steps, "Teacher, may we take five steps?" Respond with a yes or no. Continue playing until the children have reached you. Play this game indoors or out.

I Will Do Right

Do what the Lord says is good and right. Deuteronomy 6:18

Materials:

Transparency Pattern:	star (optional)
Background:	blue paper
Border:	wide white ribbon or 2" wide strips of white paper
Lettering:	red
Hands:	hands made by children in the art activity
Stars:	assorted foil wrapping paper or star stickers

Directions: Cover the board. The arms made by the children in the art activity should be mounted along the bottom edge of the board.

Add the border around the edge of the board. Mount the caption. Trace and cut out stars and mount randomly, or adhere star stickers. For positive reinforcement, add stars to the board when you "catch" children doing right.

Art—*I Will!*

Materials:
  shelf paper
  crayons

Cut a piece of shelf paper approximately 18" long for each child. Trace around one arm and hand for each child. Let children color. Older children will be able to draw sleeves, fingernails, and jewelry. Let older children write their names on their paper arms. Write names for younger children. Talk about choosing to do right as children color.

Cut out arms and mount on the bulletin board.

Active Play—*Balance the Ball*

Materials:
  ball
  masking tape
  bath towel

Use masking tape to mark a starting point and turn around point on the floor. Help each child find a partner. If there is an extra child, team up with that child. Give the first pair a towel. Each child holds one end of the towel. Place the ball in the middle of the towel. Signal the pair to walk the course to the turn around point with the ball on the towel and then back to the starting point. (It is easier to keep the ball on the towel if the towel is not taunt. If the ball does roll off, the children stop, pick it up, put it back on the towel, and continue.)

All the other children should be encouraging their classmates. Point out to the children how they have to cooperate to be able to complete the course. Talk about how good it feels when others encourage you. Remind children it is right to cooperate and encourage others.

Optional: This can be turned into a relay by dividing the children into two teams. If one team has more pairs than the other, the team with the fewer members sends one pair a second time. Lay out a two team course. Use two towels and two balls.

Song—*Jesus Wants to Be Our Friend*

Sing to the tune of "Mary Had a Little Lamb:"

Jesus wants me to obey, to obey, to obey.
Jesus wants me to obey, so I will do right.

I will do as Jesus says, Jesus says, Jesus says.
I will do as Jesus says, because I love him so.

God Loves Me

God is love. 1 John 4:8

Materials:

Background:	white paper
Border:	red scalloped
Lettering:	black
Hearts:	hearts made by children in the art activity

Directions: Cover the board and mount the border around its edge. Mount the caption across the middle of the board. Surround the caption with a collage of hearts made by the children in the art activity.

Art—*Puffy Paint Heart*

Paint Recipe:
   1 cup flour
   1 cup salt
   3/4 cup thin, red liquid tempera paint

Materials:
   heart transparency pattern
   clean plastic squeeze bottles (i.e., shampoo, catsup, or dish soap bottles)
   tagboard

Trace large hearts onto tagboard using the transparency pattern. Cut out. Mix paint ingredients. Put the paint into squeeze bottles.

Hold a bottle upside down and shake the paint to the cap. Show children how to squeeze the bottle to paint a design on the tagboard heart. Allow to dry and use on the bulletin board. Each child may need to paint more than one heart to cover the board.

Song—*God Gives Us Many Gifts*

Sing to the tune of "Looby Loo:"

Chorus
   God gives us many gifts. God gives us many gifts.
   God gives us many gifts. He gives them to us with love.

Verse
   He gives us sunny days. He gives us sunny days.
   He gives us sunny days because He loves and cares for us.

Complete the verse with any three syllables that describe the season. For fall use falling leaves, gentle winds, cooler days. In spring sing about butterflies or budding trees. For winter include falling snow or longer nights. In summer use lightening bugs, strawberries, and thunderstorms.

Circle Time—*I Know Something God Made*

Say, "I know something God made and it's yellow." Let children take turns naming yellow things God created. Name things that are round, heavy, or soft. Name animals or people. Thank God for his love and his gifts.

It Is Right to Thank God

We must always thank God. 2 Thessalonians 1:3

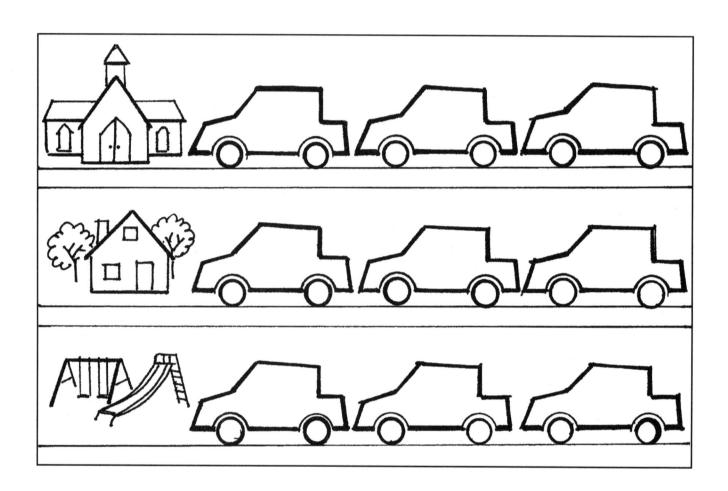

Materials:

Transparency Patterns:	church, house, playground
Background:	yellow
Border and Streets:	gray crepe paper streamer
Church, House, Playground:	assorted markers
Cars:	cars made by children in the art activity

Directions: Cover the board. Divide the board into thirds horizontally by adding three crepe paper "streets."

Trace the church, house, and playground directly onto the background with markers. Place one on each "street" on the left side of the board.

Mount the cars made by the children in the art activity on the "streets."

Art—*Thank You God for My Family*

Materials:
   car transparency pattern
   white paper
   crayons
   magazines

Trace and cut out a car for each child using the transparency pattern. (Or enlarge and print in a photocopy machine.)

First let each child color his car. Then ask children to tear out pictures from magazines to represent each person in their families (e.g., mother, father, sister, and self or mother, grandmother, two brothers, and self). Talk about families, recognizing the uniqueness of each. Glue pictures onto cars.

Mount cars on the bulletin board. Talk about where the children like to go with their families such as to God's house, to a friend's house, or to the park.

Active Play—*Hide and Seek*

Materials:
   several frozen juice can lids
   praying hands stickers (available from Standard Publishing)

Put one sticker on each lid. Hide several of the prepared lids around the room or outside. Let children search for the lids and bring them one at a time to you. Ask each child a review question from the day's Bible story, a memory verse, or one thing for which they can thank God as they turn in the lid.

Dramatic Play—*Thank You God for My House*

Materials:
   cardboard boxes
   masking tape
   old blankets or bedspreads

Ask parents to save corrugated cardboard boxes in sizes young children can carry. Tape the empty boxes closed.

Children can use the empty boxes to build houses. Help them drape blankets or bedspreads across the top for roofs. Encourage dramatic play with children assuming the roles in a caring family. Join the children inside the house. Help children think of things at home for which they can thank God.

Our Friend Jesus

Then Jesus took the children in his arms.
He put his hands on them and blessed them. Mark 10:16

Materials:

Transparency Pattern:	Jesus
Background:	light blue
Border:	color coordinated wide ribbon
Lettering:	black
Jesus:	white paper
	assorted markers
Silhouettes:	silhouettes made by children in the art activity

Directions: Cover the board and add the ribbon border. Trace and cut out Jesus. Add color as desired. Mount Jesus in the center of the board. Add the caption across Jesus.

Mount silhouettes of children made in the art activity around Jesus.

Art—*Silhouettes*

Materials:
  overhead projector
  black paper
  cardboard
  wrapping paper with a small print
  ribbon

Use an overhead transparency to shine light on a child sitting in front of black paper mounted on the wall. Trace the child's profile onto the paper and cut out. (A helper may be needed to hold heads still while you trace quickly.)

Cut an oval from cardboard and wrapping paper, slightly larger than the silhouette. Mount the silhouette on the wrapping paper and the wrapping paper onto the cardboard. Glue a ribbon loop to the back for hanging the picture.

Repeat this process for every child. Hang pictures on the bulletin board. When the board is changed, send pictures home as gifts to parents.

Table Games—*Puzzles*

Materials:
  jumbo craft sticks or tongue depressors
  pictures of Jesus from old Sunday school materials
  X-Acto knife

Trim the pictures into 6" x 6" squares. Glue craft sticks to the back of each picture. Place the sticks side by side so that the back is completely covered. Using an X-Acto knife, cut through the picture between the sticks to make the puzzle pieces. Children work the puzzles by placing the picture pieces in order side by side.

Circle Time—*Cube Roll*

Materials:
  two half gallon cardboard milk cartons
  X-Acto knife
  Con-Tact paper
  six pictures of Jesus with friends from old Sunday school materials

Cut the top off two half gallon milk cartons with an X-Acto knife so that when the two are pushed together a cube is created. Cover the cube with Con-Tact paper. Glue a picture to each side of the cube.

Take turns rolling the cube. Ask, "Who was Jesus' friend?" Talk about how Jesus was a friend to many.

I Am Important To God

He cares for you. 1 Peter 5:7

Materials:

Transparency Pattern:	star
Background:	white
Border:	green and blue crepe paper streamers
Lettering:	blue
Stars:	green paper
	assorted tissue paper
	glitter

Directions: Cover the board and use blue and green crepe paper streamers twisted together for a border.

Trace and cut out a star for each child, using the transparency pattern. Letter children's names on the stars with bottled glue. Let children sprinkle on glitter. Cut tissue paper into one inch wide strips and various lengths. Attach three strips to the back of each star.

Mount the caption across the middle of the board. Surround the caption with stars.

Finger Play—*Learning Names*

Tell children that they are important to God. He knows everything about each one of them and he knows their names. It is good for all the children in the room to know each other's name too. Recite this finger play with children standing in a circle.

Here I am at Sunday school* with new friends all around.
(Point to children around circle.)

So many names for me to learn. First, let's all sit down.
(Everyone sits.)

We will pass the beanbag and when it reaches you
(Begin passing a beanbag.)

Say your name then pass the bag. That's all you have to do.
(Have children say their own names as they take the beanbag.)

This is an especially good activity to use when there are new children in the class.

*Substitute the appropriate name for your program.

Art—*I'm Important to God*

Materials:
  6" x 10" aluminum foil
  9" x 12" colored paper
  assorted markers
  assorted paper triangles

Run a line of glue along the outer edges of the dull side of the aluminum foil. Glue foil to the center of the colored paper, shiny side up. Above the foil write "Who is important to God?" Below the foil ask each child to print his or her name. (Write the names for young children.) Decorate the border of the paper with small construction paper triangles in assorted colors.

Mount the art around the room. Ask each child, "Who is important to God?" Let children look at their reflections and reply.